DATE DUE

PRINTED IN U.S.A.

Elgin Community College Library
Elgin, IL 60123

Democracy's Reconstruction

TRANSGRESSING BOUNDARIES
Studies in Black Politics and Black Communities
Cathy J. Cohen and Frederick Harris, Series Editors

The Politics of Public Housing: Black Women's Struggles Against Urban Inequality
RHONDA Y. WILLIAMS

Keepin' It Real: School Success Beyond Black and White
PRUDENCE L. CARTER

Double Trouble: Black Mayors, Black Communities, and the Call for a Deep Democracy
J. PHILLIP THOMPSON, III

Party/Politics: Horizons in Black Political Thought
MICHAEL HANCHARD

In Search of the Black Fantastic: Politics and Popular Culture in the Post-Civil Rights Era
RICHARD ITON

Race and the Politics of Solidarity
JULIET HOOKER

I Am Your Sister: Collected and Unpublished Writings of Audre Lorde
RUDOLPH P. BYRD, JOHNNETTA BETSCH COLE, AND BEVERLY GUY-SHEFTALL, EDITORS

Democracy Remixed: Black Youth and the Future of American Politics
CATHY J. COHEN

Democracy's Reconstruction: Thinking Politically with W. E. B. Du Bois
LAWRIE BALFOUR

LAWRIE BALFOUR

Democracy's Reconstruction
Thinking Politically with W. E. B. Du Bois

2011

Oxford University Press, Inc., publishes works that further
Oxford University's objective of excellence
in research, scholarship, and education.

Oxford   New York
Auckland   Cape Town   Dar es Salaam   Hong Kong   Karachi
Kuala Lumpur   Madrid   Melbourne   Mexico City   Nairobi
New Delhi   Shanghai   Taipei   Toronto

With offices in
Argentina   Austria   Brazil   Chile   Czech Republic   France   Greece
Guatemala   Hungary   Italy   Japan   Poland   Portugal   Singapore
South Korea   Switzerland   Thailand   Turkey   Ukraine   Vietnam

Copyright © 2011 by Lawrie Balfour

Published by Oxford University Press, Inc.
198 Madison Avenue, New York, NY 10016

www.oup.com

Oxford is a registered trademark of Oxford University Press

All rights reserved. No part of this publication may be reproduced,
stored in a retrieval system, or transmitted, in any form or by any means,
electronic, mechanical, photocopying, recording, or otherwise,
without the prior permission of Oxford University Press.

Library of Congress Cataloging-in-Publication Data
Balfour, Katharine Lawrence, 1964-
Democracy's reconstruction : thinking politically with W. E. B. Du Bois
/ Lawrie Balfour.
    p. cm. — (Transgressing boundaries)
Includes bibliographical references and index.
ISBN 978-0-19-537729-3
1. Du Bois, W. E. B. (William Edward Burghardt), 1868–1963—Political and social views.
2. Du Bois, W. E. B. (William Edward Burghardt), 1868–1963—Criticism and interpretation.
3. Slavery—United States. 4. African Americans—Politics and government.
5. African Americans—Social conditions. 6. African Americans—Civil rights.
7. Critical theory—United States. 8. United States—Politics and government.
I. Title.
E185.97.D73B358   2011
303.48'4092—dc22   2010012912

9 8 7 6 5 4 3 2 1
Printed in the United States of America
on acid-free paper

For my parents

CONTENTS

Preface ix
*List of Abbreviations of Books by
W. E. B. Du Bois* xiii

ONE   Politics in the Present-Past   1

TWO   Unreconstructed Democracy and the Claim of Reparations   23

THREE   Resurrecting John Brown   47

FOUR   Practicing Critical Race Autobiography   71

FIVE   Representative Women: Slavery and the Gendered Ground of Citizenship   97

SIX   Black World, White Nation: Remapping Political Theory   115

Acknowledgments 141
Notes 143
Index of Writings of W. E. B. Du Bois 189
Index 191

PREFACE

WHEN THE MOMENT CAME FOR Martin Luther King, Jr., to memorialize W. E. B. Du Bois at a ceremony at Carnegie Hall in February 1968, he sketched a portrait of a scholar, organizer, and radical advocate of black power who embraced "humanity in all its hues."[1] Recalling the events and causes that gave shape to Du Bois's life, King likened U.S. support for a repressive regime in Vietnam to the compromise that ended the "monumental achievement" of Reconstruction in 1876; he railed against the pernicious effects of an anticommunist campaign that distorted Du Bois's memory and perverted American politics; and he reminded white Americans of the depth of their debt to a man who committed himself to undoing their ignorance of their own history. Together with King's ambitious outline for a march on Washington that he would not live to see, these observations reflect a pivotal and perilous moment in the civil rights leader's biography and reveal as much about King in his final weeks as they do about the man he came to honor.

Yet King's words also reach beyond that context in two interrelated ways. First, he insisted that Du Bois be remembered as a teacher: "He would have wanted his life to teach us something about our tasks of emancipation."[2] Chief among these lessons, King observed, was that "the keystone in the arch of oppression was the myth of inferiority."[3] Contending against degraded popular images of African Americans and a historical profession that represented slavery as a benign institution and black citizenship as a mistake, Du Bois pursued the truth about black women and men as a lifelong vocation. Second, King concluded his remarks by announcing that Du Bois's "greatest virtue was his committed empathy with all the oppressed and his divine dissatisfaction with all forms of injustice."[4] Committed empathy and divine dissatisfaction: King's emphasis on these democratic virtues indicates how we might honor *his* memory, but it also suggests why Du Bois's voice remains so vital in an era hailed by many as "postracial."

King's words resonate now, because they indicate why the particular combination of Du Bois's historical gifts with his attunement to all forms of injustice is urgently needed, even after the legal edifice of Jim Crow has been dismantled. By training his audience's attention on the political significance of Du Bois's rewriting of history and joining it to contemporary forms of subjugation, King countered the impulse to construe the passage of the major civil rights legislation of the 1960s as a signal that the quest for racial equality was finally over. Notwithstanding the accomplishments of the civil rights movement, King contrasted the uncertainty of "the date of full emancipation" with a promise that "the struggle for it will endure."[5] King's caution reminds us who bears the costs of premature declarations of a postracial or post–civil rights era. It upends the assumptions that give rise to smug statements that African Americans now have "no more excuses" and requires more searching consideration of the behavior of the privileged and unjust institutional structures that have been too readily excused.

Maybe the connection seems strained. In contrast to the tumultuous moment of King's address, the dominant images of recent years include Barack Obama's acceptance of the Democratic nomination for the presidency on the forty-fifth anniversary of the March on Washington and the scene of Americans' first African American president greeting jubilant well-wishers in front of the Capitol on January 21, 2009. Such images support the view that slavery, Jim Crow, and their legacies have lost their grip on American public life. Even if the initial wonder of the election has since given way to a more complicated reality, demanding renewed attention to racial injustice may seem ill-timed or misdirected. Not only have African Americans realized aspirations unthinkable in Du Bois's time—or King's—but preoccupation with the unfinished "tasks of emancipation" may be divisive and distracting in a time marked by violent conflict, environmental devastation, and economic crisis. Why focus now on the historical injuries of a relatively small portion of a populace in which suffering is both immediate and widespread? King's memorial address offers an answer. In his celebration of Du Bois's "priceless dedication to his people," King links that dedication to unmet challenges of poverty, exploitation, illiteracy, and imperial war that cross color lines and exceed national borders. Du Bois's particular commitments, in this light, are revealed as universal, not parochial.[6] His passion to renarrate stories of the slaves and their descendants sustains a form of democratic thinking that enables us to address contemporary concerns by working *through* the historical devaluation of nonwhite lives, rather than sidestepping that history or treating it as an aberration.

This book approaches the question of democracy by reading Du Bois's work in the spirit of King's remarks. Animated by a conviction that regarding racial injustice as a bygone problem disables contemporary efforts to address a range of political challenges, I mine Du Bois's political thought as a resource. Drawing on his vast corpus of published work, I highlight those elements of his thought that enable us to interpret the present and conceive alternative futures by regarding the past anew. Du Bois, I argue, enables us to grasp ways in which racial subjugation has been constitutive, rather than anomalous, in American history and in modern experience more broadly. He sheds light on a political inheritance that encompasses both a commitment to liberty and equality, refashioned and enlarged by generations, and a tradition of violence and disregard that has also been refashioned, and even enlarged over time. He offers us tools with which to consider a self-described democracy in which a black man can be president, but incarceration has become more common than college graduation or military service among young African American men;[7] in which an African American woman can assume the presidency of an Ivy League university, but black children are disproportionately represented in the measures of our collective failure: poor schools, unlivable housing, inadequate health care. To take Du Bois as inspiration and guide does not mean to take him unquestioningly or in all regards as an authority. The richness of his written legacy, capacious enough to contain a wealth of tensions and contradictions, invites contemporary readers to learn from and to argue with him. Through a prolonged engagement with Du Bois's thinking and his example, then, I hope to show how we might cultivate an unwillingness to accept, uncontested, a status quo in which the inheritances of slavery and segregation still matter. In other words: "Let us be dissatisfied."[8]

LIST OF ABBREVIATIONS OF BOOKS BY W. E. B. DU BOIS

BR *Black Reconstruction in America: An Essay Toward a History of the Part Which Black Folk Played in the Attempt to Reconstruct Democracy in America, 1860–1880* (1935; repr., Cleveland: Meridian, 1964).

DOD *Dusk of Dawn: An Essay Toward an Autobiography of a Race Concept* (1940; repr., New Brunswick: Transaction, 1984).

DW *Darkwater: Voices from Within the Veil* (1920; repr., Mineola, NY: Dover, 1999).

JB *John Brown*, ed. John David Smith (1909; repr., Armonk, NY: M. E. Sharpe, 1997).

SAST *The Suppression of the African Slave-Trade to the United States of America, 1638-1870* (1896; repr., Mineola, NY: Dover, 1970).

SBF *The Souls of Black Folk*, ed. David W. Blight and Robert Gooding-Williams (1903; repr., Boston: Bedford, 1997).

Democracy's Reconstruction

ONE | Politics in the Present-Past

Memory—of what has been, of acts of commission or omission, of a responsibility abdicated—affects the future conduct of power in any form. Failure to adopt some imaginative recognition of such a principle merely results in the enthronement of a political culture that appears to know no boundaries—the culture of impunity.

—Wole Soyinka, *The Burden of Memory, The Muse of Forgiveness*[1]

Facing the Worst

On January 10, 2007, members of the Virginia General Assembly introduced a controversial joint resolution, atoning for Virginia's part in the enslavement of Africans and calling for racial reconciliation. The reaction was furious. In late February, the Senate and the House of Delegates unanimously passed an amended resolution that expressed regret for slavery and for the exploitation of Native Americans and, again, called for reconciliation.[2] During the intervening weeks, as Virginians prepared to celebrate the four hundredth anniversary of the founding of Jamestown, they also debated the presence of the slave past. Many responded with outrage when Delegate Frank Hargrove complained that the time had come for African Americans to "get over" slavery. Others worried that the language of apology would trigger demands for reparations. Still others asked whether an apology without a commitment to material change amounted to an empty gesture. Although the passage of the resolution did little to put these conflicting concerns to rest, its broad endorsement signaled that the aim of reconciliation had, in some respects, been served. As Delegate Donald McEachin, one of the resolution's original sponsors, noted, the measure was the first of its kind and potentially a model for others. "This session will be remembered for a lot of things," McEachin remarked, "but 20 years hence I suspect one of those things will be the fact that we came together and passed this resolution."[3]

McEachin is surely right. The symbolic power of an official acknowledgment of slavery issuing from the former capital of the Confederacy is undeniable, and the resolution has spurred similar measures in other states, as well as the U.S. Congress.[4] Nevertheless, the political substance of the resolution is less clear-cut. One way to gauge that substance is to consider textual differences between the resolution that aroused resistance in January and the one that secured wide approval in February. In the eyes of many commentators, the crucial change was the replacement of a language of "apology" with one of "regret."[5] Where the former imputed responsibility to present-day Virginians—an imputation adamantly disavowed by those who view responsibility as a matter of identifying individual wrongdoers and victims—the new language registers a sense of sorrow for bygone crimes.[6] More significant than this change of wording, however, are other alterations that received relatively scant attention. Three issues stand out.

First, the initial resolution made direct the connections between the institution of racial slavery and contemporary racial conditions. It traced a route from the Atlantic slave trade through the decades leading up to the Civil War to the Black Codes, lynchings, disenfranchisement, and de jure segregation that followed emancipation to the present day. "In the Commonwealth, home to the first African slaves" the resolution declared, "the vestiges of slavery are ever before African American citizens," who continue to confront both "the overt racism of hate groups" and subtler obstacles in their efforts to secure decent health care, education, housing, and business opportunities. Indignities rooted in chattel slavery were thus characterized as ongoing, and "the ghosts of their collective pasts" were said to haunt both white and African American citizens.[7] Although the resolution did not directly call for material reparations to address this haunted present, it invoked "the broken promise of '40 acres and a mule'" and tied that promise to a pattern of denial "of any responsibility for the centuries of legally sanctioned deprivation of African Americans of their endowed rights or for contemporary policies that perpetuate the status quo." None of this language remains in the final resolution.

Second, the original resolution balanced its account of crimes committed against African slaves and their descendants with an account of their efforts to secure their own freedom. In addition to noting resistance by African captives and slaves, the resolution acknowledged black Americans' service during the Civil War. The final resolution, by contrast, offers a general expression of "acknowledgment and thanksgiving for the contributions of Native Americans and African Americans to the Commonwealth and this nation, and to the propagation of the ideals of liberty, justice, and democracy."[8] Where it specifies these contributions, the resolution shifts the attribution of agency to the Commonwealth itself: "In recent decades, Virginia's affirmation of the founding ideals of liberty and equality have been made evident by providing some of the nation's foremost trailblazers for civil rights and electing a grandson of slaves to the Commonwealth's highest elective office." In light of such alterations, it is worth noting that two paragraphs which survive the revision process intact recall how Africans were "sold at auction as chattel, like inanimate property or animals" and specify that "the ethos of the Africans was shattered" and their families destroyed. Although these words convey the character of the violation represented by New World slavery, to present an account of thoroughgoing cultural destruction, and especially to emphasize its effect on family life, without recognizing African or African American roles in resisting and dismantling slavery, reproduces narratives of black victimhood and hints at a legacy of cultural deficiency.

Third, changes to the structure of the two resolutions indicate a dramatic shift in political intentions. "Slavery" was the first word of the original resolution. It began by situating Virginia's history within a history of enslavement stretching back to the ancient world; it then proceeded by recalling American participation in the international slave economy through much of the nineteenth century. As it moved forward to the present, furthermore, the resolution tied the expression of atonement not only to President Bush's comments at Goree Island, Senegal, but also to apologies by European and African nations for their roles in the slave trade and more broadly to a growing consciousness that historic injustice must be reckoned with "lest the world forget."[9] The amended resolution, by contrast, enfolds the crimes perpetrated against Africans and Native Americans within a story that begins and ends in Jamestown. Indeed, slavery is not named until the fifth paragraph. The first mention of slavery now follows the observation that "despite the 'self-evident' character of these fundamental principles [articulated in the Declaration of Independence], the moral standards of liberty and equality have been transgressed during much of Virginia's and America's history, and our Commonwealth and nation are striving to fulfill the ideals proclaimed by the founders to secure the 'more perfect union' that is the aspiration of our national identity and charter." Even as the resolution describes slavery in unflinching terms, this contrast of passive and active voice insinuates that the disregard for democratic principles was an anomaly or a departure from "the ideals that bind us together as a people."[10] Slavery is thus rendered containable, its effects bounded spatially by national borders and temporally by the end of state-sanctioned racial hierarchy sometime in the past.[11] If the resolution marks a departure in a society not given to reckoning with history's underside, in other words, it stops short of allowing that that history has concrete bearing on the present. History is "both denied and heralded."[12]

In light of these alterations, the call for reconciliation is troubling. Although the measure deserves credit for enjoining the remembrance of historic injustice and aspiring to foster a sense of shared endeavor among members of a heterogeneous, and often mutually distrustful, citizenry, it raises questions that it cannot, in its present form, address. What would constitute an adequate act of coming to terms with the past? What does reconciliation require? And from whom? Does a resolution that simultaneously reopens the past and insulates present-day citizens from its effects provide the basis from which they might begin to bridge their historic divisions? Does it press beyond what William Connolly calls "the slippery language of regret without moral indictment and, more significantly, of the recognition of undeserved suffering without a plan to curtail it in the future"?[13] And if it does not, is it far-fetched to wonder whether the call for reconciliation, no matter how sincerely expressed, will be interpreted by many Virginians as a demand that black citizens "get over it"?

By raising these concerns, I do not intend to belittle the Virginia Assembly or the expression of regret. Instead, I offer the resolution as an illustration of a paradox in contemporary political life: at the very moment when Americans appear willing, finally, to talk about slavery, claims about the ongoing challenges of racial injustice and their links to the slave past are rendered publicly unspeakable. If there is a new openness to acknowledging white supremacy, it seems, the price of acknowledgment is its banishment to a prior era. Worse, even as state legislatures and other institutions rush to express their regret for historic injustice, structures of redress that were put in place during the civil rights era are being dismantled. While historical markers and monuments give new public visibility to the slaves and their descendants, there is little enthusiasm for the work of eliminating, concretely, the imprint of the past on current social and political arrangements. The uneasy coexistence of regret and evasiveness, openness and closure, that characterizes the Virginia resolution thus provides an occasion for thinking more generally about Americans' collective failure to grapple with the life and afterlife of slavery.

This book attempts to come to terms with one dimension of that failure: political theorists' reluctance to treat race and racial injustice as fundamental to the study of modern democratic life. Where legislators must heed the demands of constituents and make compromises for the sake of political outcomes, political theorists (particularly those with tenure) inhabit a relatively protected sphere in which to think hard about the continuing effects of the massive displacement, exploitation, and slaughter that characterized the African slave trade, New World slavery, and modern colonial conquest. Nevertheless, our inquiry into "the ideals of liberty, justice, and democracy" has rendered many of us insensible to their violation. This insensibility reflects a general reluctance by political theorists to probe the conditions of injustice as distinct from and worthy of attention equal to the concept of justice.[14] But it also bespeaks a more specific evasion of questions of race and racial injustice. The nonpresence of these questions in academic conferences and colloquia, in courses on modern political thought, and in the vast production of books and journal articles is striking. It is also disabling. For our inattention to the slaves' perspectives on the promise of emancipation ("Where in our history can we hope to find visions of freedom untainted by slavery?")[15] and to the deep roots of sedimented forms of inequality distorts our conception of the political world. It reinforces a view of racial hierarchy as tangential rather than fundamental to the development of our most cherished political ideals.[16]

By treating race as a specialty topic or an artifact of the past, we inhibit our capacity to understand many of the most difficult challenges of contemporary political life. We fail, in other words, to face the worst. "Facing the worst," observes George Kateb, "is surely one of the purposes of reading the canon, just as it is, of course, of reading anything worthwhile in the whole field of the humanities."[17] Kateb's aim is to raise the question of whether the texts that typically make up graduate reading lists and that are the basis for survey courses in Western political thought are capable of assisting political theorists in comprehending "the scale of humanly inflicted suffering on human beings and the mentalities that permit the initiation and implementation of such deeds."[18] It is puzzling, in this light, that generations of students of political theory have sidestepped or minimized the "scale of humanly inflicted suffering" associated with modern slavery and colonial conquest. Perhaps the puzzle is solved when we consider how many of the great modern political thinkers wrote from positions of racial privilege; if they were not themselves involved in slavery or imperial projects, they were mostly insulated from their cruelties. If the standpoint of these thinkers explains their inattention to questions of race, then expanding the canon appears to be an apt way to proceed. And I would submit that political theory will remain impoverished to the extent that it fails to wrestle with the rich traditions of black political thought and with the work of feminist, queer, postcolonial, and other subaltern thinkers operating both within and outside the bounds of the discipline. Yet it is not clear that revising or enlarging the canon is sufficient to counter the power of conceptual frames and habits of thought that continue to push slavery and its legacies to the margins.[19] The flexibility with which democratic thinkers make note of racial injustice, only to bracket it or explain it away, indicates that political theory *as a practice* remains shadowed by an unowned past. Even if we embrace a conception of political theory as "an unapologetically mongrel sub-discipline,"[20] we may still avoid confronting our indebtedness to a tradition of thought that reinvented liberty and slavery simultaneously. To the extent that we do not scrutinize this mixed inheritance, we limit our capacity to see the contours of the present.[21] And we handicap efforts to construct a democratic theory that is itself broadly democratic.

One way to begin to grapple with these challenges is to consider the American democratic experiment through the writing of W. E. B. Du Bois. Between his birth in Great Barrington, Massachusetts, in 1868, and his death in Accra, Ghana, 95 years later, Du Bois undertook the work of several lifetimes. His vocations were multiple and intertwined, as he pursued the realization of a more democratic way of life through scholarship, writing, and activism.[22] Across the arc of a career that traversed the "nadir" of African American history, through renaissance and depression, war and cold war, and drew to a close as civil rights activism at home and anticolonial struggles abroad began to bear fruit, Du Bois strove to understand the meanings of freedom, equality, leadership, citizenship, and democracy with the slave trade, slavery, and colonial conquest always in sight. Although he appreciated the value of studying history for its own sake, Du Bois perceived the political importance of the way historical stories are told. Consigning the past to oblivion, he argued, goes hand in hand with consigning the relatively powerless to civic death. Thus, he dedicated himself to the presentation of a past that was not just known but creatively reworked to sustain a critique of the present. This book examines how his efforts to craft a usable past from unspeakable loss can inspire our efforts to conceive alternative, more democratic futures.

If theory is understood as a practice of seeing and articulating what is and can be seen, Du Bois's careers offer an illuminating example of how to *see* the living legacies of slavery.[23] As Sheldon Wolin reminds us, "the way in which [political] phenomena will be visualized depends in large measure on where the viewer 'stands.'"[24] As he notes, moreover, vision is itself a double term, referring both to an "objective" perception of the world and to the artistic or religious imagination.²⁵ Such doubleness is a hallmark of Du Bois's thought, which weds empirical scholarship and literary expression. Du Bois's most famous variation on the theme of twoness and vision, his meditation on "double-consciousness" in *The Souls of Black Folk* (1903), has inspired and divided scholars for generations. When Du Bois describes the experience of existing, simultaneously, as a Negro and an American, he limns a condition of profound estrangement. "A peculiar sensation . . . [a] sense of always looking at one's self through the eyes of others, of measuring one's soul by the tape of a world that looks on in amused contempt and pity," double-consciousness can paralyze, and it can incite rage. Even as African Americans contend with the alienating force of double-consciousness, however, they are also gifted with a form of "second-sight" through which it is possible to see "this American world" more clearly (*SBF*, 38). Du Bois thus indicates how the vantage of the marginal affords possibilities for recognizing injustice and distortion that may not be readily available to the privileged. It is only a possibility, though, as Thomas Holt remarks, "The insight of the oppressed is neither innate nor inherent; it must be worked for, struggled for."²⁶ The lasting power of Du Bois's hard-won double vision not only resides in the poignancy with which he recounts the experience of alienation and thwarted desire as an African American in Jim Crow America. It also lives on in Du Bois's capacity to convey the universality of his peculiar perspective and, simultaneously, the partiality of all perspectives.²⁷ He models a way to face the worst in the present by summoning and re-viewing the past.

Political Theory in the Shadow of a Deep Disappointment

Du Bois's work is rightly celebrated for the living force of its metaphors. Among them, double-consciousness, the Veil, the color-line—perhaps the best-known images of his best-loved book—remain vital elements of the lexicon upon which contemporary social critics and scholars draw in their efforts to describe and counter the effects of white supremacy. Another central image of *Souls*, the image of the shadow, offers a powerful way of evoking our political present in relationship to the slave past.²⁸ Writing at the turn of the twentieth century, Du Bois uses this language to limn the contours of a world in which long-awaited emancipation and new citizenship gave way to disenfranchisement, debt peonage, and de jure segregation, enforced by terror in the South and inaction in the North. "Whatever of good may have come in these years of change," Du Bois says of the lost promise of Reconstruction, "the shadow of a deep disappointment rests upon the Negro people" (*SBF*, 40). The vantage he offers is not that of the wholly disinterested outsider. "By aligning his voice with that of the suffering slave,"[29] elucidating shadows visible to black Americans but unnoted by most whites, Du Bois models a theoretical vision that aspires to see the world as it looks from the perspective of "the disremembered and unaccounted for."[30] When, for instance, he interprets the meaning of Sherman's march through Georgia, "which threw the new situation in shadowy relief," he counters a tendency to "see all significance in the grim front of the destroyer" or "in the bitter sufferers of the Lost Cause" (*SBF*, 48). Where others remember only the white characters in the national drama, Du Bois alerts readers to the former slaves who followed the Union ranks. Where others attempt to make sense of the chaos of war and its aftermath by leaving African Americans largely out of account, he unsettles the conventional relationship between margin and center in political discourse.

Shadows perform multiple functions in Du Bois's thought. Sometimes they signify the weight of present injustice or the bleakness of the future. His fondness for the biblical image of the "Shadow of Death" thus both intimates the burdens weighing on Alexander Crummell, the nineteenth-century intellectual leader and missionary (*SBF*, 169),[31] and, repeated five times, expresses Du Bois's torment at seeing his young son die when white medicine was unavailable to him (*SBF*, 161). Often the image of the shadow accompanies that of the Veil, Du Bois's metaphor for the division of black and white worlds in *Souls*.[32] For example, his retelling of his first apprehension of racial prejudice and its capacity to obstruct his aspirations begins with the observation that "I remember well when the shadow swept across me" (*SBF*, 38). And his fierce elegy for his son explicitly links the two, using "the shadow of the Veil" (*SBF*, 160) to describe the fate that awaits the African American child in Jim Crow America. Conveying not only darkness but also the unknown, Du Bois's "shadows" also signal the possibility of alternative ways of living. This is the effect of his description of "Ethiopia the Shadowy," which gestures toward the lost grandeur of an African past that Du Bois can only dimly perceive; this world is hidden from him by its physical distance and its temporal remoteness from the bloody experience of western modernity (*SBF*, 39). Further, when he recounts the fleeting experience of transcending racial barriers, of rising "above the veil," Du Bois conjures "a region of blue sky and great wandering shadows" (*SBF*, 38).

Most important, Du Bois's repeated return to the language of shadows provides a way of capturing the heavy presence of a past whose suppression enables present-day crimes to reign unseen and unchecked. "The shadow of fear" cloaked "the inner thoughts of the slaves and their relations one with another" (*SBF*, 190), Du Bois observes; and, confronted by the real prospect of "a second slavery" after Reconstruction, "the very soul of the toiling, sweating black man is darkened by the shadow of a vast despair" (*SBF*, 43, 42). This shadow hangs heavily not only because the past was so awful, but also because it represents a history of evasion, of stories that could not be told and that remain untold (*SBF*, 109).

Du Bois thus dedicates much of his career to seeing through these shadows and enabling others to see with him. He recognizes that social hierarchy and political exclusion in the United States reflect not only antiblack racism but also deep misunderstanding about the history of slavery and its aftereffects. Scathing in his criticism of efforts to deny or prettify the past, he fights for more accurate representations of slavery, Reconstruction, and their legacies. To the extent that this history remains buried, Du Bois insists, citizens will be ill-equipped to assess their present circumstances.

Contemporary scholars have made similar points about the connection between historical knowledge and political possibility. Despite evidence that African Americans lag behind whites in nearly every measure of well-being, white Americans nonetheless largely believe that a state of racial equality either has been achieved or will be relatively soon.[33] Such confidence inhibits the will to respond to the racial wealth gap, to the disproportionate presence of black and brown inmates among the nation's 2.3 million prisoners, to proliferating legal and technical mechanisms of disenfranchisement, to disturbing trends in residential and educational segregation and the disadvantages they engender. Without discussion of slavery's role in the constitution of the nation and of the forms of racial injustice that outlived abolition, citizens today are likely to interpret racial inequalities as a product of poor personal choices or cultural deficiency. "In the absence of widespread public familiarity with the causal background to contemporary racial problems," offers Thomas McCarthy, "the political-cultural resources for resisting racist reframings of them are seriously impoverished."[34] The absence of historical consciousness, thus, impedes the formation of new policies and social movements.[35] But will a corrected consciousness generate support for such policies and movements? Can historical knowledge reorient U.S. citizens to *see* racial injustice and *feel* called to act?

In his early career, Du Bois maintained that "the Negro problem was . . . a matter of systematic investigation and intelligent understanding." "The world was thinking wrong about race, because it did not know" (*DOD*, 58). Over time, however, Du Bois moved toward the view that overcoming ignorance was insufficient. Without abandoning his effort to illuminate dark corners of African American life and history, Du Bois acknowledges that more accurate pictures of the present and recollections of the past would not, on their own, promote democratic purposes. If amnesia is part of the problem, he reasons, memory is not a complete solution. His perspective reverberates in Saidiya Hartman's meditation on the relationship between historical knowledge and substantive change. "By seizing hold of the past, one illuminates the broken promises and violated contracts of the present,"[36] she notes; and yet, "bluntly put, is there a necessary relation between remembering and redress? Can the creation of a collective memory of past crimes insure the end of injustice?"[37] Proliferating expressions of regret for slavery and simultaneous opposition to efforts to acknowledge and respond to its ongoing effects indicate why enhanced historical consciousness is both necessary and far from sufficient.

Du Bois understands that this tension between remembering the past and acting on that remembrance is so intense because Americans have not simply forgotten the history of slavery.[38] Thus, he begins his inquiry into "the strange meaning of being black" through the excavation of things that have been "buried" (*SBF*, 34). And *Souls* brims with allusions, not only to shadows but also to burial, silences, veils, and ghosts. Americans' desire to suppress the memories of the constitutive injustices of their past is politically salient, Du Bois recognizes, because those memories threaten to disrupt the racial order of the present. He demonstrates the prophetic power of Tocqueville's observation that "memories of slavery disgrace the race, and race perpetuates memories of slavery."[39] The marks of slavery, in other words, cannot be effaced simply by declaring the slaves free. Further, the vehemence of protests against revisiting slavery reveals why this history is threatening: not only is it painful but also, if taken to heart, it still demands an adequate response.[40]

Much more is at stake, therefore, than better histories and additional facts. Writing in the aftermath of a national reconciliation that left black Americans bereft of the future they had been promised—and for which many had given their lives—Du Bois disallows the impulse to construct a narrative about American democracy that is free from slavery's taint. Against such narratives, he offers a counterhistory of the twinned development of modern democracy and racial slavery. Aiming to "educat[e] civic perceptions,"[41] his tools are words, his words pictorial and aural:

> Across the blue waters of the Atlantic two hundred and fifty ships a year hurried to the west, with their crowded, half-suffocated cargoes. And during all this time Martin Luther had lived and died, Calvin had preached, Raphael had painted and Shakespeare and Milton sung; and

yet for four hundred years the coasts of Africa and America were strewn with the dying and the dead, four hundred years the sharks followed the scurrying ships, four hundred years Ethiopia stretched forth her hands unto God. All this you know, all this you have read many a time. *I tell it again, lest you forget.*[42]

The reminder is crucial, Du Bois maintains, because the antimnemonic orientation of his fellow citizens undergirds their willingness to embrace or at least tolerate racial hierarchy. Yet even as his work is dedicated to educating his readers, taking them to worlds they do not see, he also recognizes that they must not only see further but see differently. For as long as race remains a marker of truths many whites would rather forget, black citizens will continue to be figured as a "problem." Pointedly, he ends *The Gift of Black Folk*, his 1924 tribute to the accomplishments of black women and men, with an admonishment to the reader: "You know. You know."[43]

Part of Du Bois's task, then, is to undo the effects of buried memories by crafting narratives in which African American lives are presented as worthy of attention. To that end, he reunites the slave's memory with that of the master and twines the stories of their descendants. Du Bois effects such a reunion in one of the most magnificent and harrowing passages in *Souls*—his portrait of two emblematic figures of the post-Civil War landscape:

> Amid it all, two figures ever stand to typify that day to coming ages,— the one, a gray-haired gentleman, whose fathers had quit themselves like men, whose sons lay in nameless graves; who bowed to the evil of slavery because its abolition threatened untold ill to all; who stood at last, in the evening of life, a blighted, ruined form, with hate in his eyes;—and the other, a form hovering dark and mother-like, her awful face black with the mists of centuries, had aforetime quailed at that white master's command, had bent in love over the cradles of his sons and daughters, and closed in death the sunken eyes of his wife,—aye, too, at his behest had laid herself low to his lust, and borne a tawny man-child to the world, only to see her dark boy's limbs scattered to the winds by midnight marauders riding after 'cursed Niggers.' These were the saddest sights of that woful day; and no man clasped the hands of these two passing figures of the present-past; but, hating, they went to their long home, and, hating, their children's children live to-day (*SBF*, 54–55).

These figures accomplish more for Du Bois than merely vivifying the enduring pain of the conflict. They reframe the national iconography, undercutting the romance still clinging to the Southern aristocracy with a reminder of the violence that sustained its gentility and replacing nostalgic images of the selfless slave with a portrait of human loss and longing. Through the tableau, furthermore, Du Bois reveals the possibilities for collective life in the aftermath of slavery, war, and abolition. He sketches, in a few swift strokes, something about the relations of power and powerlessness that history produced. If the intensity of the hatred dissipates with time and through the work of sympathy, he intimates, its traces still shape the present in unacknowledged ways.

This passage makes several political theoretical points. Du Bois's appreciation for the costs exacted from all sides of the conflict enables him to resist the urge to moralize, even as he hints at the appalling crimes committed by the "gray-haired gentleman."[44] Reminding his readers that these figures inhabited a world in which such crimes were part of the fabric of ordinary life, he offers an alternative to simplistic narratives of victims and villains, criminals and innocents. Further, the discussion of violent racial mixture discredits the idea of racial purity; and if Du Bois shows sympathy for the Southerner's surrender of his white sons to unmarked graves, he is unsparing in exposing the evasion through which that father leaves another son unmarked altogether and his "dark limbs . . . scattered to the winds." Du Bois's choice of the slave mother as one of the emblematic figures of the postwar scene, moreover, exposes a striking gap or silence in many contemporary discussions of the legacies of the slave past. As a number of commentators have noted, debates about apologies and/or reparations for slavery and Jim Crow have typically neglected the gendered character of American bondage.[45] By placing the bereft slave mother alongside the Confederate father, Du Bois intimates that any transformative reckoning with the past must contend with the sexual domination at the heart of slavery and the double burden borne by African American women. Such an approach has its risks, of course, for it has too often been used to reinforce the idea that African American women need patriarchal protection, and Du Bois's own record on this score is mixed. Nonetheless, his insistence on differentiating the kinds of power relations that slavery engendered provides at least a preliminary basis for what today we might call an intersectional approach to the politics of memory.[46] Finally, the passage reveals the depth of the obstacles to any meaningful reconciliation and intimates the dangers of premature declarations of reunion. Du Bois's observation that "no man clasped the hands of these two passing figures of the present-past" (SBF, 54) rebukes anyone who presumes that society can be healed without confronting the *living* legacies of its gravest crimes.[47]

Du Bois tells this story not only to condemn. His stark painting of the "present-past" captures the felt power of historical injuries, compounded over generations, and of their capacity to foreclose democratic futures. But Du Bois both counters the view that slavery has no bearing on the present and offers an alternative. Frank Kirkland describes this alternative as an intellectual tradition that "is ever contesting a conception of modernity in which the legacy of racial enslavement as a historical condition is dismissed and thereby thrown into oblivion."[48] To that end, Du Bois returns to the history of enslavement to reflect on his own political circumstances. His meditation on the Sorrow Songs, for example, shows how attunement to the culture of the slaves not only affirms African Americans' aesthetic contributions but also deepens readers' understanding of the concept of freedom. Likewise his redescription of the fugitives' role in the Civil War as a "General Strike" in *Black Reconstruction* both highlights the economic underpinnings of the war and Reconstruction and replaces a tradition of representing black subjects as will-less with a view of them as workers and political actors. Such a perspective shows that the backward look need not present an obstacle to politics in the present. Rather, it can provide a font for new forms of political expression and practice. For thinkers struggling with the inadequacies of a civil rights discourse that evades acknowledgment of the past, Du Bois's understanding of the slave past as a generative source and his effort to write himself out of "the shadow of a deep disappointment" offer badly needed guidance.[49]

While the danger of presentism haunts any appropriation of earlier thinkers to understand current concerns, looking only to contemporary sources or imprisoning earlier thinkers in their own contexts may intensify the sense that the resources for critical political theory are diminished or unavailable. According to Mark Reinhardt, "Powerful theories of the past instruct us by leading us out of the present. The most powerful of all, however, also lead us back to it. As they distance us from the positions offered in contemporary debates, they help us to scrutinize the very framework of agreement within which these debates take place. Their challenge to contemporary priorities begins from and, in the end, returns to questions that matter now."[50] Following Du Bois's lead through the layers of history, downward from segregation to slavery and then back again, enables us to scrutinize familiar modes of thinking and argument and raise questions when race is treated as a specialty subject or excluded altogether. Looking to Du Bois's struggles against the intertwined challenges of distortions of the past, on the one hand, and inaction against injustice in his own time, on the other, is particularly fruitful at a political moment that has been described as "post-civil rights," "post-identity politics," and, simply, "dark times."

That Americans inhabit a "post-civil rights" era seems obvious. Positively, it reflects the ways that the achievements of the civil rights movement have altered the social and political landscape. Legal segregation and disenfranchisement have been officially dismantled, and American citizens, by and large, appear to embrace the principle of racial equality. When Barack Obama presides at the White House, Rosa Parks is mourned as a national heroine, and political figures on both the right and the left vie for title to the legacy of Martin Luther King, Jr., it seems clear that the United States has moved well beyond a horizon about which Du Bois could only dream. But the United States also inhabits a post-civil rights era in a second and too often disregarded sense: it is a period marked by a retreat from racial justice as a political priority. Among the most pointed examples of "how far we have come" is Americans' dwindling outrage over Hurricane Katrina and unwillingness to regard it as evidence of the persistent linkage of race, poverty, and powerlessness.[51] Even as legislatures express their regret for slavery, they have largely failed to develop policies that attack racial disparities in voting rights, education, employment, housing, incarceration, health, and a long list of other indicators of well-being. When such efforts have been implemented, furthermore, many have found an inhospitable reception in the courts.

Du Bois inhabited another post-civil rights era. His early life coincided with the short interval between the passage of the Fourteenth Amendment and the Supreme Court admonition that it was time for black citizens to "ceas[e] to be the special favorite of the laws."[52] His inquiry into the undoing of the achievements that culminated in the abolition of slavery and the brief flourishing of multiracial democracy thus offers a useful vantage from which to consider our own, quite different and yet not wholly unprecedented, situation. Du Bois's account of the double-edged character of the Thirteenth, Fourteenth, and Fifteenth amendments anticipates in illuminating ways later limitations of formal equality as a mechanism for dismantling racialized structures of power. Although he dedicated much of his life to the realization of the guarantees embodied in the Constitution, Du Bois perceived how these same guarantees enabled a kind of public forgetfulness about slavery and fed Southern fury against the former slaves. When Du Bois writes that "the War Amendments made the Negro problems of to-day" (*SBF*, 45), therefore, he exposes the paradox of the constitutional promise of rights that apply regardless of "race, color, or previous condition of servitude." Understanding that white Americans, north and south, wanted most of all to be done with the conflict and were willing to sacrifice African American interests to do so, Du Bois shows how the passage of the amendments became a vehicle for denying that there was a conflict, or at least that it had centrally concerned slavery.

These observations help us to make sense of more recent mnemonic politics. Just as slaves and black abolitionists fought hard for the measures that affirmed their citizenship after the Civil War, many of their descendants sacrificed everything to achieve the guarantees embodied in the Civil Rights Act of 1964 and the Voting Rights Act of 1965. Like other vulnerable populations, furthermore, they do not have the luxury of dispensing with the language of formal equality in which those guarantees are framed. At the same time, however, the promise enshrined in those laws has come to be interpreted in ways that allow white Americans to disown the past and its implications for the present, thereby compounding the disadvantages faced by the very people the laws were passed to protect.[53] The tenuous survival of affirmative action in higher education—and its disconnection from explicit reference to historic injustice—provides just one example of the growing distance between a rhetoric of "civil rights" and the commitment to racial justice.

A second, and related constellation of challenges confronting democratic theorists is the vexed status of "identity politics." The modern civil rights movement not only bequeathed a legacy of legislative measures and court decisions designed to undo the effects of bondage, but it also inspired the broad proliferation of social movements organized to pursue redress for identity-based injustices. The struggles of feminists, the disabled, lesbians and gays, Latino/a, Native American, and Asian American activists, and other groups indicate the lasting power of a model of politics in which historical oppression provides a basis for mobilizing group members and frames political demands. Since the late twentieth century, however, intellectuals allied with these movements have questioned the wisdom of such an approach. To what extent, they ask, does a focus on identity-based oppression depend upon and perpetuate problematic conceptions of the group? Does a preoccupation with past injuries disable the critique of unjust structures of power and the articulation of emancipatory aspirations? Have identity-based movements fragmented progressives into rival factions? Do they divide the world too neatly into victims and perpetrators?

Du Bois's work does not provide clear answers. Indeed, his understanding of identity categories, and race in particular, has generated intense scholarly disagreement. Nevertheless, I highlight those aspects of his thought that assist contemporary theorists in getting beyond the impasse produced by debates about identity politics. Against concerns that focusing on the power of identity categories risks treating them as fixed or static, I consider those dimensions of Du Bois's writings that enable contemporary readers to approach identity as a *question* to be explored rather than a foregone conclusion. That racial categories have concrete effects in the world is not subject to dispute in Du Bois's work;

but the precise nature of those categories, their origins and histories, remains open to investigation, reflection, and amendment over the course of his career.[54] Against worries that emphasizing any single identity category entails stifling others or overlooking their intersections, I turn to places in Du Bois's work where he explicitly contends with the tangled relationships of race and class and gender. Indeed, although it is too often forgotten, he demonstrates why attending to the legacies of slavery is necessarily an intersectional enterprise. Slavery was never *only* a "racial" institution; looking for its contemporary traces requires rethinking the constitution of American manhood and womanhood and addressing the raced character of class divisions.

Du Bois also parries the concern that a fixation on inherited forms of injury is politically infertile insofar as it distracts from present-day wrongs or the development of alternative futures.[55] As the discussion of his tableau of the "present-past" indicates, Du Bois's attention to the living presence of the past is not the same as living in or for the past. His reworking of received historical narratives, furthermore, reminds us that the constitution of the past is itself a political question. When, for instance, Du Bois observes that "the silently growing assumption of this age is that the probation of races is past, and that the backward races of today are of proven inefficiency and not worth the saving" (*SBF*, 192), he both challenges the racial contempt of social Darwinism and calls into question the definition of time upon which such contempt is grounded.[56] Du Bois's scathing indictment of his contemporaries and predecessors who rushed to locate slavery as "the past" just as neo-slavery was on the rise warns against a similar impulse to assert the inauguration of a "postracial" era and unsettles the view that appeals for redress of racial injustice are exclusively backward-looking.

Entwined with the theoretical and political difficulties posed by debates about the viability of civil rights and identity politics is a more general sense of foreboding about the prospects for democracy in the twenty-first century. That we live in "dark times" has become a common refrain among political theorists, particularly those on the left.[57] The close of the Cold War era not only discredited socialist dreams but also raised uneasy questions about the apparent victory of liberal democracy over competing forms of political life. Faith in the progressive realization of democratic ideals appears naive, unpersuasive in the face of new restrictions on civil liberties, waning political participation, increased surveillance, yawning inequalities, rising militancy around the world, and unchecked environmental crises. And partisan division further constricts political possibilities by "foreclosing . . . the common ground upon which we can listen and learn."[58] "We are disoriented," writes Wendy Brown, "by the literal loss of trajectory following the collapse of historical metanarratives in a present that appears fraught with injustice and misery and not only apocalyptic danger. It has become a commonplace to describe our time as pounded by undemocratic historical forces yet lacking a *forward* movement. This makes the weight of the present very heavy: all mass, no velocity."[59] Although we inhabit a political time well beyond any horizon Du Bois could see, it is nonetheless precisely because so much of his thought dwells in the space between the moment of emancipation and the withholding of freedom that followed, and because he grapples with the ways in which inherited terms of political critique and engagement proved insufficient to meet the challenges of his time, that they speak with such force to the contemporary predicament. Du Bois's early work reflects a period when faith in historical progress proved impotent in the face of the violent and racially regressive turn of events that defined the post-Reconstruction era.[60] His later work bespeaks a new confidence, particularly as he finds in Marx a theoretical system through which to wed historical consciousness to an expansive, international conception of social justice. Nonetheless, Du Bois remains ever mindful of the experience of the "nadir" of African American history, when the project of emancipation from slavery was at a dead end, but the work of freeing the former slaves and their descendants remained unfinished.

He also reminds readers that the closures of today's dark times, while novel in many respects, may yet be illuminated through attention to the evasions that supported an earlier turn from halting steps in the direction of multiracial democracy back toward racial domination. His writings may be appropriated not only to allow us to "see in the dark" but to assist us in "seeing the darkness."[61] Anne Norton's distinction helpfully captures the double task of political theory. On the one hand, the theorist has an obligation to bring to light what is hidden in the shadows, behind the Veil, as Du Bois does in his lifelong study of African American life. On the other hand, theoretical work entails the revelation of taken-for-granted ways of being and organizing our collective lives. Seeing the darkness, Du Bois demonstrates, requires more than demands for better knowledge and treatment of the subjugated, more than arguments for the extension of rights that have been denied. It entails the work of discerning the historical constitution and present pervasiveness of racial power and of reorienting our thinking accordingly.

Fugitive Pieces

Du Bois wrote prolifically on a broad array of subjects for most of his 95 years, and this book does not attempt to provide a comprehensive or summary statement of his political thought. Instead, I offer a series of interlocking essays, each of which takes up some aspect of the relationship between the heritage of racial slavery and contemporary injustice and, through a close reading of one or more texts, asks how Du Bois's work shifts our understanding of the present and opens new possibilities for the future. In doing so, I take inspiration from Du Bois's own description of the chapters that comprise *The Souls of Black Folk* as a collection of "fugitive pieces" (*DOD*, 80). Certainly, the phrase "fugitive pieces" belies the intentional character of Du Bois's masterpiece. *Souls* is not a random assemblage of writings but, as Robert Gooding-Williams observes, "a densely figurative and carefully plotted composition."[62] It is nonetheless possible and useful, I think, to adopt the spirit of Du Bois's claim as a way of characterizing an approach to some of the most vexed questions of political life. For even as Du Bois hones his essays into exquisite compositions in their own right and deliberately fits them together into a powerful whole, he emphasizes the transitory power of the images he creates and the difficulty for the reader of grasping truths that sometimes only resonate faintly as echoes. Even as he makes bold pronouncements ("The problem of the twentieth century is the problem of the colorline."), he allows that what he has to offer are "essays and sketches," and that these offerings may themselves be "in vague, uncertain outline" (*SBF*, 34).

It is telling that Du Bois so frequently reaches for the language of the essay, both as noun and verb, to describe his work. Strikingly, two of his most substantial texts—*Black Reconstruction* (1935) and *Dusk of Dawn* (1940)—are advertised as essays "toward" their subjects: the history of black participation in the effort to reconstruct American democracy, on the one hand, and "an autobiography of a race concept," on the other.[63] Du Bois's literary and intellectual mobility, his willingness to work across and through multiple genres indicates an experimental approach to the task of reaching and moving his readers. He works on them not only through the substance of his arguments and the evidence he marshals in their support but also through the content of their form. When he uses "essay" as a verb, moreover, Du Bois simultaneously conveys an understanding of his work as a process of trial or testing, an experimental approach to the pursuit of truth, and reveals the fraught conditions under which he pursues it. Whether groping for an adequate response to the epidemic of lynchings and loss of his own son at the turn of the twentieth century or, some 50 years later, standing trial for subverting U.S. interests and confronting his abandonment by the black middle class whose cause he had championed, Du Bois's life and work exemplify a process of trial and revision.

Du Bois's identification of the "fugitive" character of the writings gathered together in *Souls* is felicitous in still another sense for democratic thinking.

Not only does it intimate the difficulty of capturing in final, settled form the complex claims that Du Bois advances, but it also conveys the fleeting character of democracy itself. Wolin's observation that "democracy . . . seems destined to be a moment rather than a form" crystallizes a widespread sense of the fugitivity of those instances in which the people can actually be said to rule.[64] This way of understanding democratic life, not as an end to be accomplished once and for all but as an ongoing effort whose triumphs are always shadowed by losses and whose successes may prove to be their own undoing corresponds with Du Bois's inquiry into the experiences of African Americans. He studies the activities of black subjects and praises their staggering achievements, but he also notes the unanticipated costs of those achievements. He traces the routes by which Reconstruction gave way to Jim Crow and records the cruel reversals in which vibrant signs of intellectual promise, like that of a girl he teaches in rural Tennessee, are snuffed out by heartbreak and early death. Although Du Bois evinces a sincere conviction in the possibility of progress, that conviction is colored by his apprehension that the advancement of human capacities is not steady and inexorable but halting and "necessarily ugly" (*SBF*, 79).

The language of the "fugitive" not only captures something about the provisional character of any achievement of democracy and its attendant risks, but it also gestures toward a specific racial history. To use this language only to connote evanescence is to miss something crucial in the U.S. context. Indeed, to speak of the fugitive in the aftermath of slavery is to resuscitate the memory of those men and women whose illegality was written into a constitutional provision for the return across state lines of any of "Person held to Service or Labour," whose status was reinforced and made all the more perilous by the Fugitive Slave Act, and whose descendants were rendered outlaws when they dared to trespass against racial norms. For Du Bois, furthermore, the figure of the fugitive stands at the nexus that joins the slave past to a democratic future. "Fugitive slaves . . . spelled the doom of slavery" (*BR*, 13): their presence undercut the innocence of the antebellum North, posed a problem for Lincoln as he searched for a compromise that would hold the union together, and offered a solution, pointing the way toward emancipation and victory. Du Bois's "fugitive pieces" are thus grounded in historical experiences of bondage and flight. They provide an "opening for thought" insofar as they trouble the line between slave and free.[65] Du Bois, writing from the shadows of slavery, emphasizes the nameless and voiceless actors who make U.S. history, recognizes the attributes of citizenship in their deeds, and insists on conducting himself as a citizen despite widespread disavowal of his rights, giving pride of place to the fugitive in American public life. In this way, he translates into political expression what Stephen Best and Saidiya Hartman characterize as "black noise": "the kinds of political aspirations that are inaudible and illegible within the prevailing formulas of political rationality."[66]

The essays that follow draw on the figure of the fugitive in all of these senses. But they are also informed by the concept of pieces, elements of a complex whole that have been arranged in a particular way for particular effect. My approach to Du Bois thus highlights three interconnected themes. The first is the critical force of Du Bois's idea of a present-past. I trace Du Bois's efforts both to bring to life suppressed dimensions of American slavery and Reconstruction and to reveal how that history and its suppression exert living power. The second theme is his exploration of black exemplarity. Working through examples of African American lives, Du Bois rewrites the anomalies of slavery and Jim Crow segregation as central features of modern democracy. This is not to say that he presents African Americans, uncritically, as paragons, but that he asks how our understanding of democratic life is altered when black experiences are taken to be representative of democratic possibility. The third theme is the global reach of Du Bois's political imagination. Recently, theorists have taken note of the insufficiency of the nation-state as a framework for political inquiry; yet Du Bois demonstrates why this insufficiency is not new. To focus on modern slavery, he shows, is to engage political questions that redefine the boundaries of the political imagination.

All three themes are woven through the book, but I emphasize the first theme in chapters 2 and 3, the second in chapters 4 and 5, and the third in chapter 6. Chapters 2 and 3 thus inquire into the political theoretical lessons of Du Bois's rewriting of history. Chapter 2 looks to Du Bois's efforts to correct distorted understandings of Reconstruction, by focusing on African Americans' role in abolition and by redefining the postwar era as the nation's only genuine experiment in democracy. Examining the connections he draws between historical consciousness and the disappointments of the post-Reconstruction period, I argue, enlarges our understanding of the disappointments that followed the civil rights era or "second reconstruction." Although Du Bois does not expressly advocate reparations for the former slaves and their descendants, I turn to *The Souls of Black Folk* and *Black Reconstruction* to suggest the possibilities opened up by a shift from a political language of formal equality, which is premised on the erasure of the past, to a language that affirms and refigures the past as a vehicle for social change. And I ask how reparations might constitute such a language. The third chapter considers the political implications of Du Bois's 1909 recasting of John

Brown's life story. Written at a moment when antiblack violence was actively abetted or at least unanswered by white political leaders, *John Brown* reveals how the disavowal of the violence of the past underwrites current practices of racialized brutality and explores what it would mean to come to terms with the idea that "John Brown was right." Although the biography vindicates Brown and his campaign, I contend, it also unsettles Brown's conception of American mission and models a tragic form of historical memory that ought to inform our own reflections on race and violence in an age of terror.

Chapters 4 and 5 investigate interconnections between Du Bois's treatment of the legacies of slavery and his treatment of African American exemplarity and ask how they press on contemporary conceptions of democratic selfhood and citizenship. Without denying the importance or the undemocratic implications of Du Bois's arguments on behalf of elite racial leadership, these chapters call attention to other facets of his reflections on racial representation and the political work of the example. Chapter 4 addresses Du Bois's inquiry into his own exemplarity, his status as both an exemplar or "exception" and an example of "the Problem." I offer an interpretation of *Dusk of Dawn*, Du Bois's 1940 autobiographical exploration of his life and the life of the "race concept," as a counterpoint to William Connolly's account of identity and difference. Read together, Du Bois and Connolly demonstrate how identity categories shape democratic life; but Du Bois takes a further step, discerning those places in Connolly's work where race is elided and gesturing toward an alternative model of self-fashioning in a racially divided society. Chapter 5 focuses on the 1920 essay "The Damnation of Women," Du Bois's collective biography of African American women. Despite the masculinism that defines much of his writing, and the tensions that qualify even his strongest arguments on behalf of gender equality, this essay demands that readers grapple with the meaning of "womanhood" and "citizenship" through the lens of black women's history. Further, I argue, it reorients feminist citizenship theory in the United States by demonstrating the need to go beyond reckoning with race to confront the lingering shadows of slavery.

The sixth chapter considers how the worldly orientation of Du Bois's political thought might inform political theory as it turns toward the global. My central text in this case is an unlikely one. While scholars increasingly appreciate the extent of Du Bois's transnational activism and writing in the mid-twentieth century, this chapter concentrates on *The Suppression of the African Slave-Trade the United States of America, 1638–1870* (1896). I argue that Du Bois's first book, although thoroughly American, nonetheless demonstrates the impossibility of constructing a theory of democracy that restricts its concern within U.S. boundaries. Using a contrast between "black world" and "white nation," I suggest how a close reading of *Suppression* in conjunction with Martha Nussbaum's *For Love of Country* reveals the unacknowledged racial politics of recent appeals to cosmopolitanism, on the one hand, and civic nationalism, on the other.

It is a mistake to presume that the meanings of race and racism are constant across time or that the challenges Du Bois confronted persist unchanged. Nevertheless, we bear a responsibility to investigate those meanings and the part they play in shaping public life today. To do so with Du Bois's guidance is not to ask, "What would Du Bois say?" Although there is a canon-building dimension to this project insofar as it urges that Du Bois's work be more widely read, taught, and debated by political theorists, I quarrel with many of his views even as I profit from the living value of his insight. In this regard, I follow Toni Morrison's admonition that "there must be a way to enhance canon readings without enshrining them."[67] This means approaching Du Bois's work critically and not allowing his voice to mute others.[68] It means asking how Du Bois's words are timely without rushing to declare them timeless and pondering how our sense of democratic possibility is altered and enlarged through engagement with his double vision.

Neither is my purpose only to inquire, "What did Du Bois say?" While I take care to honor the letter and the spirit of Du Bois's writings, my objective is not simply to excavate his ideas, and I do not provide a genealogy of the political circumstances and intellectual influences that shape them.[69] Du Bois's corpus deserves far greater systematic attention than it has yet received from political theorists. A growing body of very fine work offers careful explications of Du Bois's writings, and many of these studies provide detailed accounts of his political and intellectual milieu and take up the intricate questions of how to characterize his thought—as pragmatist or idealist, integrationist or nationalist, elitist or radically democratic. I am profoundly indebted to these projects, but my end is somewhat different. Through the essays that follow, I hope to suggest why and how revisiting Du Bois's work makes a particular kind of political critique possible in the present. I ask how his tireless effort to offer a critical perspective on his own times—especially at their darkest—might shed light on our aspirations to do the same today.

TWO | Unreconstructed Democracy and the Claim of Reparations

The vestiges of slavery are ever before African Americans.

—Virginia Senate Joint Resolution No.332

Reconstruction in Dark Times

When Du Bois's essay on the achievements and shortcomings of the Freedmen's Bureau appeared as "Of the Dawn of Freedom" in *The Souls of Black Folk* in 1903, African American liberation dreams had been dispelled by grim reality.[1] Disenfranchisement, debt peonage, segregation, and subjection to widespread violence and intimidation marked what Rayford Logan calls "the nadir" of African American experience.[2] When Du Bois published *Black Reconstruction in America* 32 years later, his narrative took shape against the backdrop of a Great Depression whose burdens fell heaviest on people of color, many among them the descendants of slaves.[3] Looking backward from the vantage of the injustices of the present, Du Bois understood that prevailing historical accounts of Reconstruction, which painted the post-war experiment in black political participation as a disaster and blamed it for widespread corruption and fiscal mismanagement (*BR*, 711–29), needed to be challenged. Not only were these accounts factually wrong, but the persistence of degraded images of black citizenship in history books and the public imagination exposed Du Bois and his contemporaries to new forms of exploitation, exclusion, and brutality.[4] Today, historians credit Du Bois with changing the way that the story of Reconstruction is told. But what follows, politically, from this development? By tracing how Du Bois reconstructs the "splendid failure of Reconstruction," this chapter sketches an answer. I show how Du Bois's analysis remains vital for theorists aiming to grasp and respond to the disappointments that succeeded the triumphs of the civil rights era or "second Reconstruction."

Du Bois's interpretation of the meaning of Reconstruction as it looked from his own "post-civil rights" era offers both a correction and a warning that history not be repeated. Yet it does more than caution against amnesia or insist that his readers get the facts right. By inquiring into the missed opportunities of the past, Du Bois offers a critique of the present and reflects more generally on the requirements of multiracial democracy. As Charles Lemert observes, in writing *Black Reconstruction*, "Du Bois was, in effect, writing out of his time back into the displaced time of the Reconstruction in American history that was, for the American Negro, a deferral of Black hopes that turned out to be a deferral of national hopes, even global ones."[5] This is not simple presentism. He is less interested in passing judgment on previous generations than in recuperating the creative promise held out by black citizens' brief moment of partnership in democracy's reconstruction.

A crucial element of Du Bois's argument involves defamiliarizing familiar terms that were at the heart of the struggle over slavery and black citizenship. In his reflection on the valence of freedom, for instance, he makes visible the conflicting ways in which the events of those tumultuous years were seen and understood. Thus, Du Bois notes that "to the Negro 'Freedom' was God; to the poor white 'Freedom' was nothing—he had more than he had use for; to the planter 'Freedom' for the poor was laziness and for the rich, control of the poor worker; for the Northern business man 'Freedom' was opportunity to get rich" (*BR*, 347).[6] By resurrecting the contending visions and voices of the past, furthermore, Du Bois also enlarges the possibilities for democratic theory. If theory, as Hayden White contends, "asks us to consider what, from a specific perspective, will be permitted to count as a fact, the truth, rationality, morality, and so forth,"[7] then Du Bois's efforts to recast the history of Reconstruction also recast the theoretical lessons to be drawn from the period.

When Du Bois shows how democratic values were spoken "in different and unknown tongues" (*BR*, 347), he pays particular attention to those citizens who were systematically unheard from, the invisible actors at the center of the conflict over slavery and Reconstruction. In doing so, his work resonates with Judith Shklar's suggestion that "one way to undertake a historically rich inquiry into American citizenship is . . . to investigate what citizenship has meant to those women and men who have been denied all or some of its attributes, and who ardently wanted to be full citizens."[8] As David Blight remarks, Du Bois was a "self-conscious creator of black counter-memory";[9] "in a combination of descriptive history and theatrical pageantry, he created a new framework in which the plight of the freedpeople might be seen."[10] Consider, for example, his description of the meaning of freedom as it might have appeared from the vantage of an ex-slave:

> Free! The most piteous thing amid all the black ruin of war-time, amid the broken fortunes of the masters, the blighted hopes of mothers and maidens, and the fall of an empire,—the most piteous thing amid all this was the black freedman who threw down his hoe because the world called him free. What did such a mockery of freedom mean? Not a cent of money, not an inch of land, not a mouthful of victuals,— not even ownership of the rags on his back. Free! (*SBF*, 123)

As the passage suggests, Du Bois's preoccupation with the condition of former slaves does not indicate a narrowness of perspective. Just as the tableau of the two passing figures of the present-past dramatizes losses experienced on both sides of the Civil War, his attention here to "the broken fortunes of the masters" and "the blighted hopes of mothers and maidens" reveals an appreciation for the wider costs of American failures toward the former slaves. He gives pride of place to the freedmen and women, to be sure, but he links their fate to the prospects for democracy more generally. In this vein, Du Bois notes in a 1915 editorial in *The Crisis* that the "fiction of failure" that represents Reconstruction (and the participation of African Americans in their own government) as the low point in American democracy also provides a basis for discrediting suggestions about extending the vote to women and empowering immigrants.[11] Further, as I will discuss in more detail in chapter 6, his vision is never confined to the United States; he connects the plight of the former slaves and the distortion of their history to the brutalization and exploitation of nonwhite workers across the globe (*BR*, 728). In other words, Du Bois insists that much can be learned about the prospects for *all* citizens by understanding the lived meaning of democratic principles from the vantage of society's most vulnerable members and acknowledging the *general* benefits that follow from policies that aim to improve the circumstances of particular groups.

Although Reconstruction and its aftermath offer a touchstone for Du Bois's writing throughout his career, I focus on *The Souls of Black Folk* and *Black Reconstruction in America*.[12] Reading these texts together, I contend, reveals the chasm between the act of declaring the slaves to be free by law and reconstructing American democracy. In both texts, Du Bois draws out connections between the nation's unwillingness to confront the centrality of slavery to the Civil War and its avoidance of the question of was owed to the women and men who had been enslaved. Showing how the mnemonic orientation of his fellow citizens was directly implicated in the development of new forms of racial subjugation, Du Bois's explorations of the "present-past" illuminate three dimensions of this reticence: the absence of serious discussion about the kinds of economic reconstruction that would have ensured the former slaves their freedom; the reluctance to acknowledge what Du Bois calls the "gifts" of African Americans, their contributions to the making of the United States; and the fundamental failure to come to terms with the denial of the slaves' humanity "at the heart of slavery."[13] Together, these arguments indicate the limitations of legal abolition. They go beyond vivifying the cruel realities that defined the "dawn of freedom," prompting readers to consider the kinds of provisions that would have been necessary to bring genuine "abolition democracy" into being.[14] And they intimate the possibilities opened up by a shift from a political language of formal equality, which is premised on the erasure of the past, to a language that affirms and refigures the past as a vehicle for social change. In this chapter, I explore how reparations arguments could constitute such a language.[15]

I want to be clear that my aim is not to understate the differences between Reconstruction and the unfinished business of the civil rights revolution in the twentieth century. The years that followed Reconstruction witnessed the development of new forms of political, social, and economic oppression that, together with the organized terror of such groups as the Ku Klux Klan and the widespread practice of lynching, instituted the regime of neoslavery that prevailed in the South until the civil rights movement challenged it in the mid-twentieth century. Further, the distorted understanding of Reconstruction against which Du Bois wrote has been supplanted in professional historical circles by an understanding much closer to—and influenced by—his own.[16] In contrast to Reconstruction, the civil rights movement is viewed as a highpoint in U.S. history, and the visibility of powerful African Americans, the paeans to racial equality offered up by political leaders, and the broad euphoria that greeted the inauguration of the first African American president indicate how much has changed. Despite the obvious differences between the two reconstructions and their aftermaths, however, telling similarities remain. Although I can provide only a compressed discussion here, let me call particular attention to the ways both reconstructions were marked by inadequate commitment to a fundamental economic restructuring that might counteract generations of exploitation and discrimination, by a failure to acknowledge the crucial role of African Americans in securing their own freedom and that of their fellow citizens, and by a willingness to privilege the interests and feelings of whites over the implementation of black citizens' constitutionally guaranteed rights.[17] In both eras, moreover, the passage of civil rights legislation was followed by a backlash—often couched in the rhetoric of self-help—against attempts to give concrete substance to legal promises. Significantly, studies have shown that although white Americans are supportive of the principles of racial justice in a way that they were not during the Jim Crow era, they remain resistant to policies that might realize those principles.[18] Thus, one might reasonably conclude that the "carelessness" Du Bois discerns at the turn of the twentieth century persists a century later.

Righting Reconstruction History

Animating Du Bois's passion for retelling the story of Reconstruction is his assessment of that period as Americans' first genuine experiment in democracy. The years that followed the Civil War witnessed not only the passage of the Thirteenth, Fourteenth, and Fifteenth amendments but also the flowering of black political participation and the writing of more democratic state constitutions across the South. In light of these accomplishments, the susceptibility of Reconstruction history to distortion and glaring omission suggests to Du Bois a deeper reluctance to admit the capacity of African Americans to inhabit the mantle of citizenship. Thus, the subtitle of *Black Reconstruction* promises to correct a crucial absence from the historical record: "a history of the part which black folk played in the attempt to reconstruct democracy in America."[19] Although he recognizes that his study will inevitably reopen wounds that have barely healed, Du Bois insists that nothing is more dangerous to democracy than a history that merely flatters. By straining "to paint the South as a martyr to inescapable fate" and "to make the North the magnanimous emancipator," accepted accounts of Reconstruction prevent honest evaluation (*BR*, 723). *Souls* and *Black Reconstruction* propose by contrast to restore the memory of African Americans' role in the undoing of their bondage and of the nation's unwillingness to part entirely with the vestiges of slavery that its commitment to democracy made untenable.

Both texts make plain the boundedness of most white Americans' commitment to the emancipation of African Americans or their inclusion as equal partners in the polity. Racial slavery was the underlying cause of the Civil War, Du Bois contends, but abolition was not part of the North's original plan. Tracing attempts by the Union Army to deal with the thousands of fugitives who flooded their camps, he notes that the slaves were treated as "contraband" or returned to their masters before being recognized as "a military resource" by the Northern army (*SBF*, 46; see also *BR*, ch. 4–5). He echoes the words uttered by Frederick Douglass in 1865 to capture the deeper meaning of the conflict: "The Civil War was begun 'in the interests of slavery on both sides. The South was fighting to take slavery out of the Union, and the North fighting to keep it in the Union; the South fighting to get it beyond the limits of the United States Constitution, and the North fighting for the old guarantees;—both despising the Negro, both insulting the Negro'" (*BR*, 61). By this account, the freedom of black Americans was unintended. It was "the price of the disaster of war," according to Du Bois, and the program of reconstruction was disabled from the start (*BR*, 83).

Consequently, the end of the Civil War abandoned the four million former slaves to a nether region between freedom and the deeper hell of slavery. To tell the story of this in-between state, Du Bois marshals an enormous amount of historical and sociological evidence. He captures the challenges posed by the heritage of racial slavery and the difficulty of reconstructing American democracy with particular poignancy, however, when he distills the significance of a mass of data into a single, vivid image. Most effectively realized in *Souls*, this device reveals Du Bois's sensitivity to the complex claims that the past makes on the present and indicates the limitations of formal equality and the legal promise of freedom as a source of redress or a guarantor of future change. His stark portrayal of the "two passing figures of the present-past" provides just one example of Du Bois's deftness in limning the condition of American democracy as it entered Reconstruction. In his evocation of the violent intertwining of black and white, of past generations and future hopes, he indicates the depth and force of the obstacles preventing black Americans from escaping the limbo between slavery and citizenship.

Despite his understanding of these obstacles, Du Bois cautions that there are only two alternatives: "Either extermination root and branch, or absolute equality. There can be no compromise" (*BR*, 703).[20] What would this "absolute equality" require? In what ways did Reconstruction promise that it could be realized, and how was that promise retracted? To respond, I highlight three dimensions of Du Bois's work on the period: his argument about the relationship between economic reconstruction and democratic ideals, his delineation of the contributions of black Americans to the nation, and his insistence that a denial of black humanity is at the root of the failure either to endorse the first of these lines of argument or to recognize the second.

Treating the economic claims of *Souls* and *Black Reconstruction* together requires some caution, to be sure, for the later book is indebted to Du Bois's study of Marx in a way that the earlier one is not. Where *Souls* criticizes the self-help philosophy of Booker T. Washington and blames the nation's abandonment of political and spiritual ideals on the ascendant materialism of the Gilded Age, *Black Reconstruction* offers a full-blown analysis of the role of industrial capitalism in undoing Reconstruction.[21] Still, the germ of many of the central ideas of the later book can be found embedded in the argument of its predecessor. In both texts, the assessment of the economic dimension of Reconstruction's promise and shortcomings is informed by twin convictions: that democracy must be grounded in an economically self-sustaining citizenry and that, through their labor on the land and in the army, the former slaves had more than earned the resources necessary for their independence.

The conception of democracy that animates both texts is characterized by the absence of gross inequality or the dependency that accompanies it.[22] Democratic citizenship, for Du Bois, entails at least a basic education and the economic wherewithal to live a relatively comfortable life free from unearned debt. It encourages mutual cooperation among citizens, inculcates self-respect, and rewards such virtues as thrift and responsibility. Political institutions are served as well when economic self-sufficiency is combined with education and suffrage, Du Bois argues. Tracing the accomplishments of the Reconstruction legislatures, he shows how the entire region benefitted from the inclusion of new voices in governmental deliberation and the challenge this inclusiveness posed to the planters' oligarchical control. Although connecting economic independence and citizenship is certainly not unique to Du Bois, what is distinctive is his examination of these values in the context of Reconstruction. Thus he presents the Bureau of Refugees, Freedmen, and Abandoned Lands, or Freedmen's Bureau, as an agent of large-scale social change. With responsibilities that included the establishment of schools in the postwar South, the administration of justice, and the dispersal of abandoned lands, the Freedmen's Bureau represents for Du Bois an institution that held out the promise of a lasting independence from the domination of the planters for poor Southerners, black and white. "The Freedmen's Bureau was the most extraordinary and far-reaching institution of social uplift that America has ever attempted," Du Bois insists. "It had to do, not simply with emancipated slaves and poor whites, but also with the property of Southern planters. It was a government guardianship for the relief and guidance of white and black labor from a feudal agrarianism to modern farming and industry" (*BR*, 219).[23] Underfunded and lasting only seven years (from 1865 until 1872, with no budget after 1870), the Freedmen's Bureau was largely unable to accomplish its objectives. Things might have been otherwise, Du Bois advises. A bureau designed to last for decades and to oversee "a careful distribution of land and capital and a system of education for the children" might have translated the promise of emancipation into genuinely equal citizenship.[24] Such a bureau, moreover, might have helped to forestall the penury Du Bois encountered as a young teacher in Tennessee or that he finds in the "Black Belt" of Georgia, where black tenants struggle to keep up with rents on the "forlorn and forsaken" land once populated by plantations (*SBF*, 107).

To a great extent, Du Bois attributes Americans' inability to recognize the democratic potential of the Freedmen's Bureau to the perverse development of the "American Assumption." That assumption, the conviction that wealth is the reward for hard work and that anyone can achieve material success by dint of his or her own effort, may never have applied in the lives of most Americans (*BR*, 182–83). But Du Bois shows how, applied to the situation of freedmen and women, the American Assumption distanced successive generations from the wrong of slavery and denied that those who profited from that wrong bore any ongoing responsibility for it.[25] Tracing the rise of the Assumption to the emergence of a Cotton Kingdom predicated on slave labor, Du Bois replaces the conventional conception of individual exertion and reward with a more dynamic story of race and class. In his telling, the dismissal of the former slaves' claims to the basic equipment of citizenship appears cruelly disingenuous. "To give land to free citizens smacked of 'paternalism,'" Du Bois relates. "It came directly in opposition to the American assumption that any American could be rich if he wanted to, or at least well-to-do; and it stubbornly ignored the exceptional position of a freed slave" (*BR*, 601–02). That such gifts were "showered" on the railroads during the same period did little to alter public perceptions (*BR*, 212). What the end of the Freedmen's Bureau signifies to Du Bois, therefore, is not the triumph of a culture in which labor is rewarded but the rise of a culture that prizes wealth and power (*BR*, 182). Thus he contends that Northern industry was able to sound a death knell for Reconstruction when black emancipation no longer served its interests (*BR*, 187). This is not to say that only white Americans subscribed to the American Assumption. Of Booker T. Washington's embrace of this philosophy and his willingness to sacrifice political and civil rights in the name of economic development, Du Bois observes: "His doctrine has tended to make the whites, North and South, shift the burden of the Negro problem to the Negro's shoulders and stand aside as critical and rather pessimistic spectators; when in fact the burden belongs to the nation, and the hands of none of us are clean if we bend not our energies to righting these great wrongs" (*SBF*, 72).

It is possible to argue that the "American Assumption," strictly applied, also makes a case for the redistribution of land and other resources to the former slaves. After all, it was their exertions that transformed the land into cotton and tobacco. Not only did black labor provide an economic underpinning for the antebellum South, Du Bois maintains, but it fueled the industrial development of the northern United States and Europe (*BR*, 5). In rebuttal to the claim that the former slaves were unwilling to work without the motivation of the lash, he supplies examples of blacks' eagerness to cultivate abandoned lands. The "key to the situation," he writes, is that "the Negroes were willing to work and did work, but they wanted land to work, and they wanted to see and own the results of their toil" (*BR*, 67).[26] Furthermore, he discerns African Americans' fervent desire for economic independence in the fact that the Freedmen's Bureau—a symbol, to many white Americans, of black dependency and Northern imposition—was funded for its first year by the freedmen themselves through rents collected on the land on which they labored (*BR*, 602). Viewed in this light, the promise of "forty acres and mule" represents, not a hand-out, but "the righteous and reasonable ambition to become a landholder, which the nation had all but categorically promised the freedmen" (*SBF*, 56). It is unsurprising, then, that African American leaders repeatedly returned to the question of land distribution as a fundamental concern, despite the intransigence of most white leaders on the issue (*BR*, 368).[27] Reasonable though it may have been, this "land hunger" of the former slaves was met with "surprise and ridicule" (*BR*, 602). Whereas the idea of compensating the former *slave owners* for their losses was seriously considered by Abraham Lincoln himself, he "curiously never seemed seriously to consider the correlative loss of wage and opportunity of slave workers, the tangible results of whose exploitation had gone into planters' pockets for two centuries" (*BR*, 150).[28] Indeed, proposals to pay the former slaves were generally dismissed as a weapon to punish the South (*BR*, 602).[29]

One must be careful here not to misread Du Bois's insistence on the value of economic independence and the historical evidence of black fitness for such independence as an appeal for more scrupulous application of the American Assumption. In *Souls*, his resistance to such an appeal is most clearly manifest in his rejection of "the gospel of Work and Money" as spiritually cramped, a threat to any higher sense of human aspiration (*SBF*, 67);[30] and in *Black Reconstruction*, he exposes the inadequacy of idealizing individual effort without attending to structural forms of injustice that are part of slavery's legacy. In this regard, Du Bois departs from Jennifer Hochschild's reluctant conclusion that the best hope for a more democratic future is to accept the ideological dominance of the "American Dream," the components of which resemble Du Bois's American Assumption, and to demand that American society live up to the tenets of that dream.[31] The quest for land and education, two principle objectives of the former slaves, are not simply prerequisites for individual "success." Rather, Du Bois ties this demand—inchoately in *Souls* and explicitly in *Black Reconstruction*—to a larger aspiration to restructure American society so that no group of citizens would be excluded from the concrete promise of freedom.

Connected to Du Bois's view of the centrality of slave labor in the making of the United States are larger claims about the contributions of African Americans to the cultural, political, and physical creation of the nation. Black Americans, he argues in *Souls*, have offered their neighbors three gifts: "a gift of story and song . . .; the gift of sweat and brawn . . .; [and] . . . a gift of the Spirit" (*SBF*, 192–93). One need not embrace Du Bois's concept of racial mission to appreciate how his language of "the gifts of black folk" enables him to challenge official memories of slavery, Reconstruction, and the disappointments that followed.[32] By discerning in the culture of the slaves the gift of a deepened understanding of freedom; by finding in their labor and the work of their descendants the underpinnings of American wealth; and by delineating the extent of their part in the abolition of slavery and the effort to create a more democratic society, Du Bois upends white assumptions about black worth. And he provides a resounding answer to his own rhetorical question: "Your country? How came it yours?" (*SBF*, 192).

For Du Bois, the reconstruction of American democracy began with the initiative of the slaves, thousands of whom participated in a "General Strike" by fleeing from the plantations to the Union army camps (*BR*, ch. 4).[33] The armies of the North and South and their supporters denied the significance of slavery to the conflict, but the slaves had no such illusions about the stakes of the war. Even before they were welcomed by the Union as laborers, spies, and, finally, soldiers, their abandonment of their masters created a labor shortage that crippled the Confederacy. In *The Souls of Black Folk*, Du Bois describes the fugitives who swelled the Union camps as "a horde of starving vagabonds, homeless, helpless, and pitiable, in their dark distress" (*SBF*, 46). Yet even as he represents the fugitives as a formless mass, he also shows how their insistent flight undercut the effort to deny slavery's centrality in the conflict and forced military and political leaders to abandon their hopes of saving the Union by compromising with slavery.[34] Du Bois's later work openly affirms the magnitude of the slaves' role in their own emancipation and attributes the conclusion of the Civil War to "the largest and most successful slave revolt."[35] Peter Kolchin builds on Du Bois's analysis, concluding that "by refusing to act like slaves—blacks throughout the South struck a mortal blow to slavery."[36] This claim, which is further borne out by Lincoln's recognition of the strategic value of the Emancipation Proclamation, discredits the characterization of black Americans as helpless or the liberation produced by the war as entirely the gift of the white North. Furthermore, it exposes the danger of any discourse of self-help that obscures the enormity of what African Americans have already done to help themselves.

Du Bois goes still further. He credits black Americans with securing new freedom and more substantive equality for *all* Americans during Reconstruction. In *The Gift of Black Folk* (in a chapter entitled "The Reconstruction of Freedom") he describes the role of African Americans in reestablishing the Union, founding public schools, extending the vote to poor whites, and creating the basis for "industrial democracy in America."[37] With regard to education, for example, Du Bois notes that the idea of public education in the South, which benefitted poor whites in the region, grew out of the clamor by black Americans for access to schools (*BR*, 638). Additionally, he attributes the elimination of property qualifications for office holding and the passage of a wide array of social legislation in Southern states to the period of black political power.[38] Recording the contribution of black leaders to the elevation of politics at the national level, he observes that the words of black representatives "were, perhaps, the last clear, earnest expression of the democratic theory of American government in Congress" (*BR*, 629).

Despite the arguments in favor of providing the former slaves with the basic resources necessary to secure their freedom and the importance of acknowledging their gifts to the nation, Du Bois perceives a fundamental obstacle to democratic reconstruction: the devaluation of black life. In the note to the reader with which he begins *Black Reconstruction*, Du Bois makes the following proposition: "I am going to tell this story as though Negroes were ordinary human beings, realizing that this attitude will from the first seriously curtail my audience" (*BR*, front matter).[39] He is, in other words, warning that any understanding of American history must take seriously the view of that history from the perspective of the former slaves and that, for white Americans, this requires an openness to reevaluating their basic beliefs about the order of things. The telling of the story of Reconstruction thus becomes crucial to the work of reconstruction. Its erasure from public narratives reveals the underlying truth that white Americans see their black neighbors as "a thing apart" or a "*tertium quid*," somewhere between human beings and cattle (*BR*, 370; *SBF*, 90). Plumbing beneath the surface, Du Bois probes "the vaster and far more intricate jungle of ideas conditioned on unconscious and subconscious reflexes" (*DOD*, xxx), and he argues that a residual resistance to accepting the equal humanity of the slaves made the experiment in reconstruction unthinkable and its undoing vicious. That resistance could not be fully obliterated by the legislative commitments made to the freedmen and women, he writes, and it persists in damaging both black and white citizens.

"Never in modern times," Du Bois remarks, "has a large section of a nation so used its combined energies to the degradation of mankind. The hurt to the Negro in this era was not only his treatment in slavery; it was the wound dealt to his reputation as a human being" (*BR*, 39). Du Bois's most famous articulation of the impact of this wound is captured in his formulation of "double-consciousness." Although double-consciousness is joined to a heightened perception or second-sight, the insight it produces exacts a terrible toll. It means living with a "sense of always looking at one's self through the eyes of others, of measuring one's soul by the tape of a world that looks on in amused contempt and pity" (*SBF*, 38). For ordinary men and women, such inner turmoil can destroy their motivation to seek better lives, and it can lead to a variety of social ills. For black leaders, Du Bois argues, it is crippling.

Damaging though the "precept of black inferiority" may be to African Americans,[40] however, it is "fatal" when it infects the minds of whites (*BR*, 52, 166). To reinforce this point, Du Bois quotes a statement issued by black leaders in 1864 that goes to the heart of white Americans' stake in black subordination: "You cannot need special protection. Our degradation is not essential to your elevation, nor our peril essential to your safety" (*BR*, 235). The result of white dependency on such "special protection" is a distorted sense of self-worth and an incapacity to comprehend the gap between professed ideals and unjust social practices and structures of power. Hence the troubles that beset the Freedmen's Bureau (chief among them, lack of funds, time, or adequate force) reveal a deeper truth: "The very name of the Bureau stood for a thing in the South which for two centuries and better men had refused even to argue,—that life amid free Negroes was simply unthinkable, the maddest of experiments" (*SBF*, 54). Further, the compromise that put a premature end to the experiment did lasting harm to white Americans:

> Evil results of the revolution of 1876 have not been confined to Negroes. The reaction on the whites was just as significant. . . . Perhaps their early and fatal mistake was when they refused long before the Civil War to allow in the South differences of opinion. They would not let honest white Southerners continue to talk against slavery. They drove out the nonconformist; they would not listen to the radical. The result was that there has been built up in the South an intolerance fatal to human culture. Men act as they do in the South, they murder, they lynch, they insult, because they listen to but one side of a question.

> They seldom know by real contact Negroes who are men. They read books that laud the South and the 'Lost Cause,' but they are childish and furious when criticized, and interpret all criticism as personal attack (*BR*, 703–04).

This failure to question slavery and/or to regard its legacies "as though Negroes were ordinary human beings" not only affects white Americans individually, in other words. It stifles democratic possibility for everyone.

Thus, even though the nation embraced emancipation, and ultimately black suffrage, in response to Southern recalcitrance, that commitment proved weaker than the assumption that black Americans were less than fully human (*BR*, 329–30). This commitment to the racial order enabled a pact whereby Southern planters were able to measure their value through their continuing capacity to control the labor of others; white workers accepted the "public and psychological wage" of racial superiority in lieu of adequate payment for their labor (*BR*, 700);[41] and Northern whites convinced themselves that they had done their duty by the emancipated slaves. It produced, according to Du Bois, a kind of "phantasmagoria" that rendered the United States unfit for democracy at Reconstruction's end (*BR*, 705).

Notes toward a Third Reconstruction: The Time of Reparations

One might accept Du Bois's analysis of the opportunity lost in Reconstruction and acknowledge parallels between the disappointments of that period and those that followed the era of civil rights and still ask how they bear on contemporary democratic prospects. Is it even appropriate in the twenty-first century to claim, as Du Bois does at the dawn of the twentieth, that Americans are evasive about the importance of slavery and the Jim Crow system that followed from it? Recent scholarship answers this question with a resounding no. The prodigious outpouring of historical treatments of American slavery and Reconstruction, particularly those that focus on the activities and perspectives of the women and men in bondage, reflects an attitude far removed from the prevailing view in Du Bois's day and intimates the reach of his influence. Further, inquiry into cultural traditions that developed out of the slave experience and the reclamation of slave narratives as a treasured literary inheritance reinforce the sense that there has been a decisive break with the academic traditions of silence and misrepresentation against which Du Bois wrote. While these developments deserve celebration, however, their political significance is less clear. If we turn our attention to political life and public discourse, it appears that Americans still have little appetite to engage the fundamental questions Du Bois raises in *Black Reconstruction:* "What was slavery in the United States? Just what did it mean to the owner and the owned?" (*BR*, 715).

Implicit in those two questions is a third: What does the United States owe the former slaves and their descendants? That this question has gone largely unasked suggests a resistance to acknowledging the reach of slavery beyond abolition or the continuing effects of the forms of racial oppression to which abolition gave rise. As Boris Bittker suggests, the historical *absence* of discussion about proposals for reparations is telling.[42] It reveals, in Bill Lawson's words, a "functional lexical gap," a failure of language to express the status and experiences of black citizens.[43] Robert Westley concurs, noting that "a history of reparations for slavery would be a history of a nonevent."[44] In this section, I build on these insights to ask what Du Bois's reconstruction of U.S. history reveals about the unasked question of reparations, about how to understand a nonevent with a long, vexed history. And, conversely, I ask whether and how reparations could provide an alternative political language from which to formulate a constructive response to the lost opportunities of the two reconstructions.[45]

As these comments indicate, I use the term "reparations" quite broadly. In part, this breadth reflects the range of proposals that have been included under the umbrella of reparations; these include truth commissions, payments to individuals, payments to groups, the establishment of a trust fund, apologies, civil rights legislation, and a variety of public commemorations. Equally important, I argue, the idea of reparations ought to be understood as a vehicle for tying principles of justice to the acknowledgment of historical injustice. Reducible neither to back wages nor to a calculation of injury, the idea of reparations prods citizens to ponder *how* the stories of American democracy are told. "Rather than accepting the idea that we are living at a moment characterized by the final chapter in the unfolding story of freedom," writes Walter Johnson, "the theorists and grassroots activists of the reparations movement insist upon the presence of slavery, in both its historical guise and in more contemporary forms of exploitation and disadvantage, in the condition of blackness."[46] Reparations discourse is unique, according to Melvin Oliver and Thomas Shapiro, because it "provide[s] the political space to reclaim memory and narrative about race in America. Otherwise, discussions about the legacy of race do not occur other than in the context of some current event or crisis, and circumstances of the moment become the lens of discussion."[47] Looking to reparations as "a structure of memory and critique,"[48] my aim is not to offer specific proposals. Nor do I mean to imply that reparations alone would be a cure for racial injustice; the obligation to respond does not diminish the incompleteness of any possible response.[49] Instead, I inquire whether and how the idea of reparations might offer live alternatives to stillborn gestures that are disconnected from concrete change. Regardless of one's position on this question, furthermore, I maintain that democratic citizens have an obligation to ask it. And Du Bois shows why.

Before returning to Du Bois directly, however, let me briefly address the larger context of the reparations struggle. Although the idea of reparations is not new, the latter part of the twentieth century witnessed an explosion of demands that collective injustices be concretely memorialized through some form of redress. The era has been dubbed, with varying degrees of approval and disdain, "the age of apology."[50] The German program of reparations for victims of the Nazi regime may be the most prominent example, but other efforts include legislation to restore property stolen from indigenous peoples in North America, Australia, and New Zealand; movements to obtain apologies and compensation from Japan for crimes committed during the Second World War; truth and reconciliation commissions in South Africa and Latin America; and calls for compensation for losses sustained by Africans as a result of slavery, colonialism, and neocolonialism.[51] In addition to the Virginia resolution, examples from the United States include Florida's payments to survivors of the Rosewood massacre and their families, the federal government's reparations to victims of the Tuskegee syphilis experiment, the Senate's apology for its failure to pass anti-lynching legislation, and the Civil Liberties Act of 1988, which apologized for the internment of citizens and permanent residents of Japanese descent during World War II and allocated $20,000 apiece to survivors.

The struggle for reparations for American slaves and their descendants dates back at least to the nineteenth century, but it has more recently moved in from the margins.[52] The movement flickered, briefly, in the national news, when James Forman interrupted services at Riverside Church in April 1969 to deliver a Black Manifesto demanding redress from American churches and synagogues.[53] In the last part of the twentieth century, it acquired broader momentum. Evidence of this shift is varied and includes H.R. 40, a bill introduced by Representative John Conyers (D-MI) in every Congress since 1989 to acknowledge the horrors of slavery and establish a commission to study the idea of reparations; the publicity that followed the appearance of Randall Robinson's *The Debt: What America Owes to Blacks* in 2000;[54] the spread of grassroots initiatives, such as the establishment of the National Coalition of Blacks for Reparations in America (N'COBRA) and the Black

Radical Congress (BRC); the initiation of lawsuits against the U.S. government, corporations, and individuals who benefited from slavery; the proliferation of legislative expressions of regret for slavery and the passage of reparations-related resolutions at federal, state, and local levels; and the explosion of scholarship, particularly in legal academia, addressing the issue. That Bill Clinton and George W. Bush both visited Goree Island in Senegal during their presidencies and that they both used the occasion to decry the slave trade indicates a new openness to the revisiting the slave past.

Notwithstanding the success of movements to address historic injustice around the world and renewed attention to slavery's lingering questions in the United States, the will to enact concrete policies of redress remains weak and largely divided along the color line. Strikingly, in response to a 2000 survey by Lawrence Bobo and Michael Dawson, 96 percent of white Americans rejected the idea of monetary payments to African American descendants of slaves, and 70 per cent opposed a federal apology.[55] Perhaps more arresting is the response to a 2002 study by the *Mobile Register;* this study found that the level of white opposition to reparations in Alabama was higher than white Alabamians' opposition to integration during the civil rights era.[56] Confronting a variety of legal hurdles, including questions of standing, sovereign immunity, and statutes of limitations, demands for slavery reparations have yet to score a major victory in court. More worrisome still, from the perspective of reparations advocates, is the dismissal of a lawsuit filed on behalf of victims of the 1921 race riot in Tulsa, Oklahoma, because the time limit for filing suit had expired.[57] Unlike the slavery cases, this one involved survivors of a white rampage, abetted by the police and National Guard, that destroyed the prosperous black section of the city and left at least 100, and perhaps as many as 300, people dead. It is perhaps unsurprising that claims for reparations have had little effect, but it is nonetheless worth inquiring *why* this idea remains so inconceivable in the United States, even as our understanding of the heritage of the slave past has been transformed.

Returning to the submerged questions excavated by Du Bois's history of Reconstruction, I suggest that his analysis of Americans' refusal to come to terms with slavery's persistent political implications and his demonstration of the central role played by African Americans in the making of the United States indicate the urgency of taking seriously the idea of reparations as one element of a third attempt at democratic reconstruction. This is not to say that Du Bois himself would endorse a campaign for reparations. Indeed, he might well dismiss it as a pipe dream, much as he did in 1916, when a group of African Americans sought compensation from the U.S. Treasury for a share of the revenues from American cotton production. Of the vow by the group's attorney to seek $68 million, Du Bois scoffs: "Of course, he can claim it and anybody else can claim it and they may also claim the moon but the chance of getting the one is about as great as that of getting the other."[58] Despite Du Bois's own reservations about the costs of succumbing to "the latest craze," his examination of the "splendid failure" of Americans' first attempt to make good on their democratic commitments offers three lines of argument in support of reparations for slavery, neoslavery, and segregation.

First, reparations could respond to both strands of Du Bois's claims about the economic requirements of a genuinely reconstructed democracy. Conceived as a massive investment in black communities, rather than a per capita payment, and targeted primarily at the poorest of those communities, reparations could create a basis for attacking the deep economic inequality Du Bois understands to be incompatible with democracy. Such an approach could broaden the base of African Americans who enjoy the fruits of citizenship in a meaningful sense. Du Bois's study of the short-lived experiments that allowed former slaves to work abandoned lands during the Civil War provides a glimpse of the opportunity lost when the Freedmen's Bureau was prevented from carrying out the redistribution of Southern lands and establishing the former slaves as "peasant proprietors" (see *BR*, ch.4; *SBF*, ch.2). Furthermore, his attention to the perspectives of the former slaves enables him to articulate a critique of Reconstruction's shortcomings that speaks to the limits of recent civil rights legislation: without a significant material commitment, the Thirteenth Amendment would become part of a "legalistic formula . . . [that] did not cling to facts" (*BR*, 188). Du Bois's account of the link between the subjugation of African Americans at the close of Reconstruction and the concentration of capital in the hands of a small industrial class also serves as a reminder that any argument for reparations, although targeting African Americans specifically, should be constructed as a component of a larger commitment to eliminating disparities of wealth and power among Americans more generally.[59]

Reparations also addresses the second strand of Du Bois's economic claims by providing some recompense for the years of slave labor and for the exclusion from access to resources that succeeded abolition. By emphasizing the value of African Americans' labor under slavery and the continuities between the slave era and the Jim Crow period, Du Bois exposes the roots of present inequalities. What succeeded Reconstruction, he argues, was the disenfranchisement of black citizens, the revival of racial caste distinctions, the systematic exploitation of black workers, the deliberate impoverishment of black schools, the widespread denial of access to health care and other social services, the use of the criminal justice system as a cheap source of black labor, and the condoning of mob violence as an instrument of social control

(BR, 693–708). "We can trace the sedimented material inequality that now confronts us directly to this opprobrious past," write Oliver and Shapiro in their study of the wealth gap between white and black Americans.[60] Moreover, Du Bois's examination of the ways in which white Americans as a group profited from the oppression of blacks shows that an account of what is owed to African Americans need not reinforce the individualist framework of the "American Assumption." Anticipating recent work on the "cash value" of whiteness,[61] Du Bois's retelling of the fall of Reconstruction reveals the economic function of racial privilege, even for those white Americans who disavow it (BR, 700–01). Although it would be impossible to calculate with any exactness what is owed for uncompensated and undercompensated work and the cost to generations of black families of discrimination and restricted access to public resources, Du Bois provides an important reminder that the failure even to consider what sort of redress might be appropriate represents a kind of continuing "carelessness" and constrains the project of conceiving more democratic practices and institutions.[62]

A second way to link Du Bois's exploration of Reconstruction to an argument for reparations is to consider what he calls "the gifts of black folk." This element of the argument is crucial, for it supplements the language of apology with the language of thanksgiving. Speaking of the period after the Civil War, Du Bois insists that "Negroes deserved not only the pity of the world but the gratitude of both South and North" (BR, 188). Du Bois's comment suggests that it is imperative that the construction of a sincere and long overdue apology not reinforce conceptions of black victimhood or neediness.[63] Emphasizing black contributions as a cornerstone of the argument—through careful attention to the rhetoric promoting reparations measures, as well as the institution of museums, memorials, and educational programs—would help to allay the well-grounded fear that a campaign for reparations would be interpreted simply as an instance of special pleading. Such a public reimagining of the debt to African Americans could be revolutionary. It would discredit the assumptions that inform traditions of public "charity" for black Americans. Generous charity was, after all, commonplace even in the segregated South (SBF, 145–46), but the impetus behind programs of almsgiving was, and is, misplaced. Not only does it disguise and thereby reinforce racial hierarchies, but it also perpetuates the erasure of black accomplishments and the fear of black success that often lies behind white efforts to prevent African Americans from enjoying political, economic, or social equality (BR, 633).[64] A form of reparations acknowledging the gifts Du Bois describes, therefore, would not require that black Americans sacrifice their claims to historical agency in making their claims for the resources necessary to live a decent life.

Moreover, Du Bois's account of the contributions of African Americans to the construction and reconstruction of American democracy provides a rebuttal to charges that the demand for black reparations is necessarily "divisive." Certainly, the purpose of reparations is to advance the prospects and interests of black citizens. Yet Du Bois's historical studies expose links between the improvement in African Americans' political and economic fortunes and the protection of other vulnerable members of American society. He notes, for example, that members of Congress like Senator Blanche K. Bruce and Representative John A. Hyman, both former slaves, fought against restricting Chinese immigration and for assistance to the Cherokees, respectively (*BR*, 629). Further, the possibility that the fight for reparations might offer opportunities to bridge, rather than widen, social divisions is suggested more recently by the support of members of the Black Congressional Caucus for reparations in the Japanese-American case.[65] Without concluding that reparations for black Americans would inevitably form the basis for new coalitions, Du Bois's historical narrative discredits the claim that redress for slavery and segregation can *only* divide and reminds his readers that such a contention helps to perpetuate divisions that are patently unjust:

> Emancipation came not simply to black folk in 1863; to white Americans came slowly a new vision and a new uplift, a sudden freeing of hateful mental shadows. At last democracy was to be justified of its own children. The nation was to be purged of continual sin not indeed all of its own doing—due partly to its inheritance; and yet a sin, a negation that gave the world the right to sneer at the pretensions of this republic. At last there could really be a free commonwealth of freemen (*BR*, 125–26).

If emancipation meant the liberation of all Americans from the shadow of slavery, however, Du Bois recounts how swiftly antiblack racism contributed to Reconstruction's undoing. It may be that this third dimension of Du Bois's reconstructed history, his attention to the failure to apprehend the equal humanity of black women and men, appears unnecessary in the contemporary context. Is Du Bois's appeal for a concrete, public accounting of the crimes of racial slavery and its aftermath as an affirmation of the human worth of the slaves and their descendants still pressing? One could argue that it is precisely this worth that is reaffirmed by the passage of the Civil War amendments and the civil rights legislation of the last century. One could find still more evidence in the successes of individual African Americans, perhaps most spectacularly the rise of Barack Obama. Yet the testimony of American prisons and jails, the dwindling attention to the long-term effects of the decimation of black communities on the Mississippi Gulf Coast, and the state of predominantly black and brown public schools indicate otherwise. Although racial attitudes today do not mirror those Du Bois confronted at the turn of the twentieth century, we still have an obligation to confront the disregard that means the suffering of some citizens earns only fleeting attention or goes altogether unremarked. In other words, the persistence of dramatic racial disparities calls on all citizens to ask: "What *makes for a grievable life?*"[66] The challenge is not so much to undermine explicit arguments about racial inferiority as to confront the residual assumptions that sustain public silences and feed the resistance to action in matters of racial injustice.[67] As long as the United States is defined by significant racial inequalities, there is political value in investigating why the claim of the ex-slaves to compensation was considered laughable in the nineteenth century and what makes the suggestion (literally) outrageous in the minds of so many Americans today.

My reading of Du Bois's reconstruction of the complex entanglement of past and present suggests that filling that gap requires both reckoning with the desperate conditions of many African American communities today and reviving the memories of the "many thousands gone." Without making facile comparisons between chattel slavery and the crimes of National Socialism, Du Bois's work suggests why Theodor Adorno's reflection on "the destruction of memory" resonates in the U.S. context. The menace posed by a failure to come to terms with the past is that "the murdered are to be cheated even out of the one thing that our powerlessness can grant them: remembrance."[68] This is what W. James Booth calls "memory-justice,"[69] a responsiveness to injuries of the past and to the shared humanity of the injured. Not to be confused with individual guilt, the obligations imposed on the current generation of American citizens are better understood as an aspect of their *political inheritance*.[70] "Every generation," writes Hannah Arendt, "by virtue of being born into a historical continuum, is burdened by the sins of the fathers as it is blessed with the deeds of the ancestors."[71] To be sure, present-day political aspirations ought not to be sacrificed to a perfectionist effort to rectify every misdeed of the past. But the centrality and scale of racial slavery and segregation through most of the development of the United States weaken the force of this concern. One lesson of Du Bois's reconstruction of history, furthermore, is that automatic dismissals of reparations are themselves dangerous. "Closure is not possible. . . . Yet silence is also an unacceptable offense, a shocking implication that the perpetrators in fact succeeded, a stunning indictment that the present audience is simply the current incarnation of the silent bystanders complicit with oppressive regimes."[72] By demanding that

Americans examine the collective injustice at the core of the nation, reparations may help to prevent today's citizens from becoming "the current incarnation of the silent bystanders."

A language of reparations might, furthermore, enable a more democratic refiguration of political time. Such a refiguration is very much in keeping with Du Bois's interest in the possibilities opened up by engagement with the past and his specific reflections on how the interval between emancipation and the compromise that ended Reconstruction shaped his own present. Properly conceived, reparations for slavery and Jim Crow might dramatize "the difference between the past as bygone and the past as prologue."[73] This difference bespeaks a legacy of loss and gives rise to lamentation; it requires a political vocabulary supple enough to convey grief as well as grievance.[74] And it simultaneously helps to stretch the bounds of the thinkable by reorienting Americans to see their history from the perspective of the former slaves and their descendants. The promise of such a reorientation resides in its capacity to discredit the lingering impulse to "answer all queries concerning the Negro *a priori*" (*SBF*, 96). It reminds us of the too-ready rejection of claims for full citizenship that were forestalled, for generations, as "too soon" and undercuts the assumption that recent efforts to connect present policy to past wrongdoing are "too late."[75] Dismissed as untimely, arguments for reparations offer an alternative to the time of exceptionalism narrated as the inexorable, if bumpy, march of liberty. These arguments create an occasion to "reset time."[76] That political life is unduly constrained by conceptions of time that rule out such creative uses of the past is reinforced by the words of James Ellison, the federal judge who dismissed the Tulsa riot survivors' demands for reparations. Even as he defended his ruling that the statute of limitations barred their claims, he emphasized that his was "strictly a legal conclusion" and that it did "not speak to the tragedy of the Riot or the terrible devastation it caused."[77]

Du Bois's work also exposes dangers in pursuing claims for reparations. Most pernicious is the risk of inciting an antiblack backlash and the possibility that a monetary settlement would fix, once and for all, the public meaning of slavery and segregation, forestalling any thorough-going attempt to consider what still needs to be done to effect racial justice. One lesson of the brutality with which the achievements of Reconstruction were dismantled is that any large-scale attack on racial injustice is perilous. Du Bois's attention to the sources and effects of this brutality suggests that the aspiration to counter centuries of racial hierarchy through reparations must confront a version of Rousseau's dilemma: how is it possible to bring a free and equal society into being democratically? The relation of cause and effect is circular, Rousseau demonstrates, for it is only through socialization in such a society, obeying its laws and adopting its habits as their own, that people become capable of governing themselves. Indeed, it is only through such collective engagement that they become a people at all: "Men would have to be prior to laws what they ought to become by means of laws."[78] At the heart of reparations demands is a critique of the exclusion of African Americans from full membership in "the people," but it is precisely this same people to whom the appeal must be directed. Reparations advocates must, in other words, "make an appeal that sets the conditions for its own proper reception," by calling into being a citizenry sufficiently attuned to the harms of racial injustice to acknowledge the need for reparations.[79]

Additionally, some forms of reparations—those that aim to close the book on American racial history rather than opening it to scrutiny and revision by successive generations—might be worse than none at all. In this regard, the acceptance by some white neoconservatives of reparations as a one-time alternative to affirmative action or other forms of redress ought to give reparations advocates pause.[80] Further, Du Bois's study of the ways in which partial measures underwrite the carelessness of citizens who believe enough has been done illustrates why such measures may be counter-productive. "Without change in the material conditions of racial group life," warns Eric Yamamoto, "reparations are fraught with repressive potential. Without attitudinal and social structural transformation of a sort meaningful to recipients, reparations may be illusory, more damaging than healing. No repair. Cheap grace."[81] Beyond these concerns lie a host of technical and strategic questions that would require attention before any program of reparations could be undertaken. My aim is neither to minimize these challenges nor to imply that Du Bois's work provides answers to all of them. Rather, I read his retelling of the story of Reconstruction as a basis for reorienting present-day thinking about what democracy requires and as a reminder that today's swift dismissals of reparations are kin to, if not the direct offspring of, the disreputable denials of the past.

Although he does not expressly advocate a public commitment to reparations, then, Du Bois's rewriting of history suggests how such a commitment might call attention to Americans' halting, limited, and perpetually unfilled democratic aspirations. By opening the door to a collective exploration of the past's imprint on the present, such a commitment could create the possibility of new democratic imaginings. It might make space for redemption in the sense of "transfiguration of a legacy rather than transcendence of history."[82] That the financial and, for many white Americans, psychological costs of any meaningful program of reparations for racial slavery and segregation would be staggering, goes without saying. That no amount would provide adequate recompense for the horrors of slavery, or the forms of racial oppression that succeeded it, ought to be even more obvious. Yet the lesson of Du Bois's postmortem on the nineteenth-century democratic experiment is that the costs of choosing not to face up to the enduring legacies of racial slavery are incalculably higher. Although there is much truth to the view that fixating on the past or wallowing in guilt solves nothing, the banishment of centuries of history to the remote past, particularly when those centuries were followed by decades of deliberate policies of racial injustice, is undemocratic; and formal guarantees of racial equality, while a critical element of the move toward democracy, are not only inadequate but potentially regressive when they provide justification for continued forgetfulness. Thus, despite all that has happened since Du Bois investigated the "splendid failure" of Reconstruction, one lesson of his work is that the idea of reparations deserves a serious hearing. Despite all that has changed, his warning to his thoughtless fellow citizens still resonates: "Actively we have woven ourselves with the very warp and woof of this nation,—we fought their battles, shared their sorrow, mingled our blood with theirs, and generation after generation have pleaded with a headstrong, careless people to despise not Justice, Mercy, and Truth, lest the nation be smitten with a curse" (*SBF*, 193).

THREE | Resurrecting John Brown

It was the wild-eyed prophesies of John Brown, his willingness to spill blood and not just words on behalf of his visions, that helped force the issue of a nation half slave and half free.

—Barack Obama, *The Audacity of Hope*[1]

We do not believe in violence, neither in the despised violence of the raid nor the lauded violence of the soldier, nor the barbarous violence of the mob, but we do believe in John Brown. . . . And here on the scene of John Brown's martyrdom we reconsecrate ourselves, our honor, our property to the final emancipation of the race which John Brown died to make free.

—W. E. B. Du Bois, "The Niagara Movement: Address to the Country"[2]

Whose Usable Past?

Du Bois's retelling of the story of Reconstruction ends as a question: Would the United States embrace emancipation and thereby affirm its commitment to "Justice, Mercy, and Truth"? Or would it, alternatively, suppress the record of the slaves' existence and of their accomplishments and persist in its suppression of their aspirations to citizenship; would it "be smitten with a curse" (*SBF*, 193)? Three years after the publication of *Souls*, Du Bois revises the question with greater urgency and diminished hopefulness. Returning home to Atlanta after receiving news of a riot in which tens of thousands of white citizens killed at least 20 African Americans, wounded hundreds of others, and invaded black homes and businesses, Du Bois bewails the fate of "a mobbed and mocked and murdered people" (*DW*, 15).[3] "A Litany at Atlanta," Du Bois's literary response to the riot, rages against a silent God and posits bleak alternatives for African Americans in the shadow of Reconstruction: "Whither? North is greed and South is blood; within, the coward, and without, the liar. Whither? To death?" (*DW*, 16).

These dilemmas tore at the young Atlanta University professor, as did his sense that his fellow citizens, or at least his white fellow citizens, either failed to perceive the outrage or refused to acknowledge that it constituted a national crisis. Over the course of the years when Du Bois "tried to isolate [himself] in the ivory tower of race," nearly 2,000 men and women were lynched. None of the lynchers were punished (*DOD*, 54–55). During these years, too, his 2-year-old son died from diphtheria, compounding the sense of public menace with the experience of private loss. In particular, the 1899 killing and dismemberment of Sam Hose, a laborer who lived outside Atlanta, cut across the young social scientist's life as "a red ray which could not be ignored." "One could not be a calm, cool, and detached scientist while Negroes were lynched, murdered, and starved," Du Bois recalls (*DOD*, 67).[4] Appalled by the undeserved and publicly unmourned suffering of black citizens and disheartened by the lack of public appetite for the scientific studies of black life that he was undertaking in Atlanta, Du Bois relinquished any conviction that social change could be effected by academic means alone.

It is not surprising that Du Bois turned from the dispassion of social science toward a career of passionate advocacy in the bloody years of the early twentieth century,[5] and it is perhaps equally unsurprising that he found inspiration in the figure of John Brown. Du Bois's biography of the radical abolitionist first appeared in 1909 and was reprinted with additions in 1962. Although the autobiographical significance of Du Bois's gravitation toward Brown's life at this pivotal moment in his career deserves attention, I approach the text from a different direction. I argue that Du Bois's reconstruction of Brown's life and legacy, like his re-vision of Reconstruction history, engages the past in order to reflect on democratic possibilities in the present and to offer a vantage on both past and present that provides theoretical traction for envisioning a different future. By reviving and retelling the story of the bloody years that preceded the Civil War, Du Bois essays to understand and respond to the epidemic of antiblack violence that followed Reconstruction. Crucially, he connects that epidemic to a tradition of denial, a tradition that minimizes the brutality of slavery itself and disguises the extent of the terror that defined the South in the years following the Civil War. "Nothing in the popular Southern and national image of Reconstruction by the turn of the century caused more spirited defense or aggressive evasion," writes David Blight, "than the role of the Klan and violence in the white South's overthrow of Reconstruction."[6] By recalling a figure who waged holy war on behalf of black men and women, and did so in their company, Du Bois aims to reshape public memories of the antebellum past in order to assess the prospects for democratic action in the post-Reconstruction present. His efforts to come to terms with the meaning of a figure as divisive as Brown speak beyond Du Bois's situation, however. I aim to show how they also unsettle contemporary evasions of the history of antiblack violence and the brutality that has sometimes been required to oppose it.

Divergent treatments of Brown and his legacy display, dramatically, the phenomenon of "segregated historical memory."[7] Among African Americans, Brown has long been figured as a hero. As Benjamin Quarles notes, Brown's image has been a constant presence in the black fight for freedom and equality since 1859: his name often arose at rallies in the post-Civil War period; he inspired the "Exodusters'" to choose Kansas as their destination in the 1870s; and even militant black nationalists of the late 1960s appealed to his example.[8] Memorialized in poetry, painting, and other media by some of the most prominent black artists of the twentieth century, Brown joined such luminaries as Toussaint L'Ouverture, Harriet Tubman, and Frederick Douglass as a crucial ancestor in struggle.[9] As successive generations of African Americans fought against inherited and new forms of racial domination, notes Quarles, "Brown meant much to [them] in their search for a relevant past."[10]

White responses to Brown's life and memory, by contrast, have been mixed. Hailed as a martyr by abolitionists and immortalized in poems and essays by Northern intellectuals and artists in the Civil War era, Brown became an object of terror for whites in the South. Republicans, according to Gary Alan Fine, used Brown's memory to establish political dominance after 1859 by affirming Brown's principles while distancing themselves from his actions.[11] This "attitude of praise-the-man-but-not-the-deed" still echoes in more recent references to Brown, suggesting that what was an effective political strategy at the turn of the twentieth century has become a means of dealing with ambivalence about taking radical action against racial injustice at the turn of the twenty-first.[12] Conflict over how to memorialize Brown in his birthplace of Torrington, Connecticut, for example, indicates his continuing presence as a touchstone for such ambivalence.[13] And for democratic theorists, Brown's example still poses a challenge.

A white man who felt the injustice of slavery personally, Brown emerges as an obvious hero for antiracist politics. He departed from most white abolitionists in believing as fervently in racial equality as he did in abolition, and the extent of his self-sacrifice provides a rare counter-example to Derrick Bell's thesis that white Americans have only supported expanding African Americans' rights when it appears to serve their own interests.[14] Furthermore, Brown is exemplary in his capacity to refuse the willed blindness that prevented (and prevents) so many white Americans from appreciating the reality or the depth of slavery's impact on the United States. Brown, in James Baldwin's estimation, understood as few whites did the stakes of the fight against slavery: "What he was trying to do was liberate a *country*, not simply the black people of that country."[15]

On the other hand, there are good reasons to be wary. The act of remembering Brown need not, in itself, trouble a racially divided and stratified status quo. As Marita Sturken notes, "Cultural memory may often constitute opposition, but it is not automatically the scene of cultural resistance."[16] There is always the danger, Sacvan Bercovitch contends, that Brown's life could be folded into a triumphalist narrative that elides past crimes and present difficulties. "John Brown could join Adams, Franklin, and Jefferson in the pantheon of Revolutionary heroes when it was understood that he wanted to fulfill (rather than undermine) the American dream."[17] The risks are concretized in the bronze statue that greets visitors to John Brown's farm outside Lake Placid, New York. This muscular, larger-than-life Brown is depicted sheltering a smaller African American figure who looks up at him in apparent awe. Brown's image provides reassurance. It announces the presence of strong white men to save the republic and promises an interracial brotherhood through which African Americans can be welcomed into the national family without entirely upsetting older patterns of dominance and submission.[18]

Beyond the dangers that attend any attempt to incorporate Brown's story into a narrative of national redemption, there are further concerns arising from Brown himself. To take as inspiration for more democratic politics a man who perceived himself to be a messenger from God, a patriarch who dispensed advice to blacks and whites alike but took advice from no one, a warrior whose taste for blood sometimes seemed to exceed the demands of the antislavery cause is to risk replacing one form of tyranny with another. Indeed, much about Brown's example is deeply antidemocratic. "He did not use argument," Du Bois comments, indicating Brown's conviction that force, not moral suasion, was the only response to tyranny. "He was himself an argument" (*JB*, 173).

Keeping these concerns in view, this chapter pursues the suggestion of Lerone Bennett, Jr., that "it is to John Brown that we must go, finally, if we want to understand the possibilities and limits of our situation."[19] To what ends does Du Bois shape his account of Brown's life? Does his revival of Brown's memory serve to reinforce or undercut the kind of narrative reassurance against which Bercovitch warns? This chapter shows how Du Bois accomplishes the latter, remembering Brown as a hero without enmeshing his story in an account of triumphant Americanism. Beyond this, moreover, I draw out the ways Du Bois uses Brown's crusade to fashion a political response appropriate to the racial terror of his own time. Without making simplistic comparisons between the 1850s and the early twentieth century, or between the "nadir" of African American history and the post-civil rights period, I propose two readings of *John Brown* that ought to inform contemporary reflections on the entanglement of American democracy and racial violence. The first approach reads *John Brown* as a vindicationist text: Du Bois defends Brown against efforts to diminish his importance or dismiss his crusade, and by situating Brown's life story within a larger historical narrative about black accomplishment, Du Bois also vindicates the historical agency of African American women and men.[20] Still, insofar as it is read in the mode of heroic biography, *John Brown*'s usefulness for democratic thinking is constrained. A second reading, focuses on Du Bois's treatment of the conflict between Brown and Frederick Douglass and on his representation of the violence of Brown's antislavery campaign as simultaneously right and unjustifiable. Modeling a more complex, tragic form of historical memory, this approach to *John Brown* cautions against blanket disavowals of violence and, more acutely, against historical evasions of the forms of bloodshed that have been integral to American democracy.

"American Moses," "Saint of Gore"

Before assessing the political meanings of Du Bois's *John Brown*, it is useful to understand something about the circumstances of its subject's life and death.[21] Born in Torrington on May 9, 1800, Brown lived an undistinguished life prior to his full-time involvement in the antislavery cause. He worked as a tanner, land speculator, wool seller, and farmer, failing in virtually every business enterprise he attempted. In addition, Brown suffered enormous personal losses. His first wife died young, only 11 of his 20 children survived to adulthood, and three of his surviving sons were killed in the antislavery struggle. Although Brown's father was opposed to slavery, and Brown himself expressed a hatred for the institution and a commitment to racial equality from a young age, he did not fully dedicate himself to the cause until the

1840s. Active in the Underground Railroad in upstate New York, Brown worked with the black settlers on Gerrit Smith's land in North Elba and organized the League of Gileadites among African American residents of Springfield, Massachusetts, to resist the Fugitive Slave Act (1850). Brown's broader fame, however, grew out of his involvement in the bloody conflict over the extension of slavery to Kansas in 1855–58. There, he oversaw the massacre of five proslavery settlers at Pottawatomie Creek and then commanded a group of men in skirmishes at Ossawatomie. In 1858, he led a raid into Missouri in which one of his allies killed a slave owner as they freed 11 slaves and transported them to safety in Canada. His final act, the October 16, 1859 assault on the federal arsenal at Harpers Ferry (then part of Virginia, now West Virginia), led to his capture, trial, and hanging on December 2.

Brown was not remarkable for his opposition to slavery. But among white Americans, he was exceptional in his relationships with African Americans and his dedication to racial equality. John Brown, Du Bois comments, "worked not simply for Black Men—he worked with them" (*JB*, xxv). Indeed he provided a powerful counterexample to the condescension or outright racism of other white abolitionists. And his willingness to take concrete steps toward the realization of his principles further set him apart from whites whose contributions stopped at the line of declaring moral opposition to slavery.[22] Embracing the injunction to "remember them that are in bonds, as bound with them" (Hebrews 13:3), Brown offered himself and his family in sacrifice to the antislavery cause. Among his heroes was Toussaint L'Ouverture, the leader of the Haitian Revolution and symbol to many whites of black ruthlessness and the dangers of black political power.[23] Furthermore, Brown understood that the end of slavery would not be the end of the complex inheritance of racial injustice upon which the nation had been built.

Brown's politics were prophetic. Often compared to Oliver Cromwell, he resembled Michael Walzer's "saints," the Calvinists of sixteenth- and seventeenth-century England who waged holy war on the old order in the name of a politics that integrated sacred and secular concerns.[24] His rhetoric, which described the slaveholders' relationship to the rest of the nation as a state of war, was Lockean; but his defense of violent resistance to tyranny was always wedded to divine purpose. Brown's Calvinist upbringing ingrained in him a sense of predestination, a deep appreciation for personal sin, a commitment to struggle against the Devil, an apocalyptic imagination, and a love of the Hebrew prophets. The Bible, large portions of which he had committed to memory, served not only as Brown's guide to religious life but also as his manual for leadership.

Brown's conception of the prophetic tradition, moreover, was decidedly *American*. Dedicating himself to the Bible and the Declaration of Independence, he is quoted as saying to Ralph Waldo Emerson that it would be "better that a whole generation of men, women and children should pass away by a violent death than that a word of either should be violated in this country."[25] In *Cloudsplitter*, Russell Banks's monumental novel about Brown's life, Brown's son Owen recalls: "We were obliged to oppose slavery, then, not merely to preserve and protect the Republic, although that alone was a worthy enough task, but to defeat Satan. It was our holy, our peculiarly American obligation."[26] Indeed, this sense of national allegiance produced a rare moment of tension between Brown and his black allies. At the meeting in Chatham, Ontario, in May 1858, when Brown unveiled his plan to take the antislavery fight into Virginia, he offered for consideration a "constitution" modeled on the U.S. Constitution. With language borrowed from the Declaration, it included clauses concerning labor, property captured in battle, and the proscription of "indecent" behavior.[27] It was the 46th article that stirred controversy. In it, Brown pledged loyalty to the nation, the states, and the flag. Some members of the assembly objected, asserting that they had no reason to remain loyal to a flag that had never represented them; but Brown prevailed (*JB*, 128–32). And when, nearly 18 months after the convention, he proceeded to Harpers Ferry, Brown hoped his campaign would complete the fusion of divine purpose and American destiny articulated in the Chatham constitution.

That campaign proved disastrous, and Brown's new order remained unrealized. Nonetheless, many commentators note that Brown's great failure at Harpers Ferry gave birth to his greatest accomplishment. Captured, but not killed, Brown used the days that preceded his execution to arouse his fellow citizens and to participate in the construction of the legend that would outlive him. One measure of his success in this endeavor can be read in Henry David Thoreau's "A Plea for Captain John Brown." As Jack Turner observes, Thoreau's "Plea" is written in the past tense and is dedicated to fashioning Brown's memory, even though it was first delivered in October 1859, when Brown himself was still alive.[28] After Brown's death, furthermore, his resurrection in song and memory provided "a source of collective identity" forged in self-sacrifice and violence during the bloody years of the Civil War.[29]

Du Bois's Brown

The lure of that legacy drew Du Bois to Harpers Ferry in 1906. As founder of the Niagara Movement, which dedicated itself to the pursuit of full political, civil, and social rights for African Americans and opposed the accommodationism of Booker T. Washington, Du Bois participated in a barefoot, candlelit procession from the residence halls of Storer College to the site of Brown's capture.[30] That the civil rights organization chose the place of Brown's raid for its second annual meeting indicates Brown's presence in the consciousnesses of black activists in the early twentieth century and, more particularly, in the political imagination of the movement's leader. By bringing Brown's story to bear on the political questions of his day, Du Bois emphasizes slavery's continuing hold on the fate of the nation and the unanswered questions bequeathed by the violence necessary to abolish it. Although Du Bois's opposition to the reigning racial order took the form of nonviolent protest, his exploration of Brown's significance reveals the author's sympathy with his subject's urgent sense of outrage and discloses Du Bois's own struggle to define a politics appropriate to the horrors of his time.[31]

When Du Bois went to Harpers Ferry, he had already been commissioned to write Brown's life story as part of a series of biographies of key figures of the Civil War era. His decision to study Brown was, in one respect, accidental. Du Bois's first choice was Frederick Douglass. When he learned that Washington had claimed the job of writing Douglass's biography, Du Bois proposed a study of Nat Turner. The Brown book only emerged as an alternative after his editors confessed their ignorance about Turner's contributions to the anti-slavery cause.[32] Nevertheless, despite the circuitous route by which Du Bois came to the project, his choice of Brown was not only accidental. While there are obvious, substantial differences between Brown and Turner, Du Bois indicates that his aim is to put them to much the same use. He locates them within a tradition, stretching back to Toussaint, of men who dedicated their lives to the end of slavery and who, while generally reviled by whites, achieved heroic status among African Americans. Du Bois lays groundwork for the biography in *The Souls of Black Folk*, where he situates Brown's raid in the context of "a new period of self-assertion and self-development" among black leaders. If this period is epitomized in the figure of Douglass, the raid on Harpers Ferry is "the extreme of its logic" (*SBF*, 66).[33] Carrying the argument forward in both the address at Harpers Ferry and in *John Brown*, Du Bois implicitly links his own bold demands for political, civil, and social equality to Brown's actions.[34]

John Brown both extends and departs from Du Bois's earlier work. Not intended to break new ground historically, the biography builds on other accounts to provide, in Du Bois's words, an "interpretation" of Brown's life. Du Bois acknowledges that his is not the first version of Brown but avers that *John Brown* is distinct insofar as it considers the substance of Brown's life "from a different point of view": "that of the little known but vastly important inner development of the Negro American" (*JB*, xxv). From this perspective, Du Bois is able to trace Brown's intimate connections to African American abolitionists and to develop his own argument about the role of black actors in the antislavery struggle. Although Du Bois considered *John Brown* "one of the best things that I had done," critics did not respond as favorably (*DOD*, 269). Lyrical at times, it weds history to poetry. But the rhetoric runs to hyperbole in places, and the book as a whole suffers from its reliance on long quotations. Further, Du Bois sometimes bends Brown's life to his own purposes without much evidentiary support. For example, the treatment of Brown's business failures as evidence of a principled objection to capitalist maneuverings ("To him business was a philanthropy" [*JB*, 25]) probably better reflects Du Bois's early gravitation toward socialism than a convincing account of Brown's life.[35]

The value of the biography resides in its attempt to make sense of Brown in a way that simultaneously recalls the forms of violence that could not be spoken in narratives of national reconciliation and sheds light on racial injustices of the early twentieth century. Like his writings about Reconstruction, Du Bois's biography of Brown aspires both to right the historical record and to recast African Americans as central characters in the drama of their liberation and that of the nation. Thus, he situates Brown's activism in the context of African American resistance, discrediting prevailing theories about the passivity of black Americans under slavery.[36] Du Bois also discredits histories that smooth over the bloodiness of past generations or offer consolation in the present. The starting point from which he considers Brown's life and legacy is "the awful fact" that "remains congealed in law and indisputable record that American slavery was the foulest and filthiest blot on nineteenth century civilization. As a school of brutality and human suffering, of female prostitution and male debauchery; as a mockery of marriage and defilement of family life; as a darkening of reason, and spiritual death, it had no parallel in its day" (*JB*, 33). According to Du Bois, the effects of such a system extend beyond the nineteenth century and outside African American communities. For it was white men who participated in "male debauchery," white slaveholders—as well as their slaves—whose marriages were mocked, and, most crucially, all Americans who suffered from the "darkening of reason and spiritual death" as long as the institution of racial slavery existed.

Du Bois's attraction to Brown as a device for exploring these costs stems not only from the abolitionist's cause but also from his prophetic calling. Describing *John Brown* as "a study in the sociology of modern prophecy," Arnold Rampersad argues that even if Du Bois rejected the Bible's divine authority, he sustained a commitment to Puritan ethics and a deep faith in human sinfulness.[37] Du Bois's use of epigraphs in this regard is telling. The first five chapters, which discuss Brown's life before he crossed the threshold into violence in Kansas, are preceded by passages from the New Testament; the first four of these speak to the promised coming of a savior, and the last echoes Brown's admonition to "remember them that are in bonds as bound with them." The epigraphs for chapters 6 through 13 are from the Hebrew Bible, and all but one of these are from the book of Isaiah and deal with the restoration of Israel as part of a divine plan. The biblical allusions do not end there. "To the unraveling of human tangles we would gladly believe that God sends especial men—chosen vessels which come to the world's deliverance" (*JB*, 3), Du Bois announces in the first chapter. Throughout the text, Du Bois likens Brown to Moses, to various prophets, and to Gideon, one of Brown's heroes. The biblical resonances of what Du Bois characterizes as "the wonderful message of [Brown's] forty days in prison" recall the words of Thoreau and other antislavery activists who made much of Brown's Christ-like status and evoke the tradition of the Black Christ (*JB*, 186).[38]

Crucially, Du Bois is careful to paint Brown as a religious visionary but not a lunatic. The question of Brown's sanity was advanced as a defense strategy— a strategy which the defendant angrily rejected—and has occupied white commentators ever since.[39] Yet, as Du Bois and other black commentators note, the assumption of Brown's insanity reveals the ongoing power of the view that for a white man to perceive the black cause as his own is madness, and it obscures the inhumanity of the slave system against which Brown fought.[40] Indeed, Edward Blum contends, *John Brown* advances "a counter-theological view that sanctifie[s] white support for black folk."[41] Du Bois thereby speaks *through* Brown, prophesying that the present and future health of American democracy depend directly and concretely on the uses made of the slave past.

It is easy to see why Du Bois, having been thwarted in his plan to write about Turner, would turn to Brown as a promising vehicle for articulating African Americans' perspective on the present-past. Unlike most white Americans of his time, or Du Bois's own, Brown evinced a deep understanding of the stakes of sustaining racial slavery, and his antislavery convictions were matched by a sense of what the institution must mean to black Americans themselves. "To most Americans," Du Bois writes, "the inner striving of the Negro was a veiled and an unknown tale: they had heard of Douglass, they knew of fugitive slaves, but of the living, organized, struggling group that made both these phenomena possible they had no conception" (*JB*, 123). John Brown was different. He interacted comfortably with

African Americans and sought their involvement in his efforts. In addition to his well-known association with Frederick Douglass, Brown conferred with a wide range of leaders including Harriet Tubman, Henry Highland Garnet, and Martin Delany. Going further, Du Bois implicitly credits Brown with changing Douglass's mind about the need for violence in the elimination of slavery, by including the famous exchange between Douglass and Sojourner Truth in which the former proclaims that "because God is not dead, slavery can only end in blood" (*JB*, 56).[42] Crucially, when the time arose for self-sacrifice on behalf of abolition, Brown did not hesitate.

Yet Du Bois's portrait of Brown's relationship with black antislavery activists reveals the blindness joined to the insight. Certainly, Brown refused the luxury of seeing slavery as an abstraction, a distant problem. At the same time, Du Bois uncovers how Brown's Manichean worldview prevented him from recognizing the shortcomings of his own grasp of the complexity of the slave system or the stakes for black Americans in fighting it. Douglass, by Du Bois's account, evinced a more complicated understanding:

> . . . here two radically opposite characters saw slavery from opposite sides of the shield. Both hated it with all their strength, but one knew its physical degradation, its tremendous power and the strong sympathies and interests that buttressed it the world over; the other felt its moral evil and knowing simply that it was wrong, concluded that John Brown and God could overthrow it. . . . And this attitude of Douglass was in varying degrees and strides the attitude of the leading Negroes of his day. They believed in John Brown but not in his plan. They knew he was right, but they knew that for any failure in his project they, the black men, would probably pay the cost. And the horror of that cost none knew as they (*JB*, 50).

Although Du Bois defends Brown's "plan" as militarily sound and lays the blame for the fiasco at Harpers Ferry on Brown's associates, his position on African American reluctance to join the raid on Harpers Ferry is undecided. He intimates that Brown and Douglass were both right. The portrait of their disagreement reveals that Brown's ignorance of the living death of slavery enabled him to act as he did. Where Brown could only see the evil he was fighting, his black allies "saw what John Brown did not fully realize until the last: the tremendous meaning of sacrifice even though his enterprise failed and they were sure it would fail" (*JB*, 175). And as Du Bois points out, the call to sacrifice meant something quite different to those Americans whose entire lives had been, forcibly, dedicated to the good of others than it did to someone like Brown, who chose his risks and knew little about compulsory sacrifice (*JB*, 175). Even Brown's commitment to equality proved to be an obstacle insofar as he saw African Americans as human just like him and failed to recognize that their experiences might provide them with a distinct perspective on slavery and abolition.

"Was John Brown simply an episode, or was he an eternal truth? And if a truth, how speaks that truth to-day?" (*JB*, 190). Du Bois poses these questions in the final chapter, yet his answer can be read in the refrain, repeated with variations throughout the book, that "the cost of liberty is less than the price of repression" (*JB* 2, 3, 33, 66, 195, 200). What this means, for Du Bois, is that the cause of freedom and equality is as urgent in his own time as it was in Brown's. Although he does not evince optimism that the use of force will inevitably secure a more democratic society, he warns that injustice becomes more difficult to cure with every day's delay. This is not to say that Du Bois understates the price of antiracist violence. On the contrary, his straightforward report of the slaughter at Pottawatomie indicates Du Bois's understanding of the dangers of evading the hard reality of "the cost of freedom" through euphemism or romance. When he publishes the revised version of *John Brown*, he adds a "preface" that emphasizes the killing of the five proslavery "border ruffians" in 1856.[43] Du Bois's point is neither to explain away nor to celebrate Brown's participation in "violent murder."[44] He does not glory in the "five twisted, red and mangled corpses" or omit "the stifled wailing of widows and little children" (*JB* 68). Acknowledging that "the deed did not make Kansas free," Du Bois characterizes "the carnival of crime and rapine that ensued" as "a disgrace to civilization" (*JB* 66). All of this Du Bois readily admits; but he insists that these events, unjustifiable though they are, paved the way toward Brown's execution and toward the lasting effect of his utterances from prison. These words, Du Bois writes, "did more to shake the foundations of slavery than any single thing that ever happened in America" (*JB* 186). Neither saint nor criminal but both, Du Bois's Brown committed unspeakable acts that helped to put an end to centuries of unspeakable acts.

What does the case of John Brown tell Du Bois and his readers about the kind of political action that is warranted by the violent repression of the post-Reconstruction years? *John Brown* does not answer this question unequivocally. Du Bois does state that the cost of liberty is always worth paying—even by blood—and that slavery "had to die by revolution, not by milder means" (*JB*, 173). But he goes on to say that "revolution is not a test of capacity; it is always a loss and a lowering of ideals" (*JB*, 201), and he warns against equating blood with freedom or mistaking the willingness to expend it for leadership (*JB*, 196). Although this language, coupled with the refutation of violence in the "Address to the Country," intimates an effort to separate the righteousness of Brown's lifework from its bloodiness, Du Bois recognizes that such a distinction is impossible. In the 1962 version of *John Brown*, which looks with approval upon the revolutions in China and the Soviet Union, Du Bois adds the following claim: "But if it is a true revolution it repays all losses and results in the uplift of the human race."[45] Not even his conviction about the possibility of a "true revolution," however, puts to rest the conflict between violence and uplift, carnage and freedom. Rather than attempt to reconcile them, Du Bois points readers in another direction. By relating the story of John Brown from the vantage of African American experiences, he challenges divided memories and segregated time zones, insisting that every day's delay in the abolition of slavery compounded the violence committed against the slaves. Thus, when he repeats that "the cost of liberty is less than the price of repression," Du Bois is not simply making a point about ends and means in political life. He is radically redrawing the portrait of the American past so that it encompasses the lives of the disregarded.

This is not a new theme for Du Bois. Indeed, it is at the heart of the dissertation that became his first book, *The Suppression of the African Slave-Trade to the United States of America, 1638–1870*. There, Du Bois castigates the founding generation for failing to abolish the slave trade at a moment when it was vulnerable. This failure matters not only because it enabled the persistence of slavery for nearly another century but also because it helped to engender a political culture of evasion that undergirded the bloodshed of the 1850s and the resurgence of antiblack violence less than a half-century later.

> One cannot, to be sure, demand of whole nations exceptional moral foresight and heroism; but a certain hard common-sense in facing the complicated phenomena of political life must be expected in every progressive people. In some respects we as a nation seem to lack this; we have the somewhat inchoate idea that we are not destined to be harassed with great social questions, and that even if we are, and fail to answer them, the fault is with the question and not with us. Consequently we often congratulate ourselves more on getting rid of a problem than on solving it (*SAST*, 198–99).[46]

In Du Bois's view, then, we can only understand the significance of Brown's life against the backdrop of a tradition of denial that is tightly interwoven into political life in the United States from its earliest years. We can only understand it, furthermore, if we recall that "getting rid of a problem" has meant forgetting, sequestering, and even getting rid of the men and women whose existence is regarded as problematic.[47]

The concluding chapter of *John Brown* is instructive for contemporary political thinking insofar as its representation of Brown as a hero avoids the pitfalls of deploying Brown's example as part of a redemptive narrative of American nationalism.[48] All too aware of the capacity of such narratives to sustain and, simultaneously, disavow racial hierarchy, Du Bois resists participating in what Bercovitch calls "the ritual of consensus" that keeps the flame of revolution alive as a means of affirming the prevailing social order.[49] He manages this in two ways. First, he locates his story of Brown's life and meaning within a larger legacy of white supremacy and racist ideology that he traces to the very roots of the nation. Although Du Bois chastises other Americans for losing sight of "the foundation principles of their government," he understands that the return to those principles is not simply the recovery of a lost innocence (*JB*, 197).[50] Nor is the affirmation of principles sufficient without attention to their substantive realization in the lives of black Americans. Professing a commitment to racial equality without a confronting the twinned beginnings of slavery and freedom in North America is dangerous, according to Du Bois. "With the birth of wealth and liberty west of the seas," he reminds readers, "came slavery, and a slavery all the more cruel and hideous because it gradually built itself on a caste of race and color" (*JB*, 1). In the 1962 edition, he expands his argument to encompass a critique of American expansionism by adding a passage that redescribes the bloodshed of Kansas in colonial terms as "the last chapter of this great theft" of land from American Indians.[51]

The global orientation of Du Bois's thought provides a second bulwark against any temptation to fold Brown's life into a comforting narrative about American democracy. *John Brown* begins in Africa, whose "mystic spell . . . is and ever was over all America" (*JB*, 1). Thus, Du Bois radically challenges the idea of "America" as a clean break. The assertion that Africa and the United States are permanently tied together not only reminds readers that American democracy began in theft but also identifies an opportunity; for the United States, in his view, has much to gain from the exploration of its African inheritance. Further, Du Bois undercuts the presumption that freedom and equality are peculiarly American legacies. He notes, for instance, that Brown combined "the religion of equality and sympathy with misfortune" with "the strong influence of the social doctrines of the French Revolution with its emphasis on freedom and power in political life" (*JB*, 190). Du Bois's deliberate choice of the French Revolution as the emblem of political freedom and, more radically, his references to Haitian independence ("John Brown was born just as the shudder of Hayti was running through all the Americas" [*JB*, 33]) make it clear that Du Bois's approval of Brown's campaign stops well short of endorsing the abolitionist's reverence for the American mission.

Moreover, the chapter on Brown's legacy extends beyond the temporal and geographic borders of the Civil War era so as to enact a similar unsettling of borders defining the post-Reconstruction period. The meaning of Brown's life and cause, Du Bois writes, sheds light not only on the situation of African Americans but also on "the procuring of coolie labor, the ruling of India, the exploitation of Africa, the problem of the unemployed, and the curbing of the corporations" (*JB*, 195). Underlying all of these phenomena, he argues, is a new form of racism that emerged after Brown's time. Thus, he dedicates much of the concluding chapter to exposing the untruth of social Darwinism and its support for racialized forms of exploitation and domination. Noting that *On the Origin of Species* appeared in the same year as the raid on Harpers Ferry, Du Bois demonstrates that the end of slavery was hardly the end of racial hierarchy, and he traces the route by which perversions of evolutionary science allow the replacement of the old slave system with a global system of racial castes. The net result of such a system will not be the improvement of the species, he warns, but the hegemony of the weakest and most depraved whites over the nonwhites of the world and the suffering and loss of culture and productivity that accompany such a world order (*JB*, 190–201). Anticipating his later internationalist writings, indeed foretelling the specific terms of his critique of the imperial roots of World War I, Du Bois contends that the story of John Brown leads directly to a twentieth-century world ruled by the "morality of the club" (*JB* 194).

John Brown in an Age of Terror

To say that it is possible to affirm Brown's cause without reaffirming an uncritical Americanism is not to put to rest other troubling questions about whether and how to invoke Brown today. Indeed, his example seems inapt or dangerous in a number of obvious ways. The specific kinds of racial terror against which Brown fought, and those that threatened black communities in Du Bois's time, have been defeated. In addition, the September 11 attacks and the American-led "War on Terror" have engendered a widespread public rejection of religious crusaders who shed blood in the name of struggle and have hardened the line between what is perceived as legitimate, state-sponsored violence and the violence that threatens state power. Despite these concerns, I suggest that Du Bois's biography of Brown offers crucial resources for thinking about race in a "postracial" era and about violence and democracy when the specter of terror is used to justify brutal and repressive policies. To that end, I approach the text in two ways. The first begins from the claim that "John Brown was right" and accentuates Du Bois's effort to vindicate Brown's memory. This reading both appreciates the democratic work done by challenging racial divisions of historical memory and discloses undemocratic elements inherent in Brown's example and in the practice of heroic biography. Consequently, I offer a second reading, which stresses Du Bois's treatment of Brown's life and legacy as a constellation of conflicts and unanswered questions. I argue that this second reading, while not entirely displacing the first, provides a crucial supplement and a rich source from which to draw in reflecting on the tangled relations of race, violence, and democracy today.

"To-day at last we know: John Brown was right" (*JB* 172), Du Bois avers. Brown was right, in Du Bois's view, because his antislavery commitments were matched by his belief in human equality. He was also right insofar as he understood that any further delay in taking decisive action against slavery would only intensify the violence of its eventual end. He was right because, as Frederick Douglass remarks, "if John Brown did not end the war that ended slavery, he did, at least, begin the war that ended slavery" (*JB* 179). Despite the confidence of Du Bois's declarative sentence (and the authority of Douglass), vindicating Brown's cause is not as simple as Du Bois implies. For what he offers as a consensus view—what *we* know today—was in fact a profound challenge to all but the most radical white Americans in 1909. Taking this claim seriously in our time, furthermore, demands not only a rejection of racial hierarchy, a rejection that seems unproblematic, but also a willingness to entertain the possibility that achieving a democratic order may depend on zealots who disdain democratic procedures and institutions. One contemporary thinker who has absorbed this possibility is Barack Obama. In a meditation on the lasting import of Brown's bloody campaign, he observes: "I'm reminded that deliberation and the constitutional order may sometimes be the luxury of the powerful, and that it has sometimes been the cranks, the zealots, the prophets, the agitators, and the unreasonable—in other words, the absolutists—that have fought for a new order." And, he continues, "knowing this, I can't summarily dismiss those possessed of similar certainty today."[52] Obama's acknowledgment of his own fallibility in the face of what appears to be irrational conviction is a welcome alternative to a kind of anti-zealous zealotry that dismisses ideas simply because they are extreme.[53]

My interpretation of Du Bois presses on this insight. Taking seriously the claim that John Brown was right not only reinforces the wisdom of political humility, but it also unsettles some of democratic theorists' most dearly held convictions. Among them is the idea that the legitimacy of democratic decisions depends on a process of deliberation. Brown realized that the complex of interests, prejudices, and fear that preserved slavery was not susceptible to dissolution through reasoned debate. At the root of his quarrel with Garrison and other abolitionists who believed that moral suasion alone would eliminate slavery was an understanding of the depth of the racial gap in perception about the moral and political implications of the institution. "Prejudice and privilege do not emerge in deliberative settings as bad reasons, and they are not countered by good arguments," notes Lynn Sanders in her critique of deliberative models of democratic politics.[54] Moreover, Sanders maintains, the impulse to find a "common voice" that drives deliberative theories is likely to reinforce the exclusion of perspectives of those citizens who are taken to lack authority and is inappropriate in situations in which the expression of particular complaints ought to be privileged.[55] Surely, slavery constitutes such a situation. The idea that abolition or the question of redress for racial crimes on the scale of slavery should depend upon a debate in which all perspectives are treated as equal seems unfair, injurious even, to victims of white supremacy.

Starting from the position that "John Brown was right" also makes vivid the costs of what Michael Hanchard calls "racial time."[56] Temporizing, in the guise of moderation, perpetuates injuries sustained by some members of the polity so that others may be protected. Brown understood, and Du Bois concurs, that faith in the inevitable march of progress, where deeply ingrained social injustice exists, also underwrites a kind of criminality: the criminality of the unaroused, of the citizen as bystander. This is what Martin Luther King, Jr., calls a "tragic misconception of time."[57] In this light, reflecting on the urgency of Brown's antislavery campaign leads not only to consideration of the violent acts he committed or supported but also disallows the impulse to let those acts divert attention from the vastly greater violence that was enabled by prolonging slavery in the hope of ending it without entirely upsetting the public order.

Drawing this claim forward, Du Bois's rendering of Brown challenges those of us who enjoy the privileges of a well-ordered life to inquire into the kinds of violence perpetrated in our name. To be clear, I am not suggesting that anything like the antiblack violence of the 1850s or the turn of the twentieth century persists. What I contend, instead, is that one way of taking on board the implications of Du Bois's vindication of John Brown is to reorient ourselves to contemporary injustice so that we are compelled to ask when that injustice constitutes a crisis. Consider the unprecedented rise in incarceration. Bruce Western reports that African American men are imprisoned at a rate eight times that of white Americans, a figure that outstrips most other measures of racial inequality, and he concludes that "we can read the story of mass imprisonment as part of the evolution of African American citizenship."[58] This phenomenon is perhaps the most dramatic example of how, concretely, race matters in the post-civil rights era.[59] Drawing out the ethical and political implications of Western's research, Glenn Loury writes: "We law-abiding, middle-class Americans have made decisions about social policy and incarceration, and we benefit from those decisions, and that means from a system of suffering, rooted in state violence, meted out at our request."[60] The connection is not lost on Du Bois, who in the 1962 version of *John Brown* moves smoothly from the lynching epidemic to the overrepresentation of African Americans in U.S. prisons. "Not all America has approved or encouraged this injustice," he writes. And he continues, "Many have helped and defended the Negro, but the majority have permitted injustice without protest."[61] Du Bois's addition of this discussion to a book about John Brown is not a non sequitur; rather, it forces readers to reckon with the long reach of slavery and the antiblack violence to which it gave rise. It disallows a single-minded focus on the violence of some—Brown, terrorists, criminals—and demands that we also regard the largely invisible, unrecalled violence that the state undertakes on our behalf.

Embracing the view that John Brown was right should make Du Bois's readers more attuned to the extent and urgency of racial injustice, but Brown's example has obvious limitations, no matter the righteousness of his campaign. First, there is the question of how well his version of moral absolutism applies to the challenges of racial injustice in the contemporary context and whether it applies too well to a variety of other causes. Whereas Brown had a readily identifiable enemy in slavery and slaveholders, contemporary racism and racial injustice often assume more subtle and subterranean forms. Brown's example is less clear, then, as a guide to navigating the challenges posed by centuries of entrenched privilege or the complex of questions raised by the staggering levels of imprisonment of black and brown Americans. Further, good-versus-evil formulations are too easily mobilized for antidemocratic purposes, and anyone seeking to appropriate Brown's example must confront the fact that his contest with Satan has inspired not only critics of racial injustice but also extremists like Timothy McVeigh and Neal Horsley, creator of "Nuremberg Files," which lists the names of abortion providers online and tracks their fates.[62]

In addition to these dangers, there is the possibility that the kind of heroic politics represented by a figure like John Brown, and the biographical genre that enshrines it, may be undemocratic, whatever the ends of Brown's actions. Brown's insight into the symbolic power of African American militancy in an era in which presumptions about black docility prevailed among both pro- and antislavery whites, was revolutionary. And Du Bois not only admires Brown's perceptiveness in this regard but advances own version of the tradition of black resistance. One could point to this tradition without endorsing a politics that prizes military achievement as an indicator of humanity and fitness for freedom, but Brown makes no such distinctions. His subscription to such a view is revealed by his comments on Harriet Tubman—"General Tubman"—whom he paid the highest compliment he knew: "He (Harriet) is the most of a man, naturally, I have ever met with" (*JB*, 124). Beyond the sheer oddity of the formulation, there is the more troubling intimation that Tubman achieved honorary status only through her military exploits. Full humanity is thus revealed in a willingness to act like a "man," to go to battle for one's beliefs.

Even if it is admitted that women too can be warriors, such a notion of democratic political action obscures the wide range of battles fought daily both under slavery and under the racial regime that followed. It commends a politics focused on the pursuit of immortality and located outside the realm of necessity, thereby privileging certain forms of activity and denigrating others.[63] Although Du Bois does not take up this point directly in *John Brown*, he recognizes it elsewhere in his assessment of the developments that led to the legal recognition of black male citizenship:

> It had been a commonplace thing in the North to declare that Negroes would not fight. Even the black man's friends were skeptical about the possibility of using him as a soldier, and far from its being to the credit of black men, or any men, that they did not want to kill, the ability and willingness to take human life has always been, even in the minds of liberal men, a proof of manhood. It took in many respects a finer type of courage for the Negro to work quietly and faithfully as a slave while the world was fighting over his destiny than it did to seize a bayonet and rush mad with fury or inflamed with drink, and plunge it into the bowels of a stranger.

The remainder of the paragraph indicates the political and cultural poverty of a society that values military achievements above all others:

> He might plead his cause with the tongue of Frederick Douglass, and the nation listened almost unmoved. He might labor for the nation's wealth, and the nation took the results without thanks, and handed him as near nothing in return as would keep him alive. He was called a coward and a fool when he protected the women and children of his

master. But when he rose and fought and killed, the whole nation with one voice proclaimed him a man and a brother (*BR*, 104).[64]

Certainly, Du Bois's critique is itself premised on a notion of manhood. What he offers is an alternative, if quieter and less violent, form of manly heroism. But his suggestion that the greatest accomplishments of the slaves be measured in the daily struggle to survive against long odds points the way toward a conception of politics in which martial prowess is not the highest ideal. It offers a conception of politics that encompasses men and women excluded from military service, and equally important, those activities considered outside (or even dangerous to) what is considered properly political.[65]

Violence is not the only issue here. Even nonviolent versions of heroic politics, such as the enshrinement of Martin Luther King, Jr., as the symbol of the civil rights movement, risks effacing the contributions of the women and men who precede and follow the hero's efforts and whose work makes his prominence possible. To make too much of John Brown's example or any heroic example, then, is to reinforce an idea of democratic politics that is available only to those who are positioned to practice a certain kind of spectacular sacrifice and to train our eyes on only those venues to which they have privileged access. It is the wrong kind of memory insofar as it enables black heroes to join white ones without inquiring more deeply into the wide-ranging contributions of the men and women who fought slavery and who fight its lingering effects.

In this regard, Du Bois's *John Brown* attests to the limits of Brown's example, even as those limits appear to undercut the author's stated intentions. When David Levering Lewis remarks that Du Bois's chapter on African American history in the 1830s ("The Black Phalanx") offers "a narrative as engrossing as it was decoupled from the protagonist," he captures a problem presented by the book as a whole.[66] The impulse to vindicate Brown, to remake him as an inspiration for heroic politics, works awkwardly with the kind of broad-reaching social critique Du Bois aims to offer. Nor does the inclusion of Brown among God's elect, "especial men—chosen vessels which come to the world's deliverance," speak as eloquently to the "inner strivings" of African Americans that are supposed to be the center of the book as do Du Bois's vignettes of his own and other black Americans' experiences in *Souls* and other writings (*JB*, 3). Despite the radical challenge posed by the figuration of black resistance in whiteface, the focus on Brown's heroism distracts from the story of African Americans' internal lives, from their role in the liberation of the country from slavery, and from the analysis of the social, political, and economic costs of the institution that Brown gave his life to end.⁶⁷ Moreover, the dangers of applauding patriarchal power against an evil enemy ought to give today's democrats particular pause, in light of the recent availability of a discourse of "masculinist protection" to underwrite military adventures abroad and the truncation of civil rights inside the United States.⁶⁸

To be sure, the effect of Brown's name, which still moves many white Americans to anger or fear, suggests that there may be strategic value in reclaiming Brown as a reminder of the presence of the slave past and as an incitement to action in a period when the United States has moved away from racial justice as a political priority. But the project of adding good examples to the bad ones (John Brown joins David Duke, for instance) does little to address the broader implications of white supremacy's longevity. It makes sense in a political world inhabited by good people and bad people, racists and nonracists. In the world inhabited by actual human beings, by contrast, a preoccupation with individual acts and exemplars of racism obscures the normalcy of antiblack racism and the advantages enjoyed by white Americans as a group. It severs the historical links between current injustices and racial slavery.

This is not, however, the end of the story. If *John Brown* reveals the limits of heroic biography, it also models another kind of memorial politics. Reading *John Brown* for its tragic elements, rather than only for its homage to Brown as hero, opens other possibilities. When Du Bois warns that the "the memory of John Brown stands to-day as a mighty warning to his country" (*JB*, 196), he counsels against the belief that the questions bequeathed by centuries of slavery have been laid to rest. In other words, the biography reveals what is left unresolved—and may be unresolvable—in Brown's life story. It conjures "the simultaneity of justice and transgression, accomplishment and ruin, health and disease, insight and blindness, reason and tyranny that mark both Greek tragedy and political theory," in Peter Euben's view.⁶⁹ To flesh out what this means in relation to *John Brown*, I return to two elements of the biography discussed above: Du Bois's rendering of the dispute between Brown and Douglass and his treatment of Brown's bloodthirst.

Given that *John Brown* is at least as concerned with African American antislavery efforts as it is with the Old Man's crusade, Du Bois's discussion of Brown's and Douglass's disagreement about Harpers Ferry acquires a broader significance. At heart, the two men agreed that slavery could only be uprooted through force. Yet Douglass's opposition to the raid on the federal arsenal reveals how two friends, fully united in their assessment of what justice required, could be fundamentally divided in their understanding of what it meant to act on that assessment. For his part, Brown made his case with what George Shulman calls prophetic authority. Brown understood that "an imperative register of voice can sound (and be) despotic, but in the face of a racial regime constituted by (disavowal of) domination, acts of witness and judgment seem less symptoms of dogmatism and more conditions of political action, which entails claim-making about conduct, the reality of others, and fateful choices between commitments not readily reconciled." The dangers of such authority are real, Shulman notes, "but there is no escaping them."[70] Of course Douglass also had unanswerable authority. Although he concurred with Brown's assessment of the evil of slavery and was deeply moved by the example of Brown's sacrifice, the former slave's convictions grew out of an intimate understanding of slavery as a rule of force, rather than the belief in his own righteousness. Further, he understood something about the implications of the raid for slaves and free blacks that was beyond Brown's grasp. "Was not their whole life already a sacrifice? Were they called by any right of God or man to give more than they had already given? What more did they owe the world? Did not the world owe them an unpayable amount?" (*JB*, 176).

By giving voice to these concerns, Du Bois does not criticize Douglass or the men and women on who balked at Brown's plan. He honors them. First, Du Bois paints a portrait of African Americans with distinctive assessments of their own situation in the antebellum period. Their assessments, like Brown's, were rarely recalled in expressions of public memory; for they challenged rather than reinforced the terms of national reconciliation. Du Bois also affirms the wisdom of the view that the burdens of Brown's failure would be borne unequally. The costs of the mission fell heavily on African Americans, not only those who accompanied Brown but also those who were swept up in the bloody reaction.[71] More, by relating the conflict, Du Bois tempers the straightforward truths of heroic biography with the indeterminacy tragedy brings to life. Both men were right, Du Bois seems to say. Their differences were reconciled, but only retrospectively, in Douglass's actions and his tributes to his martyred comrade. By resurrecting their disagreement, Du Bois thus turns the story of a prophet into an unsettling portrait of the uncertainty that accompanies all political action.

Constructed in this way, the lesson of Brown's violence is not an answer but a question. Or, rather, it is a cluster of questions. My reading thus proposes a modest revision of William Cain's conclusion that "the most disturbing feature of *John Brown*, and the most provocative, alarmed tribute one can pay to it, is to say that Du Bois passionately evokes and labors to resist the inescapably violent settlement of the Negro question."[72] I contend that it is precisely the point of Du Bois's biography to highlight the violence entailed by the (ongoing) failure to settle the Negro question. I agree that Du Bois offers no final counsel as to how to understand the relationship between bloodshed and democracy, whether as necessarily bound together or perpetually at odds. He does not follow Thoreau, for example, in exalting Brown's violence.[73] But neither is he equivocal or ambivalent about the political significance of engaging all aspects of Brown's memory, of keeping alive the memory of its heights and its goriest depths. Doing so situates Du Bois permanently within an unreconciled—and unreconcilable—tension, between a renunciation of violence as a means of realizing racial justice and an appreciation that Brown's barbarism was necessary to his effectiveness as a catalyst for abolition. Failing to keep both poles of the tension alive, Du Bois realizes, helps to entrench precisely the kind of historical amnesia that covers over the violence of the present. Further, Brown's decision to take violent action against the state, in the name of the values on which it was founded, disturbs conventions about *who* has a monopoly on legitimate uses of force.

The upshot of this reading is a brief for active, critical recollection rather than revolution. *John Brown* does not offer criteria by which to judge when injustice demands immediate action or what shape that action should take. Instead, Du Bois calls on readers to adopt an orientation that keeps the violence of the past vivid in the present. He disallows the impulse to celebrate the accomplishments of the Civil War without noting equally the brutality that made it necessary and the temporizing that compounded its costs. "The majority of Americans," Du Bois insists, "seem to have forgotten the foundation principles of their government and the recklessly destructive effect of the blows meant to bind and tether their fellows" (*JB*, 197). In other words, Du Bois does more than simply call his fellow citizens back to their political origins or supplant romanticized stories of American freedom with a more accurate picture of its violation. By reuniting the principles and the blows, the lofty aspiration and the reckless destruction of human life, Du Bois opposes the evasions that sustain present-day practices of racial subordination.[74]

Evidence of the living force of such evasions abounds. The controversy that shadowed George Bush's nomination of John Ashcroft to be attorney general in 2001 provides just one example. Ashcroft was criticized for a 1998 interview for *Southern Partisan* in which he worried that the record of "Southern patriots like Lee, Jackson and Davis" would go undefended, "or else we'll be taught that these people were giving their lives, subscribing their sacred fortunes and their honor to some perverted agenda."[75] What is disturbing is not simply the confirmation of a defender of the Lost Cause to head the Justice Department. Also worrisome, I think, is the way that a public preoccupation with whether or not the nominee was a "racist" diverted the debate from deeper questions about the currency of nostalgia for a regime defined by antiblack brutality. Like the question of whether Brown was a madman, the focus on what was in Ashcroft's heart or head remakes the question of slavery and its legacies as an individual one. This is not a partisan failing. Instead, both defenders and opponents of the nominee engaged in what Ali Behdad calls "cultural deletion," the invocation of the past to obscure its violent character.[76] It reveals a continuing failure to reckon with the everydayness of brutality in the waning days of the slave era, a kind of retrospective, pious hope that slavery could be eliminated without passing on staggering costs to subsequent generations.

Perhaps these matters seem politically insubstantial, merely academic now. Reveling in the election of an African American to the presidency, the United States seems far removed from the day when Du Bois groped for words to capture the situation of a "mobbed, and mocked, and murdered people." At the same time, in a nation still recoiling from recent acts of terror, the dangers posed by a figure like Brown appear all too close. Nevertheless, it may be that we need to engage Brown now more than ever. Just as Du Bois unearths buried stories of slaves' part in the Civil War and the work of new citizens during Reconstruction, he revives Brown's campaign to lay bare the suppressed or forgotten violence of the past and to ask how that suppression or forgetting enables the unnoted violence of the present. In Du Bois's hands, the political consequence of Brown's memory is not, finally, his enshrinement as a heroic individual or guide to political action. Rather, reconsidering his life and legacy may allow us to reconsider the suppressed dilemmas that bequeathed both the progress we rightly celebrate and the human costs we prefer not to engage. Du Bois's warning is not only directed to those who keep alive the vision of a slaveless confederacy, but it equally rebukes all of us who fail to recognize the bloody traces of the past in today's liberal democratic order. John Brown, in Du Bois's hands, is a tragic figure whose actions proved both necessary and unjustifiable. He is a challenge to succeeding generations. Thus, Du Bois ends his book with a prophecy that disallows the temptation to close the book on the bloody era Brown represents: "You may dispose of me very easily—I am nearly disposed of now; but this question is still to be settled—this Negro question, I mean. The end of that is not yet" (*JB*, 201).

FOUR | Practicing Critical Race Autobiography

Strive to render oneself a question to oneself, while appreciating that your efforts will meet with partial and limited success.

—William Connolly, "Confessing Identity\Belonging to Difference"[1]

Setting an Example, Being a Problem

The power of John Brown's (and Du Bois's) question reverberates today. "The end of [this Negro] question is not yet," when Americans inhabit a post-civil rights era, but racial hierarchies persist; when identity politics claims appear regressive, but identities still matter politically; when political theorists openly worry that democracy "is in recession."[2] Where the previous chapters explored the contours and political consequences of buried memories of slavery and its legacies, the next two chapters engage Du Bois in an exchange with political theorists struggling to articulate conceptions of democratic selfhood and citizenship that might meet the challenges of these times. What resources does Du Bois provide for responding to the unsettled questions bequeathed by generations of slavery and colonial violence? How might a reading of his political thought stretch, complement, and trouble the most compelling attempts to understand what it means to live democratically today? By way of an answer, albeit a partial one, I offer a pair of exchanges through which I set Du Bois's writing in conversation with recent work in democratic theory. In the fourth chapter, I ask how Du Bois's exploration of his own identity and attempted cultivation of a more democratic readership in the 1940 autobiography, *Dusk of Dawn*, resonates with and challenges William Connolly's arguments for democratic self-fashioning. In the fifth, I mine Du Bois's essay on the "Damnation of Women" (1920) as a site for reflection on how feminist theories of citizenship might address the continuing consequences of slavery.

Both chapters focus on questions of exemplarity, tracing the ways Du Bois works and reworks the examples of African American lives to criticize the devastating effects of racial hierarchy and to seek political lessons from their experiences. As Nahum Chandler observes, "Du Bois is everywhere concerned with the character, status, and implication of the example. . . . The example exposes at once both the circumstances and the possible."[3] There are risks to such an approach. As the discussion of *John Brown* indicates, a focus on exemplary individuality can stifle democratic politics, and Du Bois's affirmation that "the Negro race, like all races, is going to be saved by its exceptional men" reinforces the suspicion that his view of exemplarity is primarily one of elite leadership.[4] Without diminishing these risks, I investigate those dimensions of Du Bois's re-presentation of African American lives as exemplary that enable his readers to imagine more democratic theories of selfhood and citizenship.

Dusk of Dawn begins with the following assessment: "My life had its significance and its only deep significance because it was part of a Problem" (*DOD*, xxix). In one sense, the claim is a noteworthy understatement of Du Bois's singularity and his accomplishments during the preceding seven decades.[5] In another, it universalizes his experiences and aspirations: "But that problem was, as I continue to think, the central problem of the greatest of the world's democracies and so the Problem of the future world" (*DOD*, xxix–xxx). This language of the "problem" is familiar to readers of Du Bois's work, and it reflects a lifelong dedication to the pursuit of solutions to social ills.[6] Yet Du Bois's intention of appraising his life in light of the "Problem" and *as* a "problem" indicates the flexibility of the term and the limitations of interpreting it only literally. In the opening of *Dusk of Dawn*, Du Bois implicitly revives the "unasked question" that opens *The Souls of Black Folk*: "How does it feel to be a problem?" (*SBF*, 37) and suggests why the "problem" is among the most fertile of the metaphors he employed across a life steeped in figurative language. The misfit between Du Bois as an individual and "the problem" disrupts thoughtless applications of the term to any and all African Americans or questions of race. "Metaphors *are* arguments," William Andrews observes. "Their success depends greatly on the capacity of the reader to accept and explore the creative dialectic of the semantic clash until new meanings emerge from the debris of old presuppositions."[7] It is this dialectic that I explore in this chapter, tracking Du Bois's investigation of his double-life as an example of the "Problem" and exemplar of its overcoming.

In a sense, the tensions that inhere in Du Bois's relationship to the "Problem" mirror the concept of exemplarity itself. Where the example is defined by the *Oxford English Dictionary* as, first and foremost, "a typical instance" whose roots are traceable to earlier forms of the word "sample," the "exemplar" denotes a "model for imitation."[8] Although each word can serve as a substitute or synonym for the other, their primary meanings diverge. As Alexander Gelley explains, exemplarity's doubleness reflects two different renderings of the Greek word *paradeigma*. One tradition, linked to Plato, establishes a vertical relationship between the example as model or standard to be emulated, on the one hand, and instantiations of the standard, on the other. The second sense, developed by Aristotle, establishes lateral relationships between one instance and others; the implied equality among them points to, without naming, a whole that must be constituted or recovered. Importantly, this incompleteness demands a judgment of the reader/listener, who aims to make sense of the example.[9] "The scandal of the example, its logical fallibility, lies in the fact that this ethical summons—the obligation to judge—is predicated not on a law or rule—thus at the level of the general or universal—but on the instance in its particularity, an instance that cannot itself suffice to justify the principle in question."[10] Kirstie McClure extends this understanding of the force of the example, exploring how the call to judgment enacted by the example can stimulate a political response. "The double movement of exemplarity," in her view, operates through representations of past deeds, which are both displayed and evaluated by the author. Without offering general rules for political emulation, exemplarity engages the reader, eliciting judgment and providing an example of judging.[11] Du Bois adds another dimension to this movement. For he is not simply recording his own past and selectively praising/blaming himself to kindle the imaginations of his readers. Rather, by playing on the breach between his status as exemplar and as mere example, his paradoxical relationship to the "Problem," he simultaneously re-presents himself as a symbol of uplift and renders palpable his experiences as one among the millions of Americans, and hundreds of millions of people around the world, who carry the mark of racial subordination.

This doubleness is reflected in Du Bois's rhetoric, which moves back and forth between the exalted and the deflationary, sometimes in a single passage. For instance, in the first chapter of *Dusk of Dawn*, he offers the following account of his life's work: "Crucified on the vast wheel of time, I flew round and round with the Zeitgeist, waving my pen and lifting faint voices to explain, expound and exhort; to foresee and prophesy, to the few who could or would listen. Thus very evidently to me and to others I did little to create my day or greatly change it; but I did exemplify it and thus for all time my life is significant for all lives of men" (*DOD*, 3–4). What does it mean to exemplify his day? To be a prophet, who interprets the Zeitgeist and yet goes unheard. To be "crucified." Not the experiences of an ordinary human being, surely. Yet *Dusk of Dawn* also details the ways in which exemplification, for Du Bois, means being vulnerable to the everyday insult of being mistaken for a Pullman porter or to the assault of the lynch mob. To live among men and women who are permanently divided from the opportunities of the white world. To be situated in a global economy in which the labor of nonwhites is systematically appropriated for the enjoyment of a small class of whites. As this second sequence suggests, it is the excluded and exploited who exemplify their time, in Du Bois's estimation. Hence, even as Du Bois depends on his readers' awareness of his own prominence to highlight the illogic of social structures that reduce him to an aspect of "the Problem," he does not conclude that the harm is simply a failure to recognize his exclusion from the ranks of the elite. On the contrary, he makes use of the relationship to a larger whole that is always implied by the example in order to raise the question of whose experiences can be representative, which lives exemplary.[12] In effect, he develops and reworks the notion of double-consciousness, setting his own life in relation to the race concept in order to engender double-vision in his readers.

In a democratic context in which identity categories are both in force and in question, Du Bois's double reconstruction of his life and the life of the race concept affirms the contingency and the potency of racial categories and, accordingly, counsels that these categories must be deconstructed, criticized, and exploited. For these reasons, *Dusk of Dawn* provides an illuminating counterpoint to recent political theoretical efforts to come to terms with the challenges of identity and difference. If political theory trails other disciplines in its willingness to confront the ongoing force of racial definitions, William Connolly is an exception. Over the last two decades, especially, Connolly has focused on the relationship between identity and the prospects for democracy, and the affinities between his work and *Dusk of Dawn* are many. Where Connolly advocates genealogical reflection and creative self-fashioning as a response to the multiplicity of identities, Du Bois's rendering of his own genealogy discloses both the contingency and the force of racial identity. Both thinkers, furthermore, share an interest in understanding and potentially shifting antidemocratic commitments and assumptions that operate below the level of consciousness. Through critique and example, they strive to work on themselves and others and to inspire nonvengeful responses to the challenges of living in heterogeneous and divided communities. Despite these resemblances, however, considering their ideas together also highlights places where the heritage of slavery and knotty questions of racial identity and difference are elided in Connolly's work. First, although animated by a sense of the deep inequalities that define U.S. society, Connolly understates the effects of asymmetries in the construction of identity and their relationship to difference. This leads, secondly, to an inattentiveness to the ways in which the cultivation of a democratic ethos may impose unequal burdens on racially differentiated individuals. Thirdly, Connolly's emphasis on individual selfhood and keen awareness of the dangers of collective identity comes at the cost of adequately acknowledging the democratic possibilities that may emerge from the embrace of collective identity by marginalized women and men. Connolly has dedicated much of his career to thinking through the intricacies of identity and its relationship to democratic life. That his work nevertheless falls short when confronting the ongoing force of racial categories reveals the difficulty of reckoning with those categories and indicates how *Dusk of Dawn* can spur democratic reflection today.[13]

"Mere Autobiography"

In the "Apology" that opens *Dusk of Dawn*, Du Bois allows that, for him, "autobiographies have had little lure" (*DOD*, xxix). Given that this is the third of several books to deal extensively with Du Bois's life and the first of two full-length autobiographies, the reader is immediately confronted with a puzzle: why dedicate so much energy to such an unpromising genre? A hint is offered in the subtitle, *An Essay toward an Autobiography of a Race Concept*. Perhaps, then, this is not an autobiography at all. It certainly lacks much of the personal detail that conventionally defines the telling of a life. Furthermore, Du Bois explicitly shifts readers' attention away from the personal: "I have written . . . what is meant to be not so much my autobiography as the autobiography of a concept of race, elucidated, magnified and doubtless distorted in the thoughts and deeds which were mine" (*DOD*, xxx). In other words, Du Bois suggests, his life is the vehicle, or the example through which to test his ideas about race. By marrying an act of creative self-constitution to an inquiry into the constitution of the modern concept of race in this way, he offers a layered account of racial power and the possibility of freedom. Yet Du Bois is no mere example, and he trades on his readers' awareness of that fact. At 70 years of age, he is a prominent, if embattled, political figure and an established scholar and writer. My reading of *Dusk of Dawn* calls attention to the ways in which Du Bois exploits that ambiguity, the fissure between his status as a member of a dishonored caste and his role as a "race leader" and how he uses it to press readers to reexamine their convictions.

Perhaps most obviously, *Dusk of Dawn* cannot function as autobiography in any simple way because Du Bois specifically ties his retelling to larger purposes. Chapter titles—including "Science and Empire," "The Concept of Race, "Propaganda and World War," and, finally, "Revolution" —advertise political stakes beyond the narrative of a single life. That he continually sets the phases of his development against a broader historical backdrop (pairing his boyhood in New England with the vast drama of Reconstruction, for instance) reinforces this point. Further, as the chapter titles intimate, *Dusk of Dawn* advances a constellation of political claims. Just as Du Bois links his biography of John Brown to the global phenomena of slavery, colonialism, and their legacies, he deploys his own life to similar ends. And even as he explicitly distances himself from the Communist Party, Du Bois uses the survey of his experiences as an occasion for endorsing the basic humanity of Marx's ideas, conveying his admiration for the ideals of the Soviet experiment, and expressing confidence in capitalism's imminent collapse. He also elaborates on his controversial defense of improving segregated institutions in black communities and encouraging some level of economic autonomy as a response to continued exploitation and exclusion. Finally, *Dusk of Dawn* criticizes Du Bois's earlier belief that overcoming ignorance was the key to racial justice and explicitly contemplates the unconscious and subconscious sources of racial hierarchy.

There is still another sense in which Du Bois does not, and cannot, offer "mere autobiography." Du Bois's choice of his own story as a medium for thinking about the race concept situates him within an African American literary tradition, in the company of the fugitives and their descendants, whose capacity to translate lives into words was essential to establishing their humanity against a tradition of denial. "It is doubtful," observes Arnold Rampersad, "whether any single genre holds sway over a culture as powerfully as does autobiography over Afro-American literary expression."[14] Toni Morrison suggests why: "The autobiographical form is classic in Black American or Afro-American literature because it provided an instance in which a writer could be representative, could say, 'My single solitary and individual life is like the lives of the tribe; it differs in these specific ways, but it is a balanced life because it is both solitary and representative.'"[15] Set against a backdrop in which the lives and doings of African Americans have been not only rendered invisible but actively "disremembered and unaccounted for,"[16] the idea of presenting oneself as both solitary and representative has important political implications. It serves both as an expression of what Andrews calls "that irrepressible strain of freedom,"[17] and unlike individualistic conceptions of freedom, asserts the interrelation of individual and collective life.

If autobiography is often regarded as a paradigmatic form in African American letters, it is no less crucial to Du Bois's work. As Thomas Holt observes, Du Bois's "own life became the text, the point of departure, for each of his major explorations of race, culture, and politics."[18] Autobiography is Du Bois's "characteristic literary mode," remarks Andrews, "not only in his straightforwardly autobiographical books but in his contributions to periodicals and other writings as well."[19] Accordingly, in *Dusk of Dawn*, Du Bois describes himself as someone whose ambition is always "to seek through the written word the expression of my relation to the world and of the world to me" (*DOD*, 268). This ambition is not without its dangers. Autobiography, according to Sidonie Smith and Julia Watson, often serves a disciplinary function by constructing a model of normal subjectivity and reinforcing national mythologies.[20] "Generic clothes have made the man, so to speak," writes Smith. "Making men in specific ways, these practices [of autobiography and biography] reinforce dominant ideologies, official histories, and founding mythologies of the subject."[21] Indeed, some critics have suggested that autobiography, as distinct from other forms of personal narrative, must always be regarded as politically suspect.[22]

Certainly, there are aspects of *Dusk of Dawn* that reinforce such suspicion. One can read this narrative as the journey of a heroic individual, whose trajectory from darkness to enlightenment unfolds in Du Bois's account of how his early enthusiasm for European imperialism was gradually supplanted by a dawning recognition of the relationship between race, history, and the global economy, or in his characterization of an ever more complex understanding of the causes of racial hierarchy. Although I agree with Rampersad that Du Bois does not exaggerate his accomplishments,[23] *Dusk of Dawn* nonetheless strives to establish Du Bois as a kind of standard-bearer for the race and for thinking individuals more generally. Furthermore, the text is marked by gaps and silences, particularly with regard to questions of gender and to the female leaders with whom Du Bois worked, which reveal a desire to promote his own experiences as normative.[24] This is hardly surprising from someone who cultivated an "exceptional regard for the individual"[25]; who wrote in a prophetic idiom; and who, as the founder and editor of the NAACP's *Crisis* magazine could claim to be the voice of many black Americans for decades. Together, these features of Du Bois's temperament and career reinforce Kathryne Lindberg's conclusion that Du Bois could not "renounce a certain oppressiveness in speaking for others (and the Other)."[26]

Crucial though it is to attend to these dangers, however, it is equally important not to allow them to diminish the significance of those moments in *Dusk of Dawn* that may yet serve as resources for democratic thinking. Like Du Bois's work in many other literary forms, *Dusk of Dawn* simultaneously operates within and challenges generic expectations. Moreover, even as Du Bois appears to embrace the heroic possibilities of the autobiographical form, he also uses it to undercut the idea of the great man at its heart.[27] Such ambiguity befits a text composed during what was "probably the most uncertain period of his life."[28] Du Bois, after all, describes *Dusk of Dawn* as "an essay," and the repetition of that language throughout the book stresses that it is something attempted or tested, rather than the revelation of self-evident or uncontestable truths. Indeed, he characterizes *Souls, Darkwater*, and *Dusk of Dawn* as "three sets of thought," not as definitive statements about his own life, that of black Americans, or human existence in general (*DOD*, xxix). Du Bois's insistence in defining his autobiography in this way reinforces Shamoon Zamir's remark that "[Du Bois] resists essentializing both epistemology and self-consciousness and struggles instead to describe the shape of a life's imaginative investigations of its own contexts. Only such description can be simultaneously open to the unique and the universal, which together constitute the imaginative life."[29]

Du Bois's characterization of his life story as an "essay" also reflects a twofold sense of his own limitations. On the one hand, it gestures toward the finitude that bounds all human expression. As Du Bois comments at the beginning of his posthumously published final autobiography, "Autobiographies do not form indisputable authorities"; they are too susceptible to lapses in memory and intrusions of self-interest.[30] Even if Du Bois sometimes describes his vocation in exalted terms as "one who tells the truth and exposes evil and seeks with beauty and for beauty to set the world right,"[31] his writing is replete with reflections on the inevitable shortcomings that accompany such ambition. His emphasis on the dimness of his vision reinforces this point. Consider the title of *Dusk of Dawn*. While the reference to dawn evinces hopefulness and light,[32] Du Bois qualifies that sense by giving equal place to shadows and darkness. The juxtaposition of dusk and dawn may indicate that dawn is almost over, giving way to a new day. But it also suggests the obscurity, rather than the transparency, of the medium through which Du Bois regards his life. As Du Bois observes, his own dawning consciousness of the significance of racial caste did not bring with it a new clarity: "My 'way was cloudy' and the approach to its high goals by no means straight and clear" (*DOD*, 130). Perhaps the cloudiness will produce its own insight and allow Du Bois to project what Joan Scott calls "a vision beyond the visible,"[33] but there are no guarantees. On the other hand, Du Bois also points to a second sense in which his offering can only be an attempted account of his life and of a concept of race. His own limitations are joined to those of his audience; for readers are no less susceptible than writers to self-interested interpretation. Keenly aware that his readers seek confirmation of their own commitments and identities, he struggles against the different kinds of resistance mounted by black and white audiences. As Du Bois presses black readers to loosen the grip of their own racial certitudes and, in places, posits an unflattering portrait of "the colored world," he simultaneously fights what he perceives to be the central obstacle to social change: whites' "fear of the Truth" (*DOD*, 151).

Without ignoring those elements of *Dusk of Dawn* that portray the author, unproblematically, as an exceptional man and role model, this chapter accentuates those elements that identify it as a species of what Caren Kaplan calls an "out-law" genre. The mark of the "out-law," Kaplan argues, is that it undermines conventional distinctions between autobiographical criticism and autobiography itself by incorporating the two within a single narrative.[34] The effect of this mixing is to produce a text that is more self-conscious about the conditions—and the politics—of its own production. Du Bois's narrative does not fit neatly into the categories of transnational feminist autobiographical literature Kaplan examines, yet even where he presents his life as the chronological development of his singularity, Du Bois's awareness of the situatedness of his perspective reflects critically on both the practice of autobiography and the constitution of selfhood in the world he inhabits. His attention to the interrelation between his own life and global political and economic conditions, moreover, accords with Kaplan's embrace of the connections between out-law writing and a "politics of location."[35]

Consider Du Bois's rendering of caste segregation through the image of the cave. In Du Bois's description, African Americans are "entombed," separated from the rest of the world by an impenetrable layer of plate glass. This image both conveys something of black experiences in general and vivifies the obstacles that confront Du Bois's own efforts at self-expression:

> It is as though one, looking out from a dark cave in a side of an impending mountain, sees the world passing and speaks to it; speaks courteously and persuasively, showing them how these entombed souls are hindered in their natural movement, expression, and development; and how their loosening from prison would be a matter not simply of

courtesy, sympathy, and help to them, but aid to all the world. One talks on evenly and logically in this way, but notices that the passing throng does not even turn its head, or if it does, glances curiously and walks on. It gradually penetrates the minds of the prisoners that the people passing do not hear; that some thick sheet of invisible but horribly tangible plate glass is between them and the world (*DOD*, 130–31).

As an autobiographer who shares the prisoners' situation, who is himself one of European civilization's "rejected parts," Du Bois both claims for himself and questions the condition of free selfhood. Regardless of his own aspirations, this passage serves as a reminder to Du Bois's readers that no individual can simply transcend caste imprisonment. No amount of rational argument, furthermore, will convince the men and women outside the cave of the humanity of the people trapped inside. In such circumstances, Du Bois dryly comments, "it is hard . . . to be philosophical and calm" (*DOD*, 131). Further, disaster is the likely result for the prisoners who try to make themselves heard in other ways. Screaming makes no difference, and, if they "here and there, break through in blood and disfigurement, [they] find themselves faced by a horrified, implacable, and quite overwhelming mob of people frightened for their own very existence" (*DOD*, 131). *Dusk of Dawn* thus starkly illustrates the situation of African Americans, whose word has limited or no authority and whose only recourse may be "mayhem and assassination" (*DOD*, 182). At the same time, it attempts, through words, to redefine the outlook of its readers.

Genealogy of a Problem

One way to approach this work is through genealogy. It is unsurprising that an autobiography would offer genealogical information, and at first glance, *Dusk of Dawn* appears to provide a conventional, family tree-type recounting of marriages and births and national origins. The conservatism implied in this sort of genealogy is reinforced by Du Bois's own sense of the symbolic importance of his life, and a reader might be tempted to view it primarily as an account of how he came to be a great man and "credit to his race." Still, such an approach misses the critical, theoretical work Du Bois undertakes in exploring his lineage. Du Bois's account of the accident and racial mixture that shape his background reveals little about the author personally, but it does provide a starting point for a conception of race that is fluid, historically constituted, and political. If Du Bois's genealogy resonates in some ways with old-fashioned narratives of individual heritage, it also resonates with the work of Connolly and other political theorists who have turned to Nietzsche and Foucault to develop genealogical strategies that draw on the past to defamiliarize or problematize the terms that frame political debates in the present. Its political potential emerges from the ways in which Du Bois uses his own life to "liste[n] to history."[36]

Dusk of Dawn makes note of Du Bois's mixed racial ancestry from the outset. Although this emphasis on mixture could be read to affirm the value of whiteness and his own claim to a share in it, Du Bois proceeds along another route. In the chapter on "The Concept of Race," he most effectively exploits his lineage to trace and to trouble the hold of racial categories on his life. When he writes about his maternal great-great-grandfather, for example, Du Bois relates that family speculation located him in Africa, and his own "youthful imagination painted him as certainly the son of a tribal chief" (*DOD*, 110). The truth is far less clear. Indeed, Du Bois allows that "with Africa I had only one direct cultural connection and that was the African melody that my great-grandmother Violet used to sing" (*DOD*, 114). Though tenuous, however, this connection has real effects. Further, Du Bois notes that his upbringing in the midst of the black Burghardt family both "determined largely my life and 'race'" (*DOD*, 114) and revealed this determination to be incomplete. For even if he was "black" from birth, it was only as a college student in the South that he "became a member of a closed racial group with rites and loyalties, with a history and a corporate future, with an art and philosophy" (*DOD*, 101).

This interplay of accident and fixity that produces racial identity emerges even more starkly in Du Bois's description of his paternal grandfather. Alexander Du Bois lived on both sides of the color line; born in the West Indies, he was raised as a white child but ultimately classified as black upon the death of his white father. "There is nothing unusual about this interracial history" (*DOD*, 103), Du Bois asserts; it is but one example among thousands of similar stories. Indeed, after retracing his grandfather's life path, Du Bois slyly notes: "If Alexander Du Bois, following the footsteps of Alexander Hamilton, had come from the West Indies to the United States, stayed with the white group and married and begotten children among them, anyone in after years who had suggested his Negro descent would have been laughed to scorn, or sued for libel" (*DOD*, 106). Not content to confine these ruminations to questions of individual experience, furthermore, Du Bois directly ties these examples to a history of the economic imperatives that drove the development of modern race (*DOD*, 103), thereby revealing the twisting and uneven paths by which accidents of identity are sedimented into structures of power.

As suggested above, "The Concept of Race" not only tracks Du Bois's bloodline but also provides a genealogy of Du Bois's kinship with Africa. Movingly, Du Bois recounts his first sighting of Africa in 1923, when he arrived by moonlight to be the "Envoy Extraordinary and Minister Plenipotentiary to Liberia." The moment lends itself to sentimentality, and Du Bois's title to self-importance, but he works against both temptations by pairing his account with another story. The second tale of reclaimed origins lays bare the politics of genealogy by describing the absurd situation in which his membership in the Massachusetts Society of the Sons of the American Revolution was revoked because, as a descendant of slaves, he could not provide adequate proof of his genetic title to inclusion (*DOD*, 115). In the pages leading up to the account of his dramatic arrival in the land of his African ancestors, Du Bois explains:

> My African racial feeling was then purely a matter of my own later learning and reaction; my recoil from the assumptions of the whites; my experience in the South at Fisk. But it was none the less real and a large determinant of my life and character. I felt myself African by 'race' and by that token was African and an integral member of the group of dark Americans who were called Negroes (*DOD*, 115).

What is striking here is Du Bois's capacity to convey his very deep sense of connection to Africa and his acknowledgment that he has virtually no direct family tie to the continent. From this tension, Du Bois elaborates an alternative conception of kinship:

> One thing is sure and that is the fact that since the fifteenth century these ancestors of mine and their other descendants have had a common history; have suffered a common disaster and have one long memory. The actual ties of heritage between the individuals of this group, vary with the ancestors that they have in common and many others: Europeans and Semites, perhaps Mongolians, certainly American Indians. But the physical bond is least and the badge of color relatively unimportant save as a badge; the real essence of this kinship is its social heritage of slavery; the discrimination and insult; and this heritage binds together not simply the children of Africa, but extends through yellow Asia and into the South Seas. It is this unity that draws me to Africa (*DOD*, 117).

As this passage suggests, Du Bois's genealogy is not a search for origins, not an excavation of old bloodlines for clues to his essential or authentic identity. Instead, Du Bois disturbs the very idea of racial identity at the same time that he affirms its lived importance. He raises questions about what it means to speak "as a black man" at the same time that he indicates why he is compelled to do so.[37] In this way, the very personal practice of tracing his genealogy becomes a medium for redefining the present relationship between nonwhites around the world, a relationship from which he hopes new political movements and new theoretical insights will be born.

In Dialogue

Du Bois concludes his genealogical exploration by questioning the idea of the race concept. "Perhaps it is wrong to speak of it at all as a 'concept' rather than as a group of contradictory forces, facts and tendencies," he allows (*DOD*, 133). Nonetheless, he presses forward. He builds on his inquiry into these "illogical trends and irreconcilable tendencies" and attempts to show his readers what they have meant in his life. In lieu of simply turning back to his own history, accumulating details, Du Bois departs from the role of autobiographer as reporter by constructing three imagined dialogues. Appearing in the chapters entitled "The White World" and "The Colored World Within," these exchanges are pivotal to understanding how Du Bois intertwines an examination of his exemplarity with the story of the race concept. Calling attention to the constructed, writerly character of all autobiography, these dialogues give Du Bois an opportunity to explore the meanings of racial identity from multiple perspectives. But they also introduce new hazards: "Exposing the necessary fiction at the roots of fact and the interests behind disinterested empiricism places autobiography in a difficult position. What is it that autobiography actually captures? How much does it record and how much does it create?"[38] This difficulty is compounded for African American autobiographers, whose authority (and authorship) has been historically subject to question.

Rather than evade the difficulty, however, Du Bois embraces it. Indeed, he precedes the dialogues with an admission of his own failure to find terms adequate to describe the workings of race in his own life and in the lives of other black Americans (*DOD*, 139–40). Seeking another avenue, he integrates these fictions into the telling of his life. The first relates an encounter between a white man named Roger Van Dieman, who is described as "quite companionable" apart from his obsession with race (*DOD*, 140), and a character who stands in for Du Bois himself. The second involves "Du Bois" and another white friend, who is unable to come to terms with the conflicting demands of his identity. The third, in which "Du Bois" does not appear, relates a conversation that takes place as a small group of middle-class African Americans express their frustration and disdain for the black "masses" during an evening of bridge. That the truth of *Dusk of Dawn* does not reside simply in the authenticity of Du Bois's transcription of his experience is made plain in the liberties he takes in supplying words for his characters.

The first dialogue begins by explicitly examining and playing with Du Bois's role as exemplar/example. Describing Van Dieman, he writes: "He has a way of putting an excessive amount of pity in his look and of stating as a general and incontrovertible fact that it is 'horrible' to be an Exception. By this he means me. He is more than certain that I prove the rule" (*DOD*, 140).[39] In other words, "How does it feel to be an exception?" The simple substitution in this rewriting of the "unasked question" enables Du Bois to capture something of Van Dieman's mind-set and to engage in a parallel dialogue with *The Souls of Black Folk*. Recalling the language of pity from the earlier text, Du Bois exposes the symbiosis of the "exception" and the "problem," thereby undermining the pretense that racial categories can simply be overcome through strategies of uplift. The continuing power of this pretense is reflected in Patricia Williams's observation that "every generation of my family has been a first black something or other, an experimental black, a 'different' black—a hope, a candle, a credit to our race."[40] It suggests, furthermore, why the emergence of Barack Obama as "the first mainstream African-American who is articulate and bright and clean and a nice-looking guy" marks both a departure and a cliché in American public life.[41] In *Dusk of Dawn*, Du Bois refuses this honorary status as a bad bargain. He challenges the illusory comfort of an exemplarity that merely serves to disguise and reinforce racial power. By highlighting white shortcomings and black contributions, furthermore, he inverts a representative logic whereby the dominant group is exemplified by the best within it, by its representative men, and the oppressed group is exemplified by its worst. The use of humor is crucial here, too. Disavowing bitterness, Du Bois's alter ego uses a kind of gentle irony to lay bare the chauvinism of his friend's perspective (not with any hope, it must be said, that the friend will catch on) and also to offer commentary on the rest of the text.

The dialogue unfolds as the characters debate racial superiority. Against Van Dieman's list of white accomplishments, "Du Bois" proffers a broadly comparative and historical recounting of the achievements of the non-European world and of the reliance of white civilization on slavery, colonialism, and the exploitation of workers of all colors to make its own grandeur possible. "I hand the first vast conception of the solar system to the Africanized Egyptians," "Du Bois" declares, "the creation of Art to the Chinese, the highest conception of Religion to the Asiatic Semites, and then let Europe rave over the Factory system" (*DOD*, 144). Throughout the exchange, furthermore, "Du Bois" reverses prevailing explanations for racial hierarchies, undermining the presumption that inequality can be read as proxy for innate inferiority. Insisting instead that there is both greatness and weakness in every group, "Du Bois" ponders the basis for white claims to exemplarity and black lack of achievement. "To be sure, good seed proves itself in the flower and the fruit," "Du Bois" grants Van Dieman, "but the failure of the seed to sprout is no proof that it is not good. It may be proof simply of the absence of manure—or its excessive presence" (*DOD*, 145). A subtle suggestion, in other words, that white civilization is full of shit.

Although there is much more to say about the exchange, I turn now to the last two pages. "The greatest and most immediate danger of white culture, perhaps least sensed," "Du Bois" declares, "is its fear of the Truth" (*DOD*, 151). To this Van Dieman retorts: "In other words, according to you, white folks are about the meanest and lowest on earth" (*DOD*, 152). "Du Bois's" answer, tellingly, is to resist the temptation to moral superiority. He embraces whites, noting that "they are human, even as you and I," an inversion of a comment from *The Souls of Black Folk* in which he suggests to readers that the "masses" of black folk are human "even as you and I" (*SBF*, 122). Moreover, while he criticizes the spread of white supremacy across the globe, he also admits that he too is implicated: "I am as bad as they are. In fact, I am related to them and they have much that belongs to me—this land, for instance, for which my fathers starved and fought; I share their sins; in fine, I am related to them" (*DOD*, 152). When Van Dieman takes "Du Bois's" declaration of a blood relation to the white world as a disavowal of all distinct racial histories and perspectives, "Du Bois" returns to the idea that blacks hold the key to salvation:

> Race is a cultural, sometimes an historical fact. And all that I really have been trying to say is that a certain group that I know and to which I belong, as contrasted with the group you know and to which you belong, and in which you fanatically and glorifyingly believe, bears in its bosom just now the spiritual hope of this land because of the persons who compose it and not by divine command (*DOD*, 153).

In response, Van Dieman asks, innocently, "But what is this group; and how do you differentiate it; and how can you call it 'black' when you admit it is not black?" To this "Du Bois" makes his famous reply: "The black man is a person who must ride 'Jim Crow' in Georgia" (*DOD*, 153).

Throughout the dialogue's intricate dance, "Du Bois" uses his status as exception/problem (exemplar/example) to move his partner into impossible positions and draw out their inner contradictions. With Socratic deftness, he presses Van Dieman's ideas until their illogic emerges. In this way, *Dusk of Dawn* investigates what I have elsewhere described as "white double-consciousness."[42] The effect of this double-consciousness is that "the average reasonable, conscientious, and fairly intelligent white American faces continuing paradox" (*DOD*, 153). Du Bois fleshes out what this means through a second imagined dialogue with another fictitious white friend, who "represents the way in which my environing white group distorts and frustrates itself even as it strives toward Justice and all because of me" (*DOD*, 153). This friend confronts something like a "quadri-lemma," aspiring simultaneously to live up to the ideals of Christianity, gentlemanly comportment, American patriotism, and white masculinity. Unable to resolve the contradictions that inhere in his own self-understanding, he becomes suspicious, resentful, defensive. Through the exchange, "Du Bois" elicits these contradictions. He presses his companion, and the reader, to feel the tear of one who is both moved by the promise of peace and goodwill issued from the pulpit and terrified of giving up a way of life that depends on inequality and exploitation. Du Bois also uses the exchange to undercut the pretense of realism that justifies the maintenance of a global color line ("'Honest to God, what do you think Asia and Africa would do to us, if they got a chance?'" asks the white friend) and shows how it is connected to a social order in which fully human black subjects must remain exceptional ("'Skin us alive,' I answer cheerfully, loving the 'us'") (*DOD*, 167). Like the dialogue with Van Dieman, this one exposes the irrationality of class and racial divisions that are upheld by claims to benevolence or scientific truth. These divisions, Du Bois observes, are the product of "conditioned reflexes; of long followed habits, customs and folkways; of subconscious trains of reasoning and unconscious nervous reflexes" (*DOD*, 172). By introducing fictional characters and a fictionalized version of himself into his autobiography, then, Du Bois discloses the contradictions that inhere in white American identities and uses imaginary elenctic exchanges to reshape the sensibilities of his readers.

Dusk of Dawn does not stop with this portrait of the white world. An adequate account of the pressures that impede democratic selfhood, Du Bois insists, entails consideration of the women and men who are simultaneously enfolded in and excluded from that world. In his view, "the colored world . . . must be seen as existing not simply for itself but as a group whose insistent cry may yet become the warning which awakens the world to its truer self and its wider destiny" (*DOD*, 172). Du Bois then sketches the contours of "the colored world" in a brief vignette. Unlike the previous two interchanges, this one is comprised of a series of comments without any extended back-and-forth. It focuses, inevitably, on "the problem," and it begins on a jarring note: "'Just like niggers!'" (*DOD*, 175). In just a few pages, Du Bois moves from provocation to portrait, limning the "double environment" of African American professionals who are both hemmed in by a white world that will not allow them admission and repulsed by what they see as the degradation of their black neighbors. He thus remakes the description of a bridge party into a complex account of the heterogeneity that defines "the colored world," of the structural constraints that hobble African American aspirations, and of the entanglement of righteous critique and prejudice in black self-definition. He also uses this vignette as the point of departure for a defense of the self-development (economic, educational, cultural) of black communities. If men and women like the members of the bridge party can turn their energies toward group uplift, if they resist "the flight of class from mass" that defined Du Bois's own early formulations of leadership by a "Talented Tenth," they might find "sources of strength in common memories of suffering in the past; in present threats of degradation and extinction; in common ambitions and ideals; in emulation and the determination to prove ability and desert" *DOD*, 219).[43]

Making the most of this common experience, furthermore, Du Bois believes African Americans are poised to transform their experience as examples of "the problem" into exemplars of an alternative way of being, "to teach industrial and cultural democracy to a world that bitterly needs it" (*DOD*, 219). Du Bois's "third path of advance," his alternative to the paths of direct struggle and emigration, is only thinly described. He readily admits that there are obstacles to his vision of a planned economy for African America, and while the bridge-table dialogue holds up intragroup prejudices for critical scrutiny, Du Bois's vision of group leadership risks reinforcing antidemocratic "boundaries of blackness."[44] I agree with Kenneth Mostern, that *Dusk of Dawn* is significantly less helpful in getting us to the point where we can understand the workings of bloc formation that identity politics depends upon, than it is in helping us understand the meanings of racial identity.[45] Still, despite these qualifications, Du Bois's sketch remains valuable as an attempt to think through the relationship between a fluid and contingent "concept of race" and the political urgency of formulating a response to a social and political milieu in which the effects of that concept are hard and unyielding.

Arts of the Racialized Self

By recounting events from his life and setting them against the backdrop of larger historical developments, by entwining a story of genealogical roots with an account of the fortuitous routes through which he became black and American, by constructing fictional dialogues to test racial conventions, Du Bois puts autobiography to the service of democratic thinking. Throughout *Dusk of Dawn*, he models what William Connolly describes as the work of "self-conscious practitioners of theory today," who "may, first, concede that they have not to date pulled themselves above the world of partisanship by their own bootstraps; second, seek to enact their theories in political life; and, third, recoil back upon their perspectives with a degree of relational self-modesty."[46] Indeed, Du Bois's autobiographical writings have much in common with Connolly's efforts to conceive an alternative to an "American pluralist imagination . . . [that] remains too stingy, cramped, and defensive for the world we now inhabit."[47] Both challenge fixed forms of identity that generate suffering and relations of domination. Both investigate our attachment to identity categories, plumbing not only conscious beliefs and passions but also subconscious forces that work on and through us. Both believe that these forces can be countered through creative efforts to work on the self and others through practices that Connolly calls "micropolitics." In spite of these broad areas of commonality, however, engaging Du Bois and Connolly together reveals why, when the long shadow of slavery and colonial conquest slips from view, some elements of Connolly's work may reinforce rather than undermine the hierarchies he seeks to oppose.

Beginning from an acknowledgment of the contingency, ambiguity, and paradox that define contemporary existence, Connolly argues that it is crucial to learn to live with the contestability of all identity claims and the ever-present possibility of the emergence of new and unexpected forms of identity. To say that social identities are constructed, contingent, and relational, he contends, is neither to minimize their lived significance, nor to eliminate the antagonisms they sustain. As Connolly emphasizes, questions of identity are politically salient because they involve both depth *and* contingency.[48] His work thus uncovers the ways in which efforts to fix identity amounts to a kind of "ontological compensation," a defensive attempt to shore up old sureties that can no longer be sustained.[49] Importantly, Connolly pays special attention to the defensiveness of privileged or established identities against the claims of marginalized or vulnerable citizens. He notes that the resentments of the comfortable emerge with particular ferocity when claims arising from old injuries or the constitution of new identities are at issue. Pointedly, he asks: "How do so many whites remain so aggressively righteous about juridical practices of legal violence against a growing warehouse of young, racialized convicts disenfranchised from speaking on their own behalf?"[50]

Du Bois likewise vivifies the accidental character of identity and the tenaciousness of its power by unpacking the circuitous paths through which he came to be marked as black and by tracking the changes in his own conception of race. "Anticipatory, critical, and self-revisionary,"[51] Du Bois's account of his relationship to the race concept uncovers his own blindness and remarks on the contingency of its overcoming. Recalling that, as a young man, "I was blithely European and imperialist in outlook; democratic as democracy was conceived in America" (*DOD*, 32), Du Bois explains that what saved him from being "simply the current product of [his] day" (*DOD*, 26) was neither innate intelligence nor strength of character. Rather, it was his situation as an example of the "Problem" that enabled him to reflect critically on this conventional worldview. Yet even as he discloses the insight that is born of experience as a member of a dishonored caste, he challenges "the history of tribes and clans, of social classes and all nations, and of race antipathies in our own world," all of which represent the "fight against equality and inability even to picture its possibility" (*DOD*, 134). And the "spiritual provincialism" (*DOD*, 139) that he attacks for its power to reinvest racial categories with injurious significance is recognizable as a predecessor of the forms of fundamentalism Connolly opposes.

In their attention to subconscious sources of human belief and behavior, Du Bois and Connolly are also in accord. Calling on readers to attune themselves downward, through the layers of thinking that connect culture, brain, and body in unpredictable ways, and outward beyond the territorially defined bounds of the nation, Connolly inquires into "the layered character of being."[52] Inquiring how democratic citizens might make themselves more open to alterity and insecurity in a society increasingly defined by plural ways of living, furthermore, he embraces a conception of "the practice of self as 'work of art.'"[53] Building on Nietzsche and Foucault, he explores tactics through which individuals can work to render themselves more open to the contingency of their own formation and become less prone to demonizing others. This process, he contends, "involves strategic mixings of word, image, movement, posture, touch and sound to try to alter something in your previous sensibility." And its reach extends beyond the self: "Micropolitics applies such strategic mixtures to the ethos of larger constituencies."[54] According to Connolly, the sites of such politics are many: "television talk shows, programming of cop shows, everyday gossip, letters to the editor, and computer networks."[55] To this list one might add autobiography.

At first glance, the self-fashioning Connolly endorses appears remote from the kinds of concrete political questions taken up by *Dusk of Dawn*. Yet reading Du Bois and Connolly for their points of intersection illuminates those elements of *Dusk of Dawn* that essay to understand the hold of racial categories below the level of conscious conviction alone and to dislodge hierarchical commitments from those deeper layers of being. "Not simply knowledge, not simply direct repression of evil, will reform the world," Du Bois muses. "In long, indirect pressure and action of various and intricate sorts, the actions of men which are not due to lack of knowledge nor to evil intent, must be changed by influencing folkways, habits, customs and subconscious deeds" (*DOD*, 222). Du Bois calls this effort "propaganda," and through it he hopes to bring the world to its senses about the reality of racial injustice. The language of propaganda, and Du Bois's insistence that it be "carefully planned and scientific" (*DOD*, 172), disguise the nuance of his understanding of a relationship between art, politics, and persuasion that is oriented toward not only exposing readers to the truth but also affecting them so that they can absorb that truth.[56] In the dialogic passages of *Dusk of Dawn*, especially, Du Bois uses imaginative reconstruction to provoke his readers in ways that straightforward exposition might not. Insofar as these creative efforts are directed toward effecting changes in his readers, they might be described as micropolitical techniques of multiracial citizenship. Du Bois not only presents a point of view. He works on his white fellow citizens so that they can *see* the injustice of black suffering and the beauty of black accomplishment; and he attempts to activate in black readers a sense of racial solidarity that might engender resistance to the injustice and magnify the accomplishment.

Consider the phenomenon of racial resentment. When Du Bois begins the chapter on "The White World" by pronouncing that "the majority of men resent and always have resented the idea of equality with most of their fellow men" (*DOD*, 134), he sounds a note close to Connolly's. Further, he comments that this reaction to equality is, paradoxically, both opposed and intimately connected to human aspirations toward self-realization. For Du Bois, however, this paradox must be understood in relationship to race and inherited structures of racial power. When he bares the workings of white resentments in his two interracial dialogues, he exposes an impossible conception of selfhood that is predicated on hierarchies it simultaneously disavows. When he supplies words for his fictional black characters as they heap scorn upon their neighbors and bewail the direct and indirect threats to their every attempt to carve out a decent life, Du Bois conveys how those hierarchies both feed and thwart the aspiration to responsible selfhood among black Americans. Their relationship to this aspiration is doubly problematic. Not only do they share white Americans' dream of a sovereign agency that is perpetually promised and out of reach, but they are also expected to bear responsibility for those citizens who carry the same racial markers and for the history conjured by those markers.[57] Reading Du Bois's imaginative exercises with and against Connolly brings to life, but crucially revises, the latter's observation that "the porous category of responsible agency provides perhaps the largest container into which the spirit of revenge is poured in contemporary moral and legal practices."[58]

As a consequence of their sensitivity to power of resentment and the desire for vengeance, both Du Bois and Connolly emphasize the importance of accepting and even embracing the insecurity that accompanies the acknowledgment of difference and the contingency of identity. Accordingly, Du Bois shares Connolly's enthusiasm for generosity toward others as a way of countering such resentments and helping to constitute a more capacious sense of democracy. As both writers admit, such an affirmative response is not easy to cultivate. "The entombed," Du Bois notes, "find themselves not simply trying to make the outer world understand their essential and common humanity but even more, as they become inured the their experience, they have to keep reminding themselves that the great and oppressing world outside is also real and human and in its essence honest" (*DOD*, 131). In a gesture that finds its echo in Connolly's discussion of what it means to work on the self, and in turn to work on others, Du Bois continues: "All my life I have had continually to haul my soul back and say, 'All white folk are not scoundrels nor murderers. They are, even as I am, painfully human'" (*DOD*, 131–32). Repeatedly, *Dusk of Dawn* displays Du Bois's efforts to "haul [his] soul back" from the brink of demonization, and it offers an account of social critique that abjures the temptation to moralize from a position of innocence.[59] Such vigilance is vital, Du Bois and Connolly would agree, for the difficult work of democratic coexistence.

Notwithstanding the affinities and overlapping commitments that join their thought, Du Bois's autobiographical writing calls attention to the limitations of a democratic theory that does not concern itself fundamentally with what he calls the race concept. Where *Dusk of Dawn* works through conceptions of identity and difference that are unintelligible apart from modern slavery and colonial conquest, Connolly offers a general explication of "the logic of identity and difference." This is not to say that Connolly ignores colonialism or slavery. On the contrary, he offers a devastating account of the lingering power of the genocide of American Indians—and the subsequent disavowal of that genocide—for American political culture. Still, these concerns do not *frame* his discussion of identity.[60] Instead, he argues:

> An identity is established in relation to a series of differences that have become socially recognized. These differences are essential to its being.

> If they did not coexist as differences, it would not exist in its distinctness and solidity. Entrenched in this indispensable relation is a second set of tendencies . . . to congeal established identities into fixed forms, thought and lived as if their structure expressed the true order of things. . . . Identity requires difference in order to be, and it converts difference into otherness in order to secure its own self-certainty.[61]

Here Connolly offers a compelling answer to the question of how identities are formed and why they matter. This answer, furthermore, allows readers to grapple at a deeper level with Du Bois's accounts of the resentments that sustain inter- and intraracial divisions. It offers, I think, a particularly apt way of understanding the power of whiteness, an identity category whose value resides in its exclusiveness.[62]

More, it speaks forcefully to the relationship between whiteness and Americanness, and the dependence of the latter on the contrast with a range of racially and otherwise dishonored others. As Toni Morrison notes, this dynamic of identity and difference is generative, not only policing the boundaries of fixed categories but also producing a distinctive culture from them:

> Black slavery enriched the country's creative possibilities. For in that construction of blackness *and* enslavement could be found not only the not-free but also, with the dramatic polarity created by skin color, the projection of the not-me. The result was a playground for the imagination. What rose up out of collective needs to allay internal fears and to rationalize external exploitation was an American Africanism—a fabricated brew of darkness, otherness, alarm, and desire that is uniquely American.[63]

Morrison's exploration of the conjunction of blackness and enslavement not only illustrates how the dynamic of identity\difference has worked in the American context, but it also reveals what gets lost in any effort to understand the constitution of whiteness and blackness apart from the history of racial slavery.

To say that all identities are contestable, in other words, is only a first step. Du Bois, like Morrison, demonstrates why it is also crucial to specify that identities are not always contestable in the same ways or to the same degree. Connolly does not deny this claim. Yet his work does not take the step that would allow him to account for the asymmetries of identities and to counter the stubbornness of antiblack racism and the racialized social structures that have evolved from Americans' slave inheritance. By starting from a doubled vantage, one that both contests settled racial categories and affirms their constitutive asymmetries, Du Bois goes further. Even as he claims for himself "that anarchy of the spirit which is inevitably the goal of consciousness" (*DOD*, 134), he also insists "this fact of racial distinction based on color was the greatest thing in my life and absolutely determined it" (*DOD*, 136). This lived contradiction indicates why it is crucial not only to recognize "the constitutive role of difference in identity itself"[64] but also to work through the very different dynamics operating in the relationship between imposition and self-definition in the experiences of whites and nonwhites.[65]

Under such conditions, the virtues of presumptive generosity and receptivity that Connolly advocates may have antidemocratic implications that he does not pursue. Calls for gratitude for the abundance of being, for responsiveness, and for generosity gain their force from Connolly's understanding that resentments will be directed at the most vulnerable members of society. And, as his discussion of the racialized character of punishment makes clear, the argument is animated by alarm at the ways in which (normal) citizenship is defined through the policing of racially identified outsiders. Thus, Connolly writes: "If, as Etienne Balibar contends, the cultural marker of 'class-race' identifies 'populations . . . collectively destined for capitalist exploitation,' it also marks the same constituencies as available targets of accumulated desires for social revenge through the legal rubrics of crime, agency, and responsibility."[66] In this light, Connolly's call for presumptive generosity on the part of the privileged, his efforts to engender new openness toward those citizens who have been marked for exploitation, control, and punishment, is deeply democratic.

But how does Connolly's insight apply to women and men who are the likely objects of what he calls "the desire to punish"? As *Dusk of Dawn* shows, vulnerability does not make these citizens immune to resentment or to punitive attitudes toward less "respectable" members of the group. If the call for generosity and forbearance ought rightly to include these men and women, it may nonetheless be the case that they will pay a higher price in answering it. For these qualities, or the semblance of them, have been historically expected of African Americans as the price of inclusion. Indeed, they are too often the price of survival and might, with justification, be received with some suspicion by those individuals and groups whose historical injuries have been, in part, sustained through a demand that they be open, grateful, and generous.[67] Consider a moment in Du Bois's second dialogue in which the white interlocutor grumbles that "servants must be cheap and willing and the mean ought not to be so sensitive" (*DOD*, 166). Clearly this portrait is meant to skewer a view at odds with Connolly's own. Nonetheless, outside a context of equal or shared vulnerability, the notion of reciprocity may not only make unequal demands on differently located citizens but also occlude the degree to which some citizens have historically borne the brunt of accommodation.[68] Attention to these asymmetries is crucial in a post-civil rights context, when claims of racial injustice are often refuted defensively or interpreted as instances of whining.[69] Further, although Du Bois does not make this point explicitly, his two interracial dialogues intimate that the display of these virtues, far from eliciting a reciprocal openness from white Americans, may engender precisely the kinds of resentment Connolly's work criticizes.[70]

Du Bois's autobiographical practice presents another challenge by connecting his imagination of the self to the fate of other African Americans and nonwhite people around the world. Although Connolly recognizes that "identity is relational and collective," his work gives priority to exploration of the ways in which individuals, qua individuals, can modify themselves to respond more democratically to the demands of an increasingly pluralized world. And his list of possible identity categories—"white, male, American, a sports fan, and so on"[71]—fails to contend adequately with the force of the relationship Du Bois describes when he writes that women and men of African descent "have suffered a common disaster and have one long memory" (*DOD*, 117). As Stuart Hall remarks, "identities are names we give to the different ways we are positioned by, and position ourselves within the narratives of the past."[72] The past that haunts *Dusk of Dawn*—like the present it describes—is defined by lynching and the ever-present possibility of violence, by exploitation and the vulnerability to exploitation, by public invisibility and hypervisibility, by political voicelessness. "Black identity," notes Robert-Gooding Williams, "is a collective predicament."[73]

Yet it is not only a predicament. Out of the disaster and fueled by long memory, African Americans have also nurtured alternative cultural and political possibilities. Du Bois emphasizes this point toward the conclusion of the dialogue with Van Dieman, when his alter ego asserts that his group "bears in its bosom just now the spiritual hope of this land because of the persons who compose it and not by divine command" (*DOD*, 153). There is nothing innately "black" about this hope; it is the product of African Americans' particular history of struggle. Even if allegiances are shifting, provisional, and always subject to critical scrutiny, even if one recognizes the dangers of fundamentalist forms of allegiance and the violence they entail, Du Bois illustrates why attachment to *this* set of common involvements can nurture democratic possibilities in a way that other attachments do not.

Politically, this means that overcoming the sedimented effects of racial privilege and subordination may entail creative measures that work with and through racial categories rather than seeking primarily to destabilize them.[74]

Thus, even as Du Bois would welcome the kinds of openness and engagement Connolly cultivates, when he ponders the limitations of white leadership in the cause of African American freedom, Du Bois notes a tendency "to misinterpret and compromise and complicate matters, even with the best of will" (*DOD*, 132). This is not a claim of timeless or fundamental racial difference. Nor are his recommendations for improving segregated schools, his proposals for black economic development, or his efforts on behalf of Pan-African solidarity necessarily indicators of a more rigid understanding of identity or a spirit of antiwhite vengeance. Instead they reflect an approach that favors the creative exploitation of extant identity categories through micro- and macropolitical action to constitute more democratic forms of existence in the face of durable racial hierarchies.

To turn to *Dusk of Dawn* as a resource with which to interpret and respond to racial injuries, then, is not to make a brief for the existence of a singular, authentic black self standing opposed to an equally stable, hostile white world. Du Bois aims instead to convey black experiences in a way that discredits the idea of permanent racial categories even as it limns the operation of those categories. Nor does a reading of Du Bois's life story serve to advance the view that expressions of first-person experience are unmediated and uncontestable. Indeed, one of the distinguishing features of *Dusk of Dawn* is the degree to which it is a writer's autobiography; that is, Du Bois makes little effort to disguise the heavy work of interpretation and selection in fashioning the story. Like Connolly's political thought, it "testifies to the indispensability of interpretation and to the ambiguity of its ground."[75] The living value in Du Bois's narrative resides in its capacity both to concretize the meanings of racial identity and, at the same time, to put that identity in question. While this could be said of other texts in Du Bois's long career, autobiography has at least one unique generic virtue: no matter how determinedly Du Bois, like many theorists, strives to speak in an immortal voice or, like other autobiographers, to portray himself as an exceptional man, he is fundamentally at a disadvantage vis-à-vis his readers, who get to see how (some) things turn out. As he reflects in *Dusk of Dawn*'s closing sentence: "Life has its pain and evil—its bitter disappointments; but I like a good novel and in healthful length of days, there is infinite joy in seeing the World, the most interesting of continued stories, unfold, even though one misses THE END" (*DOD*, 326).[76]

FIVE | Representative Women: Slavery and the Gendered Ground of Citizenship

My country needs me, and if I were not here, I would have to be invented.

—Hortense J. Spillers, "Mama's Baby, Papa's Maybe"[1]

Setting Another Example

Among the most potent images in Du Bois's repertoire, the portrait of the "two passing figures of the present-past" in *The Souls of Black Folk* prophesies the perdurance of slavery's injuries well beyond the horizon of abolition. The blighted Confederate father and bereft slave mother stand in stark contrast to heroic figures such as John Brown and Du Bois himself, whose sacrifices for democratic ideals confirm their exemplarity. Indeed, Marlon Ross observes that "rather than being emulative models, ["the passing figures"] are counterexamples."[2] And of the two, commentators have noted, the characterization of the "form hovering dark and motherlike" indicates Du Bois's particular inability to envision a future that is led by African American women.[3] Still, *Souls* is not Du Bois's last word on the subject. If slavery is the crucible out of which American democracy will be forged, Du Bois's 1920 essay "The Damnation of Women" locates slave women at the heart of the story of slavery and its aftermath. Not only did these women bear the brunt of bondage, in Du Bois's estimation, but "Damnation" looks to their daughters for "the up-working of new revolutionary ideals, which must in time have vast influence on the thought and action of this land" (*DW*, 107).[4] Through a kind of collective biography of African American women, "Damnation" thus extends Du Bois's argument about the ways that the traces of racial slavery permeate the present and, simultaneously, presses against his own tendency to figure the future in masculine terms.[5] Equally importantly, the essay also presses against American feminist theories of citizenship that fail to come to terms with the legacies of slavery.

The ferocity of contemporary battles over the boundaries of citizenship and a growing sense of citizens' relative powerlessness in the face of corporate and governmental authority indicates the urgency of thinking anew about democratic citizenship. Indeed, as the possibilities for meaningful political action appeared increasingly circumscribed, the 1990s witnessed "an explosion of interest in the concept of citizenship among political theorists."[6] Such scholarly focus shows no sign of abating today, as democratic thinkers, in various ways, echo Mary Dietz's question: "Can we find resources for the invigoration of the work of politics and the action of citizens that so many of us now fear are lost?"[7] The stakes are not just theoretical. As Ruth Lister explains, the revival of citizenship studies reflects international political trends, including the redrawing of national boundaries and massive migrations, and their coincidence with worries about political participation in democratic states and growing resistance to social citizenship rights.[8] In the United States, contested understandings of citizenship fuel a range of ferocious debates about questions including the status of immigrants in an age of homeland security, the future of welfare, the rights of prisoners and former prisoners, and the relationship between patriotism and criticism. All of these debates reflect a paradox at the core of democratic citizenship: how to make genuinely inclusive a concept whose binding force is itself premised on various forms of exclusion.[9] In all of these controversies, moreover, "the languages of citizenship," which demarcate full members of society from those ineligible for such membership, are intertwined with definitions of race and gender.[10]

While it may seem obvious that definitions of U.S. citizenship cannot be disentangled from questions of race, and the rich tradition of black feminist theory offers ample evidence of interconnections between slavery and the white supremacist dimensions of patriarchy, the power of these interconnections is not addressed consistently by leading white feminists. With regard to the relationship of citizenship and motherhood, in particular, this omission is disabling. As Patricia Hill Collins observes, recent debates about issues ranging from affirmative action to "family values" to immigration reform are linked to struggles over national identity that are themselves connected to questions abut the kind of women fit to be "mothers of the nation."[11] The Personal Responsibility and Work Opportunity Act of 1996 offers a telling example. The degree to which welfare reform relied on racial images with roots in slavery—images that served to assure the health of the citizenry through the containment of those citizens deemed pathological— reminds us that slavery has not been completely erased from the American political imagination.[12] Through such images, an ideal of democratic citizenship is used to define many poor, nonwhite women as noncitizens by denying them access to paying work, to the wherewithal required to have and raise children, to privacy, to the ballot.[13] And it signals the continuing force of "the equation of dark skin with debased labor" (in both its productive and reproductive senses).[14] Consequently, feminist theorists, and indeed all democratic theorists, need to wrestle with the core of American citizenship: "the enduring impact of slavery not merely on black Americans and on the Civil War generation generally, but also on the imagination and fears of those who were neither threatened by enslavement nor deeply and actively opposed to it."[15] To elide differences between the historical "dependent citizenship" of white women and "anticitizenship" of slaves is to risk neglecting, and thereby reinforcing, the "contextual, institutional, and political" relations and practices through which contemporary forms of anticitizenship are constituted.[16]

This chapter argues that Du Bois's 1920 narration of African American women's experiences exposes and corrects some of these elisions. If the phrase "as a woman" functions as "the Trojan Horse of feminist ethnocentrism" when uttered from a position of privilege,[17] Du Bois explores how its meaning can carry an entirely different political charge when the "woman" in question is not white. That "The Damnation of Women" identifies its subject without modifier and proceeds to analyze the situation of "women" through a retelling of black women's history announces Du Bois's subversive intentions. He demands revaluation of *which* women are eligible to be representative, *whose* lives are of universal significance. To be sure, Du Bois's essay is rife with tensions. It vacillates between admiration for the resistance of enslaved and poor women and praise of the delicacy and beauty of "a finer type of black woman"; and it is torn between a radical conception of freedom and a conventional ideal of "uplift."[18] The aim of this chapter is not to minimize these tensions. Rather, I approach Du Bois's work contrapuntally, setting his views in relation to ongoing debates about the nature of democratic citizenship, in order to explore the ways in which this inspiring and problematic work of feminist theory can challenge and enlarge those debates.

"Damnation's" contribution to a feminist theory of citizenship emerges from Du Bois's interweaving of three themes. First, he builds from the history of black women's sexual exploitation an expansive notion of sexual freedom that includes the freedom to have and to raise children regardless of one's marital circumstances. Second, he celebrates the economic independence achieved by African American women, making it a model, rather than a cautionary tale, for other women, and he does so without reinforcing bootstrap narratives of individual success. Third and finally, "Damnation" both advocates the inclusion of African American women as full citizens and acknowledges their historical importance as political actors, even in the absence of recognition by the polity. Read against arguments advanced by Dietz and Jean Bethke Elshtain, Du Bois's essay does more than call attention to the invisibility of black women. It gestures toward what Hortense Spillers calls "the insurgent ground" of an alternative female subjectivity, and with it, alternative possible conceptions of democratic citizenship.[19]

Du Bois's Woman Question

The question of Du Bois's feminism is surely a question.[20] On the one hand, commentators note that Du Bois was not only ahead of his time but also in many respects ahead of ours. Decades before the terminology of "intersectionality" became part of the feminist lexicon, Du Bois ventured into "the place where African-American women live, a political vacuum of erasure and contradiction maintained by the almost routine polarization of 'blacks and women' into separate and competing political camps."[21] A reading of his editorials in *The Crisis*, for example, reveals his dedication to bridging the divide between the fight for women's suffrage and the black struggle for freedom and equality.[22] According to Cheryl Townsend Gilkes, "[Du Bois's] work is the earliest self-consciously sociological interpretation of the role of African American women as agents of social change."[23] And "Damnation," whose appearance coincided with the ratification of the Nineteenth Amendment, is hailed by David Levering Lewis as "a document of such radiance as to place it among the worthiest feminist texts."[24] That so many of the pieces in *Darkwater* exhibit a preoccupation with the past, present, and future meanings of black women's experiences indicates the importance of those experiences to Du Bois's thinking at the height of his popular influence.[25]

Du Bois's obvious commitments to women's equality notwithstanding, "Damnation" also comes perilously close to submersion in what might be called "the quicksands of representation."[26] Notoriously, the essay quotes Anna Julia Cooper's proclamation that "only the black woman can say 'when and where I enter, . . . then and there the whole Negro race enters with me'" but fails to name Cooper as its source (*DW*, 100–01).[27] Du Bois's double move, simultaneously giving voice to and silencing Cooper, indicates an intention to present himself as spokesman. Furthermore, readers of "Damnation" are confronted not only with Cooper's unattributed words but also with the absence, altogether, of Ida B. Wells-Barnett, whose antilynching campaign was pivotal for Du Bois's own efforts. Thus, despite his gender egalitarianism, Du Bois's acceptance of patriarchal norms and his aspiration to offer himself as the representative African American intellectual/leader lend weight to Hazel Carby's argument that "gendered structures of thought and feeling" account for his "complete failure to imagine black women as intellectuals and race leaders."[28]

Any reading of "Damnation" must, therefore, be alert to the meanings of Du Bois's ventriloquism and to a "propensity to ventriloquize" on the part of the reader who would appropriate his essay for her own purposes.[29] There is the very real danger that engaging Du Bois's arguments—in lieu of those of Cooper, or Wells-Barnett, or any of his female contemporaries—simply reinforces their absence from a canon composed of male elites.[30] Nevertheless, to assume that only African American women can relate this history is to risk reproducing demeaning assumptions that it is not worthy of discussion by *all* political thinkers. Further, turning directly to the texts of black women is no inoculation against the presumption of a kind of proprietary intimacy with them.[31] In this regard, Ann DuCille warns: "To be valid—to be true—black womanhood must be legible as white or male; the texts of black women must be readable as maps, indexes to someone else's experience, subject to a seemingly endless process of translation and transference."[32] Two questions to keep in mind, then, are the following: To what extent does Du Bois succeed and how does he fail to narrate African American women's history without either silencing the women themselves or making them a vehicle for purposes at odds with their own? What might a reader learn from those successes and failures?

"Damnation" raises further concerns about Du Bois's representational politics. It is telling, Joy James writes, that Du Bois's nonfiction writings about women are characterized by their "nonspecificity"; in contrast to the detail he provides about particular male elites, black women (and workers) appear generically.[33] Where specific women are identified, furthermore, they are often put to the service of a typology that reinforces prevailing class and gender norms. Thus, Sojourner Truth and Harriet Tubman stand for "strong, primitive types of Negro womanhood in America," while Phillis Wheatley, Mary Shadd, and others call to mind "a not more worthy, but a finer type of black woman wherein trembles all of that delicate sense of beauty and striving for self-realization, which is as characteristic of the Negro soul as is its quaint strength and sweet laughter" (*DW*, 102–03). Here Du Bois is caught in several contradictions: between the demand for equality and the celebration of conventional understandings of difference, between the value of autonomy and the demand for protection, between the critique of society's preoccupation with women's beauty and assertions of the beauty of blackness.[34] Moreover, a lingering attachment to what Evelyn Brooks Higginbotham calls the "politics of respectability," with its emphasis on middle-class norms of propriety,[35] betrays him even as he celebrates the heroism of figures like Tubman and Truth. These conflicts remain not only unresolved but largely unexplored in "Damnation."

Clearly, making a case for the importance, today, of a text like "Damnation" involves the feminist theorist in a series of paradoxes. Even as Du Bois substitutes his own authority for Cooper's, he also develops an argument that takes Cooper's claim literally and explicitly locates African American women at the center of American democracy. Even as he draws upon conventional gender and class norms to describe his heroines, he undermines prevailing beliefs about the role of African American women in American history. His account both succumbs to and resists the temptation to contain the challenge this history poses not only to white supremacy but also to his own authority. Yet it makes its lasting contribution precisely to the extent that it does not attempt simply to represent the perspective of the margins. Rather, "Damnation" demonstrates the importance, for all Americans, of disrupting received understandings of the relationship between margin and center in American life. The women in the essay are not simply figured as the "other," whether exotic or degraded; they are not the winners of a perverse contest of relative victimization. Nor does Du Bois appear to be substituting a monolithic, simple-mindedly heroic story of black women's experience in compensation for generations of negative press; his intellectual and political commitments make him wary of efforts to produce histories that promise "pleasant reading" (*BR*, 713). Instead, when he asks, "What is the message of these black women to America and to the world?" (*DW*, 105), Du Bois indicates the importance of testing feminist ideas about citizenship against the stories of women whose "freedom [was] thrust contemptuously upon them" and who have, nonetheless, aspired to create from it "an untrammeled independence" (*DW*, 107). In light of the frequency with which echoes of this contempt still resound in policy debates, and the ease with which black women's independence is denied or pathologized, I show why Du Bois's essay, with all of its flaws, remains crucial reading.

Reading "Damnation"

The most passionate element of the essay is Du Bois's attack on the sexual violence at the heart of slavery. "I shall forgive the white South much in its final judgment day," he writes. "But one thing I shall never forgive, neither in this world nor the world to come: its wanton and continued and persistent insulting of the black womanhood which it sought and seeks to prostitute to its lust" (*DW*, 100). Isolated from the rest of the text, this claim echoes the tradition of slave narratives, written largely by men, in which women's history is largely absent and women appear primarily as sexual victims.[36] Yet "Damnation" resists such a reading in two ways. First, the rape of black women, as Du Bois presents it, cannot be uncoupled from the main story line of white aspirations for economic and political supremacy.[37] It is an aspect of what Lauren Berlant calls a "national sexuality." Du Bois's study of African American women is an account of "subaltern survival in a nation where coerced sexualization is both banal and a terrorizing strategy of control in the interstices of democracy."[38] And he insists on the importance, for all citizens, of confronting the centrality of racialized sexual brutality in American political development, the importance of rape—although legally not recognized as such—in perpetuating social hierarchy.[39]

Second, Du Bois refuses the impulse to reduce black women to the violence enacted on their bodies and to interpret that violence primarily as a crime against the masculine prerogatives of African American men. "To the limited extent that sexual victimization of black women is symbolically represented within our collective memory," observes Kimberlé Crenshaw, "it is as tragic characters whose vulnerability illustrates the racist emasculation of black men."[40] In contrast, the "daughters of sorrow" (*DW*, 96) of Du Bois's description are hardly passive. For the same dynamic that subjected African American women to white men's desire both during slavery and beyond, "has also," according to Du Bois, "given the world an efficient womanhood, whose strength lies in its freedom and whose chastity was won in the teeth of temptation and not in prison and swaddling clothes" (*DW*, 100). The emphasis on strength stands in sharp contrast to the virtues of white womanhood, which Du Bois reveals to be the product of incarceration and infantilization. It intervenes in and chastens a discourse that represented black women migrating from the rural South to northern cities as a "threat" to both white middle-class values and black middle-class aspirations and that inspired "moral panic" across the color line.[41] And it dovetails with Du Bois's political commitments, in particular, his support for legal access to birth control and opposition to sterilization programs.[42] Rather than arguing that black women, too, should be enthroned as queens of a tightly circumscribed domestic sphere, he defends the importance of sexual freedom for any meaningful conception of women as free citizens.

Du Bois elaborates on this point in the essay's opening paragraph. Musing on his childhood, he exposes the sexual dimension of the "regimes of representation" through which black women's lives were rendered intelligible.[43] The "four women of my boyhood" are Du Bois's mother, his cousin Inez, and two women from his town—one black and one white. In his early apprehension of these women, Du Bois notes, "they were not beings, they were relations and these relations were enfilmed with mystery and secrecy" (*DW*, 95). Socially, they were figured as "the problem of the widow, the wife, the maiden, and the outcast" (*DW*, 95). Of his mother, he remembers, they "were good chums" (*DW*, 95). Yet even as he acknowledges how little he knew her, he goes beyond registering the profundity of his loss at her early death to inquire into the interplay of ignorance and moral judgment that confined the possibilities of Inez, whose marriage brought with it "a litter of children, poverty, a drunken, cruel companion, sickness, and death"; of Emma, who survived by killing her passion for life; and of Ide Fuller, the white "awful outcast of the town," who "stood to us as embodied filth and wrong,—but whose filth, whose wrong?" (*DW*, 95) He questions a representational politics in which such labels not only constrain but also disguise the constraints within which black women and white women, like Ide Fuller—who is, ironically, the one whose example most obviously fits stereotypical images of black women's sexuality—live and die. From these snapshots, Du Bois concludes that "only at the sacrifice of intelligence and the chance to do their best work can the majority of modern women bear children. This is the damnation of women" (*DW*, 96). "All womanhood," he continues, "is hampered today because the world on which it is emerging is a world that tries to worship both virgins and mothers and in the end despises motherhood and despoils virgins" (*DW*, 96).

As Du Bois's accent on the degradation of motherhood suggests, ending the damnation of women entails more than the right to sexual expression. It also entails the freedom to choose parenthood—"even when the sneaking father shirks his duty" (*DW*, 107). Du Bois's earlier work has been justly criticized for linking the "degradation" of black family life to the privations of slavery and laying the intellectual foundations for the Moynihan Report and recent attacks on the character and culture of black women.[44] Perhaps Kenneth Warren is right that Du Bois "never entirely jettisoned the racial pathology argument from his arsenal of social beliefs."[45] Nevertheless, "Damnation" also provides ammunition against such arguments. Although Du Bois expresses his preference for married parenthood (and nowhere even mentions sexuality outside the bounds of heterosexual relationships[46]), the essay describes a world in which structural constraints of race and class, not moral or cultural depravity, explain its absence. Reproducing the text of slave era advertisements that uncover "the hell beneath the system" (*DW*, 98–99), Du Bois calls attention to the long centuries when, for black women, "there was no legal marriage, no legal family, no legal control over children" (*DW*, 98). A world in which, according to Spillers, "'kinship' loses meaning since it can be invaded at any given and arbitrary moment by the property relations."[47] From that history, Du Bois asks: "What sort of black women could be born into the world of today?" And he immediately sets himself against "those who hasten to answer this query in scathing terms and who say lightly and repeatedly that out of black slavery came nothing decent in womanhood; that adultery and uncleanness were their heritage and are their continued portion" (*DW*, 99). "Damnation" does not moralize about the cultural deficiencies of poor black women. In deliberate contrast to the defenders of (white) motherly virtue, it declares:

> God send us a world with woman's freedom and married motherhood inextricably wed, but until He sends it, I see more of a future promise in the betrayed girl-mothers of the black belt than in the childless wives of the white North, and I have more respect for the colored servant who yields to her frank longing for motherhood than for her white sister who offers up children for clothes (*DW*, 107).

In his celebration of marriage and black women's hard-won chastity, it appears that, at some level, Du Bois joins his peers in "shudder[ing]" at the "sex freedom" represented by the unmarried mothers he lauds. In spite of this, he nonetheless demands women's right to make such choices. Moreover, he expands the meaning of reproductive liberty in two ways that anticipate the arguments of scholars like critical race theorist Dorothy Roberts: he underscores the point that "reproductive politics in America inevitably involves racial politics,"[48] and he provides support for the view that the infringement on black women's reproductive freedom has been at least as much bound up with the right to have and to raise children as it has with access to contraception and abortion. This view resonates, as well, with welfare activists' understanding of "dignity" as including the right to make decisions about when and how to include men in their lives and to raise their children.[49] In this regard, he challenges feminists who have neglected these points, not only to recognize the roots of present-day gender subordination in racial slavery but also to consider how prevailing theoretical formulations and political agendas perpetuate white privilege.

Further evidence of the radicalism of Du Bois's argument emerges from a claim that "Damnation" does *not* make. Although Du Bois places great stock in the relationship between social improvement and a good home-life, the essay does not suggest that women's entry into the ranks of citizenship ought to come by virtue of their service as moral guardians of the next generation. The African American women he offers as models are both mothers and not. Their contributions may be linked to, but do not depend upon, a sense of women's distinctive capacity for motherhood. Du Bois's silence on this point speaks loudly in light of the ways that the idea of motherhood as a kind of public service figured in feminist discourse in the 1920s.[50] It indicates his recognition that prevailing American norms of motherhood celebrated the service of black women to other women's offspring but denigrated any dedication to their own children as shiftlessness.[51] At a time when both black and white activists deployed maternal imagery (albeit to differing ends) and staked women's entry into public life on their experiences as social caretakers, Du Bois's demand for a right to motherhood without strings and his appreciation for women's work both within and against prevailing conventions, is striking.[52]

The economic dimension of Du Bois's argument is intimately related to his unsettling of sexual norms. When he declares that "the present mincing horror at free womanhood must pass if we are ever to be rid of the bestiality of free manhood"(*DW*, 96), it is not only woman's sexual freedom but their economic independence he defends. And when he notes that black women's economic success has outstripped that of black men and that the breakdown of two-parent families is one result, Du Bois does not build from this evidence a case for a decent family wage or the importance of male breadwinning. He cautions against the effort to shore up an ideal of family life that "harks back to the sheltered harem with the mother emerging at first as nurse and homemaker, while the man remains the sole breadwinner" (*DW*, 104).[53] Black women should not cede the autonomy they have wrung from their centuries of hard labor, in Du Bois's view. "These, then, are a group of workers, fighting for their daily bread like men; independent and approaching economic freedom!" (*DW*, 104).[54] Indeed: "The future woman must have a life work and economic independence. She must have knowledge. She must have the right of motherhood at her own discretion" (*DW*, 96). This description joins the demand for reproductive rights to the kind of economic independence that he advocates in his reflections on Reconstruction. As I note in chapter 2, Du Bois insists that the realization of a democratic society requires the restructuring of the economy such that all members have the wherewithal to sustain a decent life. Thus, when he offers black women's economic history as a microcosm of "the industrial history of labor in the nineteenth and twentieth centuries" (*DW*, 105), he celebrates their accomplishments without reinforcing what, in *Black Reconstruction*, he calls "the American Assumption." Although "Damnation" does not explicitly name the "Assumption," Du Bois's rendering of the story of black women's economic successes refutes narratives about the capacity of the individual to rise above the past through her own efforts alone. It emphasizes instead a notion of womanhood whose power can only be understood by considering a larger context of communal opposition to the privations of slavery and Jim Crow.

Foregrounding African American women's history also enables Du Bois to formulate the beginnings of an argument for an alternative to individualist conceptions of citizenship without reinforcing the sex-typing of roles and occupations. Read in conjunction with "'The Servant in the House,'" another of the essays in *Darkwater*, "Damnation" points toward an "ethic of care" that challenges the assumption that "service" is the feminine form of "work." It does so in two ways. First, Du Bois elevates service to the highest human calling. Indeed, the "Credo" with which *Darkwater* begins uses the term interchangeably with "work" and equates the job of the bootblack with the "whitening of souls" (*DW*, 1). In "'The Servant in the House,'" he elaborates, connecting the ideal of service to a range of relationships conventionally thought of as both male and female. Service, he says, is illustrated in the meaning of the word "Friend" and the relationships of mother to child and daughter to mother; it is also evident in the codes of the men who attended the kings of the past.[55] In all of these examples, he finds nothing more pure or holy than "the personal aid of man to man" (*DW*, 67–68). Such praise of service might be dangerous, a cover for exploitative relationships, but Du Bois does not stop there: his ideal is "a world of Service without Servants" (*DW*, 69).[56] Nor does he fail to criticize the sex segregation of jobs often underwritten by celebrations of "service." Thus his second point: at the same time that it is crucial to recognize the real value of nursing and housework, "we cannot imprison women again in a home or require them all on pain of death to be nurses and housekeepers" (*DW*, 105).

Entwined with these ideas is another set of claims about the political significance of black women's history and their status as representative citizens. Writing at a moment when woman suffrage was at hand, Du Bois does not rehearse the case for extending the franchise. Instead, he challenges a version of American history that presents black political activity, where it is acknowledged at all, as no less depraved than black family life (*BR*, 711–29). It is possible to discern, in "Damnation's" counterhistory, four strands of argument about the significance of African American women's exclusion from and contributions to American political life. One strand consists of the claim that the measure of any democracy is the treatment of its least privileged citizens. As he says in "Of the Ruling of Men," also in *Darkwater*, "the willingness to consider as 'men' the crankiest, humblest and poorest and blackest peoples, must be the real key to the consent of the governed" (*DW*, 88). Where *Souls* identifies African Americans as the authentic interpreters of the meaning of freedom in the U.S. and posits their circumstances as "a concrete test of the underlying principles of the great republic" (*SBF*, 43–44), "Damnation" distills the claim further. The measure of American democracy, Du Bois avers, can be taken from the willingness to extend the benefits of citizenship to black women. Thus the observation that these women "had freedom thrust contemptuously upon them" has a double meaning (*DW*, 107). On the one hand, it signals an internal contradiction in American political values, for freedom "thrust contemptuously upon" a person is hardly worthy of the name. And, on the other, it reveals a distortion of the record. Crucial to Du Bois's historical reconstruction is the exposure and celebration of what African American women have in fact done to liberate themselves.

Like Cooper before him, Du Bois also gestures toward a second argument (also fleshed out in "Of the Ruling of Men") that the denial of so significant a portion of the nation's intelligence runs counter to its flourishing. A version of this argument will be familiar to readers of John Stuart Mill's *On Liberty*, although Du Bois pushes it in a direction that Mill, even in his feminist writing, does not anticipate: the silencing of *black women* is politically disabling not only because of the harm it causes them but because of the ways it inhibits the possibility of progress for everyone. "The message of these black women to America and to the world," according to Du Bois, is that "the uplift of women is, next to the problem of the color line and the peace movement, our greatest modern cause" (*DW*, 105). Although his situation of "the woman question" *next* to the others is ambiguous—is it their equal, or does it come after them? —the ambiguity does not undermine Du Bois's strong sense of the "deep meaning" of black women's claims on the polity (*DW*, 105).[57] Without attention to that meaning, he suggests, the cause of democracy is seriously, perhaps fatally, diminished.

A third political argument emerges from Du Bois's allusions to "the mother-idea" that he traces to African roots. There is, to be sure, a great deal of romance in Du Bois's genealogy, which stretches from the primal mother "through dusky Cleopatras, dark Candaces, and darker, fiercer Zinghas, to our own day and our own land" (*DW*, 97). The very notion of a "mother-idea" at the heart of African life smacks of gender and cultural essentialism.[58] Even as "Damnation" advances the image of African American women as liberated/

liberators, notes Vilashini Cooppan, "it concatenates, in a kind of rhetorical juggernaut, woman, Africa, mother."[59] My aim is not to dispute this point, but to direct attention to another that may be obscured by it. The maternity Du Bois idolizes is that of women whose power is expressed both through the keeping of homes and raising of children and through their critical role as leaders and participants in African public life. "The crushing weight of slavery" (*DW*, 98), by this reading, burdens black women not only by denying them maternal rights and womanly dignity but, at least as important, by depriving them of political status. When he traces the descendants of these African women, therefore, Du Bois consciously connects their actions to the political fortunes of American democracy. For example, his admiration for Tubman is based on her presence at antislavery events, her heroism in the Underground Railroad, her service to the Union cause in the Civil War, and her role as advisor to John Brown. Despite comments about Tubman's comportment and her reputation for drifting off at meetings, what comes through most clearly is Du Bois's appreciation for her contributions as a "dissident citizen."[60] Similarly, writing about his grandmother's cousin, "whom Western Massachusetts remembers as 'Mum Bett,'" Du Bois not only identifies her life as an example of personal sacrifice—she sustained a lifelong injury "in defense of a sister"—but also explicitly situates her memory in the context of her pursuit of freedom under the Massachusetts Bill of Rights of 1780 (*DW*, 101). By offering such an account of African American women's past political activities, he lays the groundwork for a fourth set of claims about their work in securing a democratic future.

When Du Bois says that "it is the five million women of my race who really count," he elaborates as follows:

> Black women (and women whose grandmothers were black) are today furnishing our teachers; they are the main pillars of those social settlements which we call churches; and they have with small doubt raised three-fourths of our church property. If we have today, as seems likely, over a billion dollars of accumulated goods, who shall say how much of it has been wrung from the hearts of servant girls and washerwomen and women toilers in the fields? (*DW*, 104)

Although the passage goes on to praise black women's contributions as homemakers, it does not look to the home for the political meaning of their history. First, in light of Du Bois's longstanding commitment to education as a cornerstone of social change, the political significance of the tribute to black women teachers is difficult to overstate. Second, and more interestingly, his assessment of the contributions of African American churchwomen shifts attention away from the ministers who are often the focus in accounts of the political role of black churches. In his appreciation for the centrality of women in sustaining these institutions, Du Bois identifies them as political actors. For the church, he recognizes, is not simply a place of worship but also a crucial site for the formation of what would now be called a "black counterpublic." Thus, Du Bois's work gives additional weight to recent scholarship that builds on Jürgen Habermas's conception of the "public sphere," particularly as amended by Nancy Fraser and by the Black Public Sphere Collective, to develop an account of the rich and varied forms of African American political life.[61] According to Michael Dawson, "the black counterpublic sphere is the product of *both* the historically imposed separation of blacks from whites throughout most of American history (which was associated with exclusion from the 'official' public sphere) and the embracing of the concept of black autonomy as both an institutional principle and an ideological orientation."[62] Black women were critical to the development in churches of newspapers and magazines, schools at a range of academic levels, and an expansive array of social welfare programs. Within both the churches and the larger religious conventions to which they belonged, furthermore, these women took advantage of or created opportunities for engagement in such civic activities as deliberation, voting, and agenda setting.[63] Du Bois's tribute, then, is no mere acknowledgment of their religiosity.[64] It offers a foretaste of recent work that shifts attention away from highly visible male leadership and focuses on the critical role of black women in the organizations and institutions that made possible the successes of the civil rights era. Finally, Du Bois's account of the resources "wrung from" black women's labor points toward the kinds of sacrifice—often invisible and rarely honored—that Danielle Allen discerns at the heart of democratic citizenship.[65]

Just as *Black Reconstruction* makes the case that emancipation was the product of African Americans working—by fleeing, fighting, and otherwise improvising—on their own behalf, "Damnation" offers black women as model citizens who forge their independence in the absence of public recognition. In this regard, it models what Bonnie Honig calls "democratic takings." Writing about the ways in which immigrants have rewritten American mythologies of citizenship, Honig draws on Jacques Rancière's accounts of how excluded populations have responded through the "staging of a nonexistent right."[66] Thus, she observes:

> We have here a story of illegitimate demands made by people with no standing to make them, a story of people so far outside the circle of who 'counts' that they cannot make claims within the existing frames

of claim making. They make room for themselves by staging nonexistent rights, and by way of such stagings, sometimes, new rights, powers, and visions come into being.[67]

Certainly, the story of African American women's experiences in slavery and its aftermath is a story of illegitimacy. Black women have been used repeatedly to epitomize illegitimacy in the national imagination; responsibility for rape and for poverty and for fatherless households is displaced, assigned to black women themselves. In his narration of their collective biography, by contrast, Du Bois revises readers' understanding of African American women's past, present, and future. He confounds expectations about illegitimacy and exemplarity by recording a history of accomplishment in the face of violent exclusion.

"Context Is All": Legacies of Slavery and Feminist Theories of Citizenship

"For a concept of citizenship," writes Mary Dietz, "feminists should turn to relations and practices that are expressly contextual, institutional, and political, informed by and situated within particular cultures and histories, and oriented toward action."[68] Dietz's call to action provides an appealing alternative to liberal notions of citizens as self-interested bearers of rights, on the one hand, and maternalist assertions of the virtues associated with motherhood, on the other. In *Turning Operations*, Dietz offers revised versions of two landmark essays—"Context is All: Reconsidering Feminism and Citizenship" and "Citizenship with a Feminist Face: More Problems with Maternal Thinking." Although dedicated to investigating the limitations of "maternalist" feminism, these pieces praise scholars such as Jean Bethke Elshtain for three contributions: calling attention to "the moral attributes of citizenship . . . and the content of feminist political consciousness," challenging rights-based theories of justice, and articulating an alternative, positive account of politics built on a thick conception of human relationships.[69] At the same time, however, Dietz contends that maternalism trades on traditional notions of women's roles and moral character; it inverts, without displacing, binaries of equality and difference, public and private. While it is beyond the scope of this chapter to provide adequate commentary on the rich set of arguments offered by Dietz or Elshtain, or on the literature their disagreements have generated, a selective reading of their essays against "Damnation" reveals a shared failure to confront the challenges that arise from thinking about citizenship in the context of white supremacy. Du Bois's examination of slavery and its legacies, in contrast, goes beyond the demand for inclusion to suggest how a focus on the lives of those women whose sexuality, economic activity, and political engagements have been defined outside the frame of the "normal" might provide insight into the importance of thinking of slavery when theorizing citizenship.[70]

A reader might expect that Du Bois would find much to endorse in Elshtain's account of "social feminism." The black mothers of Du Bois's description could rightly be described as "Antigone's daughters" in their efforts to defend themselves, their families, and communities against a state that was deeply invested in their powerlessness; their survival against enormous odds signals rebellion. And although Du Bois fought hard for suffrage, he would surely second Elshtain's view that feminists should be skeptical about the impulse "to discover in the state the new 'Mr. Right,' and to wed themselves thereby, for better or for worse, to a public identity inseparable from the exigencies of state power and policy."[71] The alternative offered in "Damnation" and in "Antigone's Daughters" is a theory that "begin[s] from the standpoint of women within their everyday reality."[72] But how to describe "the social world" of women? In Elshtain's view, it is grounded in relationships and practices that go deeper than those of political or economic life.[73] Du Bois, by contrast, raises questions about this account of "women's traditional identities," particularly about the possibility of understanding these identities not "tainted by relations of domination."[74] The "attentive love" of mother for child that Elshtain takes to be a given of maternal experience and that she advocates as the basis for a critique of social injustice thus appears less promising when it is recalled how often, in white middle-class households, this love has been predicated on the work of nonwhite women.[75] If feminists focus on the concrete lives of women, as Elshtain urges, then it is critical to remember that poor women's demands for the resources necessary to attend to their own children are regularly interpreted as an unwillingness to work.[76] Furthermore, although Du Bois spent a great deal of ink defending the virtues of black mothers, his scathing rejection of white norms of womanhood resists the conclusion that what he seeks is black women's inclusion in a traditional conception of the maternal. On the contrary, his account of African American women as workers and political actors, as well as mothers, undermines the idea that their challenge to liberal individualist notions of citizenship is, or ought to be, derived from a social world outside the public sphere.

Reading "Damnation" alongside Dietz's arguments suggests that her alternative to Elshtain similarly employs a race- and class-bound conception of maternal identity and activities that leaves little room for the women of Du Bois's description.[77] "Mothering," according to Dietz, is an inappropriate basis for theorizing democratic citizenship insofar as it "is an intimate, exclusive, dualistic, and particularistic activity within which the mother is directed toward the preservation of the child."[78] In contrast, she describes democratic politics as "a condition in which the many aim at acting as peers and equals."[79] And she rightly warns against the depoliticizing effects of "familizing" metaphors.[80] But does the recognition of the dangers of attempting to provide a theoretical conception of "women" that is based on motherhood mean dispensing entirely with motherhood as one among the crucial dimensions of citizens' lives? "Damnation" suggests not. For the exclusion from citizenship Du Bois describes was effected in large part through a denial of kinship under slavery and a devaluation of black family life in the exploitative working conditions of the Jim Crow era. His arguments indicate why a conception of democratic citizenship that ignores the crucial role played by images of African American mothers as anticitizens is unlikely to be genuinely "collective, inclusive, and generalized."[81]

To claim the importance of motherhood to some women's political identity, then, is not necessarily to appeal to the normative superiority of mothers or to view the family as detached from political life. Du Bois's arguments resonate with those advanced by advocates for the rights of black mothers, such as the National Welfare Rights Organization, and by critical race theorists who recognize that motherhood for many women is not a private matter, and whose activism and scholarship are grounded in a conception of motherhood as a vocation that should be freely chosen and available to all women.[82] As Anna Marie Smith notes, "For the poor black woman or poor Latina in our contemporary conditions, caring for one's family often represents one of the few self-affirming activities that are available to her."[83] Indeed, women's political organizing in defense of a conception of citizenship that values caregiving activities, regardless of the caregiver's race, class, or marital status, seems to be precisely the kind of public action Dietz admires. Paying specific attention to "relations and practices that are expressly contextual, institutional, and political," relations and practices that emerge from slavery and segregation, could expand the category of citizenship to include citizen-mothers without reasserting problematic gender norms.

"Damnation," finally, is a text that troubles contemporary practices of feminist theory—and critical theories of democracy more generally. The tensions that define the essay both indicate why the omission of slavery impedes feminist efforts to rethink citizenship in the United States and display the difficulties that attend any attempt to give that history its due. To the twenty-first-century reader, these difficulties may appear all too evident when Du Bois offers his own voice in the stead of those presumed to have been voiceless, or domesticates the meaning of his heroines' lives by reducing them to types that reinforce middle-class norms. Readers may, furthermore, be tempted to dismiss the piece as a whole when Du Bois concludes with a sentimental, or "chivalric" paean to black women's beauty and value.[84] After proposing that his essay is "a little thing" to the "memory and inspiration" of "the daughters of my black mothers," Du Bois declares: "None have I known more sweetly feminine, more unswervingly loyal, more desperately earnest, and more instinctively pure in body and in soul" (*DW*, 108).

Yet alongside this sort of tribute, and equally significantly, "Damnation" spells out both the structural constraints on African American women's activity and the multiple stages on which they have acted as agents of social change. Du Bois's focus on sexual, economic, and political meanings of the damnation and the achievements of *these* women enacts the kind of critical decentering of white experiences without which democratic aspirations are perpetually hobbled. Reading "Damnation" thus provides a powerful reminder of the importance, for any feminist theory of citizenship, of a broader conception of reproductive freedom, of a celebration of women's work that simultaneously calls into question the virtues of capitalism, and of a reconstructed history of political action in the United States. In doing so, it goes beyond simply decrying the exclusion of black women. It urges theorists to defy conventional frameworks and consider the possibilities that are opened when the lives of those Americans against whom American citizenship has been (and is) defined are taken to be representative of democratic citizenship in general.

SIX | Black World, White Nation: Remapping Political Theory

Modern life begins with slavery.

—Toni Morrison, "Living Memory"[1]

Du Bois Reaches Out

"Once upon a time in my younger years and in the dawn of this century I wrote: 'The problem of the Twentieth Century is the problem of the color line.'"[2] Du Bois's reexamination of his famous claim—which appeared in *Foreign Affairs* in 1925 as "Worlds of Color" and then, in amended form, as "The Negro Mind Reaches Out," in Alain Locke's landmark anthology, *The New Negro*—reminds his audience that he has, from the beginning, understood the color line in global terms. In this essay, he looks back at "the catastrophe" of world war and both affirms and enlarges his earlier apprehension of the entanglement of the American experiment with "the relation of the darker to the lighter races of men in Asia and Africa, in America and the islands of the sea" (*SBF*, 45). He also revisits the trope of the shadow and shows how it, like the color line, is amenable to reworking. When *Souls* registers the fugitive impressions of "a mighty Negro past," the lingering traces of "Ethiopia the Shadowy" (*SBF*, 39), it signals Du Bois's consciousness of the world beyond U.S. borders yet fails to accord Africa anything like the concrete, historical substance that it attributes to the shadows of the slave past.

In the 1925 essay, by contrast, African shadows manifest themselves in less mystical terms as indicators of the global labor problem produced through centuries of white power.[3] Discerning the "colonial shadows" that loom over European attempts at recovery, Du Bois reverses conventional wisdom about what is real, politically, and what is myth. He addresses the African roots of war to reveal that "the vision of the Glory of Sacrifice" that honored the slaughter of so many white men and boys in Europe and the United States is itself only a "faint shadow," "a mirage."[4] Further, after tracing the African shadows of Portugal, Belgium, France, and England, Du Bois turns to what he calls "the shadow of shadows" to imagine an oppositional force that might emerge from the heterogeneous peoples who comprise "the darker world."[5]

I draw attention to this essay not only to highlight Du Bois's act of self-revision and the new significance with which he invests familiar tropes but also to emphasize the theoretical angle of vision that he urges upon his readers. "Step within these shadows," Du Bois exhorts, and "looking backward, view the European and white American labor problem from this external vantage ground—or, better, ground of disadvantage."[6] As the essay makes clear, the double vision Du Bois advocates effects a shift away from the assumption that is possible to understand the character of democracy or problems of race within a framework that posits the United States as its singular concern. It is a vision that not only contends with double-consciousness at the level of the individual but also reaches out, asking readers of *Foreign Affairs* to reach out with him and acknowledge the links that join the political and economic challenges that consume them to the fate of Europe's colonies and the future of nonwhite laborers across the globe. This is not a departure for Du Bois but an elaboration on a central theme of his work. As I have noted in passing in previous chapters, Du Bois relentlessly connects the possibilities for democracy's reconstruction in the United States to a modern world order begotten through racial slavery and colonial conquest.

I pick up this thread now, reflecting on the global reach of Du Bois's political thought and the vantage it offers to contemporary political theory. My aim is not to advance anything like a comprehensive account of the shifts and changes in Du Bois's global consciousness over the course of more than seven decades as a writer, thinker, and activist. Nor will I provide a full-blown, critical analysis of his evolving relationship to Africa. Instead, I make the more modest observation that one of the signal contributions of Du Bois's work resides in the ways in which his mind presses beyond the national frame and behind the common sense of the present in order to imagine both what might have been and what might yet be, if the humanity of enslaved and colonized subjects and their descendants were the starting point for political thinking. For theorists grappling with the prospects for democracy in the United States and with Americans' broader responsibilities toward women and men beyond our borders, I argue, Du Bois redraws the map of moral and political concern in ways that demand attention.

Difficult though it is to summarize a career as long and as varied as Du Bois's, one might safely argue that it is defined throughout by a global orientation. As a student in Berlin in the late nineteenth century, an architect of Pan-Africanism in the twentieth, a novelist who imagined global redemption through the romantic union of an African American and an Indian princess, a peripatetic peace activist and, ultimately, an exile from the United States who spent his last days in Ghana, Du Bois refused to be bound, physically or intellectually, by the limits of American nationhood. He was internationalist, insofar as he envisioned the realization of democratic ideals through the actions of states both independently and in concert; yet he also stressed transnational connection, particularly among the men and women whose shared experiences of exploitation and domination would provide a counterweight to the broad reach of white supremacy.[7] These commitments shape Du Bois's political thought in ways that exceed the aims of this chapter. They are evident in Ethiopianist dreams of the rise of a mighty Africa,[8] in successive efforts to correct narratives of world history that exclude or diminish African accomplishment,[9] in attempts to articulate a form of socialism that would reflect the common interests of the darker world and to produce a poetics that might arouse the consciousness of that world.

Given the range and variety of Du Bois's efforts to "think globally," it is little wonder that he has inspired an outpouring of studies by scholars in history, literature, anthropology, philosophy, cultural studies, and other fields. Nevertheless, this dimension of his thought remains relatively neglected by political theorists.[10] Such inattention deserves remedy not only because it obscures a fundamental feature of Du Bois's work but, perhaps more importantly, because that work speaks to global concerns that have come to preoccupy so many scholars of politics. As Nancy Fraser argues, "globalization has put the question of the frame squarely on the political agenda."[11] As political, environmental, economic, military, and cultural connections have bound the world more tightly, and theorists' responsibility to think beyond national borders becomes ever more difficult to gainsay, I argue that the shadows Du Bois discerns haunt conversations in which they are rarely named.

To that end, I offer a comparative reading of two texts separated by 100 years. The first, *The Suppression of the African Slave Trade to the United States of America, 1638–1870* (1896), is Du Bois's earliest book and among the least studied works in his corpus. It may appear to be an inapt choice, far less radically democratic than his anti-imperial and anticolonial writings of the twentieth century. Yet to overlook this early work is to miss something crucial about *how* Du Bois's mind reaches out. Mindful of Amy Kaplan's insight that "in his journey to the concept of Pan-Africa, Du Bois appears at his most American," I turn this formulation around.[12] Through an examination of one of his most "American" texts, we see Du Bois's thoroughgoing worldliness. And we glimpse the possibilities that are opened up when political theorists consider the prospects for democracy in America from a globally constituted "ground of disadvantage."

In conjunction with this reading of *Suppression*, I examine *For Love of Country*, the spirited collection of short essays sparked by Martha Nussbaum's argument for cosmopolitanism. These essays provide a window into the controversies that occupy political theorists and philosophers attempting to weigh competing claims of national attachment and human obligation at a moment when the political status of national boundaries is subject to intense questions: What, if anything, do the citizens of relatively wealthy liberal democratic states owe to people in far corners of the world, and on what grounds? Is it possible to defend the priority of local loyalties over cosmopolitan duties? How should we weigh the relative merits and dangers of an array of possibilities that include but are not limited to world citizenship, rooted cosmopolitanism, patriotism, constitutional patriotism, civic nationalism, liberal nationalism? My intent here is not to survey these efforts. Rather, I suggest that Du Bois's history of the suppression of the international slave trade uncovers concerns that often go unvoiced in these debates. Contrasting *Suppression* against Nussbaum's cosmopolitanism and Benjamin Barber's "constitutional faith," I indicate the limitation of any political theoretical vision that elides the traces of slavery, the slave trade, and European colonialism.

To that end, I approach these texts through a heuristic device, a contrast between black world and white nation. The first term is a modification of Du Bois's own worldly language, his account of "worlds of color" and of "a darker world" that encompasses western members of the African diaspora, along with Africans and Asians as a potential political force.[13] "In this age, when the ends of the world are being brought so near together," Du Bois declared in his 1900 address to the Pan-African Conference in London, the fate of European and American ideals depends on their extension to the nonwhites, who comprise "over half the world."[14] That same year, moreover, he advised the American Negro Academy that African Americans could ill afford to remain aloof from the fate of this dark world: "The colored population of our land is, through the new imperial policy, about to be doubled by our own ownership of Porto [sic] Rico, and Hawaii, our protectorate of Cuba, and conquest of the Philippines."[15] In both addresses, Du Bois signals his early apprehension of the links between African Americans and the larger nonwhite world, on the one hand, and between western democratic aspirations and the future of that world, on the other.

Over time, Du Bois develops these insights into a full-blown conception of "black worldliness." "The counter-tradition of America's most marked exclusion, [black worldliness] is perhaps this country's only consistent universalism," argues Nikhil Singh. Examining the work of intellectuals and activists in the 1940s who connected racial injustice in the United States to global struggles against white supremacy, Singh demonstrates that black worldliness is universal in two senses.[16] First, by discerning a relationship between Jim Crow and the imposition of colonial power and framing their aspirations in global terms, these women and men exhibit an appreciation for what Etienne Balibar calls "real universality." In a world defined by complex webs of interdependency, they recognize that patterns of injustice are not confined within national borders and that antidotes cannot be sought through exclusively domestic measures.[17] Second, they build from the particularity of black experiences a conception of democracy far more capacious than conventional "American" notions of universalism. Countering prevailing views of the United States as already, if imperfectly, democratic, they emphasize the struggles of the excluded, the work of those Americans who have fought to give living meaning to bromides about freedom and equality.[18] Shifting and changing over the course of Du Bois's long career, this interest in plumbing the idea of a black world is a defining mark of his political thought. As I will argue, furthermore, even his preliminary and limited gestures toward such an alternative universality in *Suppression* redraws the map of political theoretical concern in ways that have yet to be properly absorbed.

The second term is inspired by Du Bois's critical appreciation of the kinship of whiteness and national identity in the United States and Europe. This connection, too, evolves over the course of Du Bois's career. In the early years, it is manifest in Du Bois's resistance to cultural assimilation, his reluctance to "bleach his Negro soul in a flood of white Americanism" (*SBF* 39); later it reemerges in more caustic observations about whiteness and American aspirations "to make the 'World Safe for Democracy'" in "The Souls of White Folk" (*DW*, 19–20). And it provides the implicit background for Du Bois's arguments on behalf of voluntary segregation in essays like "A Negro Nation within the Nation" (1935) and in *Dusk of Dawn*.[19] For my purposes, the critical power of the term "white nation" is not that it discredits all forms of civic attachment in the United States as intrinsically racist. Instead, it provides a lens through which we can see how Du Bois challenges readers to scrutinize the assumption that American identity and the articulation of American political ideals can simply be detached from the conception of whiteness they mean to discredit.[20] Together, then, the terms "black world" and "white nation" situate the accomplishments and shortcomings of U.S. democracy within a global context in which whites are not a majority and convey the difficulty of articulating an American conception of nationhood that does not privilege white experiences and history.[21] Through them, I hope to flesh out the significance of those instances in the preceding chapters that only gesture outward beyond U.S. borders in order to understand how Du Bois's twining of modern democratic ideals with the global legacies of slavery and colonial power might assist political theorists in confronting today's "dark times."

Regarding Slavery in the Age of Revolution

Originally Du Bois's doctoral dissertation, *Suppression* appeared in 1896 as the initial monograph in the Harvard Historical Studies series. It was generally well received at the time of publication, and, nearly 60 years after its initial appearance, Du Bois pronounced himself still satisfied with the accuracy of this prodigious synthesis of colonial, state, federal, and international law, official reports, congressional records, and other documentary materials.[22] Although recent critics have noted its significance as an early formulation of Du Bois's critique of imperialism, colonialism, and capitalism,[23] and Manning Marable declares that "the importance [of *Suppression*] . . . cannot be overemphasized,"[24] very few analyses of Du Bois's thought consider this text at any length.

There are good reasons *not* to turn to *Suppression* to address contemporary political questions, and three are worth noting from the outset. First, as I have indicated above, Du Bois's internationalist outlook in 1896 was not what it would be by the middle of the next century. Although *Suppression* allows that the question of how the slave trade was (not) suppressed is entangled with larger questions of the rise and nature of American slavery and European colonialism, Du Bois defines the scope of his monograph narrowly. His intent, he writes, is to produce "a small contribution to the scientific study of slavery and the American Negro" (*SAST*, ix). More fundamentally, Du Bois formulated this project before fully absorbing the implication that the slave trade and colonial expansion were integral to, rather than merely violations of, the fundamental commitments of western modernity and the

American democratic experiment. Thus, he attacks the economic motives that sustained the slave trade, without pursuing links between the trade and the emergence of capitalism; and he decries the dehumanization of slavery without discrediting evolutionary distinctions between advanced and backward peoples or the possibility that primitive societies will ultimately benefit from western encroachments.[25]

Second, apart from the discussion of Toussaint L'Ouverture, readers must look carefully to find hints of Du Bois's later emphasis on the pivotal role of black women and men in freeing themselves from slavery, and even close scrutiny yields no insight into the interior lives of these women and men. While *Suppression* makes the slaves' history central to U.S. history, their role is nonetheless largely a silent one. And while Du Bois's conception of the black world as a *political* force, "a conscious social organism, aware of itself and its parts,"[26] builds upon the analysis in *Suppression*, his conception of that world only emerges in the next century.

Third, Du Bois's first book displays the author's confidence that overcoming ignorance is the crux of the battle against injustice and that the recitation of facts with a dose of moralism might be sufficient to bring about change.[27] At this point in his career, notes Arnold Rampersad, Du Bois's "respect for truth was still almost fundamentalist."[28] And his appreciation for the subconscious play of interests, fears, and delusions that buttress white power was underdeveloped. Du Bois anticipates these concerns in the "Apologia" that precedes the 1954 edition of *Suppression*. Hampered by a lack of familiarity with Freud and Marx, Du Bois observes, his early writing focuses too much on the moral failings of the founding generation and neglects both "the vaster and far more intricate jungle of ideas conditioned on unconscious and subconscious reflexes of living things" (*DOD*, xxx) and the intimate connection between the trade in human chattel and the rise of global capitalism.[29]

These limitations, though substantial, ought not to dissuade contemporary readers from seeking in *Suppression* a rich site for thinking through questions about the scope of democratic belonging and the proper borders of moral and political responsibility. Du Bois's earliest book, I argue, is more than a valuable catalogue of statutes and treaties concerning the slave trade or an artifact primarily of interest to Du Bois scholars and intellectual historians. My reading emphasizes how Du Bois's history of the trade not only situates the United States within the world of what Charles Mills calls the "racial contract" but also points toward an account of the normative significance of the struggles of the enslaved and colonized. The vantage afforded by close attention to this international setting and these struggles, I contend, provides a fertile resource for democratic theory that is overlooked by race-blind cosmopolitanism or appeals to the (white) American experiment. To that end, I highlight Du Bois's retelling of two intertwined stories not generally acknowledged by conventional narratives of the nation's founding and early decades: the persistence of the international slave-trade through much of the nineteenth century and the impact of *another* American revolution—the liberation of Haitian slaves from French rule—on U.S. involvement in the trade.

On its surface, *Suppression* relates precisely what the title advertises: the history of efforts to end U.S. participation in the international slave trade. At a second level, however, it also conveys how efforts to contain that participation or question its crucial role in the making of the United States were themselves suppressed. The irony, as the title makes plain, is that the second suppression proved more effective than the first. By marking 1870 as the end point of his study, Du Bois undermines any assurance that the international trade ended with the passage of prohibitionist laws, announcing instead that its abolition was only accomplished through the bloodshed of the Civil War. In doing so, *Suppression* does not explicitly examine the practice of history; there is no hint of the kind of blistering critique that he will later advance in the final chapter of *Black Reconstruction*. Still, this earliest book indicates Du Bois's sensitivity to the power of a history denied on politics in the present. It disallows the temptation to see slavery either as a misfortune imposed on European Americans, a passive inheritance from a feudal past, or as a regional institution whose significance was tangential to the formation of the nation as a whole. By linking this history to events in Haiti, furthermore, Du Bois not only thwarts efforts to insulate American political development from the iniquities of the slave trade but also opposes U.S. claims to revolutionary preeminence by suggesting that the true revolutionaries of the day were not white.

In Du Bois's telling, the abolition of the slave trade is not the story of a progressive movement toward freedom. While his commitment to the meliorating effects of the scientific study of history bespeaks a confidence in such a movement, the record Du Bois sets down offers little evidence that such confidence is warranted. Throughout the text, Du Bois details the factors—geographic, climatic, cultural—that affected the character of slavery in the different colonies and states and discredits the impulse to regard the end of the trade as a straightforward story of moral improvement. During much of the colonial period, he observes, abolishing the importation of slaves was unthinkable: "that the slave-trade was the very life of the colonies had, by 1700, become an almost unquestioned axiom in British practical economics" (*SAST*, 4). Where the axiom was questioned, furthermore, the challenge to it was uneven and only partially animated by Americans' commitment to liberty. For example, Du Bois notes that opposition to slavery in the Mid-Atlantic and New England during the colonial period had little effect on New Englanders' enthusiastic participation in the slave trade. And he identifies revolutionary ideals as only one of six primary reasons for the momentum against the slave trade that nearly effected the end of slavery during the struggle for independence. The others are: the impracticality of slavery in New England and the Mid-Atlantic, the fear of slave insurrections, an oversupply of slaves in American markets, the recognition that the trade would be largely curtailed by the war in any case, and the conviction that ending commerce with England was the colonies' most effective means of achieving independence (*SAST*, 41–42). Together, these factors produced the declaration on July 4, 1775, that "we will neither import or purchase any Slave imported from Africa, or elsewhere, after this day" (*SAST*, 46).

If the motives for such a resolution were mixed, the resolve to uphold it proved temporary. "The whole movement," Du Bois concludes, "served as a sort of social test of the power and importance of the slave-trade, which proved to be far more powerful than the platitudes of many of the Revolutionists had assumed" (*SAST*, 47). Despite a trajectory of legislation in the Northeast and the Middle Atlantic that implied an imminent end to the trade and to slavery itself, the economic picture had changed substantially enough by the time of the Constitutional Convention that moral arguments could be successfully blocked by the South. Thus, a Constitution emerged with a provision that barred congressional interference with the trade at least until 1808. Congress did pass such legislation in 1807, and there were flurries of anti-slave trade activity in the nineteenth century, particularly in response to the Haitian Revolution. Nevertheless, Du Bois argues, lax enforcement crippled the effort, and Southerners moved further away from the idea that slavery would be a temporary institution. Meanwhile, international campaigns against the trade were also ineffective against U.S. resistance to cooperation. Du Bois's portrait of such efforts captures a United States that led other states in declaring the slave trade to be piracy and simultaneously rebuffed efforts at suppression that were thought to impinge on American sovereignty. Unwilling to allow the boarding of American ships by foreign patrollers, even when the flag was flown fraudulently, the United States in effect transformed Old Glory into a symbol of the trade, the sign under which slave ships could enjoy their safest passage in the decades prior to the Civil War (*SAST*, 136–50). Thus, in a dramatic reversal of progressive logic that presages his reading of Reconstruction's undoing in "Of the Dawn of

Freedom," Du Bois undercuts a narrative trajectory in which the end of the slave trade paved the way for the steady rise of moral resistance against slavery. He concludes, instead, that only the abolition of slavery through civil war put a conclusive end to the trade (*SAST*, 197).[30]

How did the slave trade prove so resilient? One answer, Du Bois demonstrates, can be found in the ways in which explicit discussions of slavery and the slave trade were evaded through strategic silences and indirection. For example, he notes that attempts to shut down the slave trade with England in the years preceding the revolution scrupulously avoided explicit mention of slavery (*SAST*, 42). His treatment of the drafting of the Declaration of Independence reveals an American relationship to human trafficking that was doubly suppressed. In the section famously deleted from the final draft, the colonists took King George to task for imposing on them the evils of slavery and the trade and for exposing them to the dangers of insurrection. The omission of this section was required not only to satisfy the demands of colonists in South Carolina and Georgia but also to appease Northerners who, according to Thomas Jefferson, "felt a little tender under those censures; for though their people had very few slaves themselves, yet they had been pretty considerable carriers of them to others" (*SAST*, 49). Had the section remained, however, it would still have represented an act of historical evasion insofar as it laid responsibility at the feet of the king.[31] This trend continued, Du Bois writes, in a Constitutional Convention that failed entirely to address the larger question of the justifications for slavery in a democratic society. As a consequence, any deep disagreements underlying the crafting of the 21-year ban on federal limits to the slave trade were effaced in the bland prohibition against congressional interference with "the Migration or Importation of such Persons as any of the States now existing shall think proper to admit" (*SAST*, 61). Without saying so directly, *Suppression* leads readers to the conclusion that "racial omission is a literal part of original intent."[32]

Additionally, Du Bois unsettles any confidence that legal abolition would be sufficient, drawing instead a disheartening portrait of the economic motives that undergirded fluctuations in efforts to control the slave trade and the unintended consequences of those laws that did pass. The failure to suppress the slave trade, Du Bois discloses, was due as much to Americans' lack of will to enforce the laws as it was to the resistance of the South against their passage in the first place. "If slave labor was an economic god, then the slave trade was its strong right arm," writes Du Bois in an 1891 paper delivered to the American Historical Association. "And with Southern planters recognizing this and Northern capital unfettered by a conscience it was almost like legislating against economic laws to attempt to abolish the slave trade by statutes."[33] The measures that did pass were "poorly conceived, loosely drawn, and wretchedly enforced." They were "negative signs," registering a range of motives among the American public, rather than "positive efforts" to put a definitive end to the trade (*SAST*, 196). More ominously even, Du Bois makes note of the role of anti-slave trade legislation in *enabling* the persistence of slavery. He concludes, for example, that individual states' efforts to restrict the trade by law during the period of the Confederation "did so much to blind the nation as to the strong hold which slavery still had on the country" (*SAST*, 52).

By marrying memories of slavery to memories of the international trade, Du Bois also complicates figurations of slavery as America's "original sin,"[34] indicating why it is crucial to acknowledge the ways in which the sin was also not original or exceptional, not containable within a national frame. *Suppression* urges upon readers a vantage that considers how the United States did *not* break from Europe and the degree to which it was bound up with Africa and the Caribbean through its participation in the international slave trade. Such an approach casts new light on the abolition of slavery in New England by linking it to the continuing role of traders from the region in the international traffic in human beings: "This trade no moral suasion, not even the strong 'Liberty' cry of the revolution, was able wholly to suppress, until the closing of the West Indian and Southern markets cut off the demand for slaves" (*SAST*, 38). Du Bois thereby uncovers the *national* collaboration that kept both slavery and the trade in human beings alive and recalls the *international* scope of that collaboration.

With a keen ear for what is left unsaid and an eye for what cannot be seen, Du Bois shows how the trade could survive even fierce moral challenges in a nation happily "lulled . . . to sleep" (*SAST*, 62), defined by its "lethargy" toward these violations of the ideals so passionately reaffirmed in the 2007 Virginia resolution (*SAST*, 196).[35] Once the moment at which the United States might have abolished slavery was allowed to pass, he writes, "the twenty-one years of *laissez-faire* were confirmed by the States, and the nation entered upon the constitutional period with the slave-trade legal in three States, and with a feeling of quiescence toward it in the rest of the Union" (*SAST*, 69). Crucially, the effects were not confined to the United States or to the period of the constitutional ban. Not only did American carelessness redefine life for blacks in Africa and the West Indies, but as Du Bois explains in *The Souls of Black Folk*, it continued to typify "this happy-go-lucky nation which goes blundering along with its Reconstruction tragedies, its Spanish war interludes and Philippines matinees, just as though God were really dead" (*SBF*, 125).

If *Suppression* unearths a deliberately untold story of the entanglement of slave trading and independence in the United States, perhaps the most radical challenge posed by this story is Du Bois's assessment of the significance of an American revolution to the south. Writing at a time when the achievements of Africans and their descendants remained segregated from the telling of modern history, Du Bois's insertion of Haiti into his account of U.S. involvement in the slave trade demands a fundamental reorientation from many readers.[36] Not only does it restore this revolution to the history of the modern West, but it also reveals a United States that was engaged with and responsive to a nonwhite world whose significance it sought to deny.[37] By focusing on what Michel-Rolph Trouillot describes as the "unthinkable" revolution, Du Bois unsettles the view that liberty and equality have their birth in the colonists' struggle against England and in the French overthrow of the *Ancien Regime*. "The Haitian revolution," remarks Trouillot, "was the ultimate test to the universalist pretensions of both the French and the American revolutions. And they both failed."[38] Furthermore, *Suppression* intimates that American independence from the slave trade is in some sense derivative of the Haitians' liberation insofar as the fear of spreading insurrection gave new life to antitrade activism. Yet more radically, he hints that this antislavery revolution is a model from which the United States might learn a positive lesson about the meaning of democracy; as he writes elsewhere: "Black Haiti not only freed itself but helped to kindle liberty all through America."[39] In 1945, he goes further: "The rise of Haiti has been a splendid triumph of unlettered slaves against the world. History has no parallel of equal accomplishment."[40] Thus, he undoes white Americans' claims to an "exceptional" history.

While the slaves remain largely invisible in *Suppression*, it is striking that the only chapter in which an individual is named is dedicated to "Toussaint L'Ouverture and Anti-Slavery Effort." Du Bois's appreciation of the importance of one former slave thereby directly counters a historical record in which the political significance of black action goes unnoted.

> The rôle which the great Negro Toussaint, called L'Ouverture, played in the history of the United States has seldom been fully appreciated. *Representing the age of revolution in America*, he rose to leadership through a bloody terror, which contrived a Negro 'problem' for the Western Hemisphere, intensified and defined the anti-slavery movement, became one of the causes, and probably the prime one, which led Napoleon to sell Louisiana for a song, and finally, through the interworking of all these effects, rendered more certain the final prohibition of the slave-trade by the United States in 1807 (*SAST*, 70 [emphasis added]).

This attention to "the greatest of American Negroes"[41] is perhaps unsurprising from someone whose affection for "great men" is widely noted. That Toussaint is embraced as an *American* hero, however, indicates the profundity of Du Bois's challenge to his readers' self-understanding. Even as the chapter stresses the works of a singular individual rather than the struggles of the masses, Du Bois radically rereads the "Age of Revolution" by identifying a black man and former slave as its exemplary figure. Indeed, we might say that by locating the source of the prohibition on the slave trade in a person who could not be credited as a revolutionary hero, Du Bois identifies Toussaint as a kind of "foreign founder." He is the stranger who unsettles and reconstitutes the polity.[42]

Yet the revolutionary aims that Du Bois sketches in this chapter cannot be realized through the actions of Toussaint alone. To the contrary, Du Bois credits the combined effects of "the wild revolt of despised slaves, the rise of a noble black leader, and the birth of a new nation of Negro freemen" as a crucial force in enabling antitrade activists in the United States to accomplish at least some of their ends. It was not only Toussaint's greatness but the fact of *slave revolution*, he argues, that produced sufficient fear to enable the passage of a Quaker-backed anti-slave trade law in 1794 (*SAST*, 80–81). This claim, moreover, lends additional weight to Du Bois's passing allusions to domestic slave insurrections. Is it a stretch to detect an inchoate account of black political activity in Du Bois's observation that "the fact that the slaves, by pillage, flight, and actual fighting, had become so reduced in numbers during the war that an urgent demand for more laborers was felt in the South" (*SAST*, 49)? Or to ask how the reading of Toussaint paves the way for Du Bois's later arguments for African American exemplarity as democratic citizens? By my reading, the answer is a resounding no. Du Bois's appropriation of Toussaint's example for an account of anti-slave trade efforts in the United States provides an opening in his own political imagination through which more robust formulations of transnational or "nonterritorial" democratic politics might enter.[43] Further, I want to suggest, Du Bois's audacious proposition that the common good and the future of American democracy might be read in the doings of slaves who never set foot in the United States opens the possibility of an alternative universalism, one that is "black-led and race centered."[44]

Alongside the specter of a black world on the rise, *Suppression* also sketches the features of what might be called an emergent white nation. The discussion of Haiti provides the occasion for Du Bois to indicate the effects of slavery on white American consciousnesses and political culture. When the slaves of Saint-Domingue asserted that the rights of man applied to them, Du Bois observes, "a wave of horror and fear swept over the South, which even the powerful slave-traders of Georgia did not dare withstand; the Middle States saw their worst dreams realized, and the mercenary trade interests of the East lost their control of the New England conscience" (*SAST*, 71). It was in the wake of this reaction that the Quakers succeeded in pressing a 1794 petition into the first national law against the trade in slaves. Still, even that achievement was deliberately circumscribed. "Congress might willingly restrain the country from feeding West Indian turbulence," Du Bois remarks, "and yet be furious at a petition like that of 1797, calling attention to 'the oppressed state of our brethren of the African race' in this country, and to the interstate slave trade" (*SAST*, 81). The desire to protect the United States from black incursions also produced, according to Du Bois, the Act of 1803, which confiscated the ship of anyone who brought "any negro, mulatto, or other person of color" into a state that prohibited the entry of such persons (*SAST*, 84–85). Explaining the genesis of this law, in the aftermath of the Haitian Revolution, Du Bois notes, "The frightened feeling in the South, when freedmen from the West Indies began to arrive in various ports, may well be imagined" (*SAST*, 84). Du Bois further explains that the protection of the United States went beyond Southern desires to keep out unwanted black men and women. The growing popularity of the idea of colonization—an idea that commanded Abraham Lincoln's support as late as December 1862[45]—gave rise to the inclusion in an 1819 supplement to the 1807 law of a provision for the removal of people of color illegally brought to the United States and their relocation in Africa (*SAST*, 121). *Suppression*'s account of the reverberations of the Haitian Revolution in Southern consciousnesses not only internationalizes the story of America's "original sin," but it also gives readers a foretaste of the portrait, sketched masterfully in *Souls*, of the anguish engendered in white Americans by the possibility of black independence on U.S. soil.

If Du Bois published *Suppression* at a time when he thought that Americanism, for all its flaws, was worth fixing, the story he tells suggests otherwise. His history is one that makes the slave trade and slavery central, not tangential, to the history of democracy in the United States; that depicts a U.S. flag once prized for the safe passage it promised slave ships; that enables readers to see how the compromises which kept the slavers sailing foreshadowed another compromise in which the sacrifice of the former slaves was deemed an acceptable price for national reconciliation; that makes the audacious suggestion that the unique achievement of the American Revolution should be displaced by the revolt of the slaves of Saint-Domingue; and that warns against the dangers of American attempts to avert our eyes from this history. Such a reading of *Suppression* asks how the story of the slave trade enables a shift of imagination away from the conviction that hope for a democratic future resides in the transcendence of this history and toward the possibility that it might be more fruitfully sought by grappling with the proposition that "a belief in humanity means a belief in colored men."[46]

Black World, White Nation

Suppression thus marks an early instance of Du Bois's effort to remap relationships of white and nonwhite, metropole and periphery, democracy and empire, slavery and freedom. Turning now to *For Love of Country*, it is possible to see how even this preliminary formulation of Du Bois's international orientation puts pressure on recent struggles to articulate the boundaries of political theoretical concern. On the one hand, Du Bois's account of the historical connections forged by the international slave trade offers a critical rejoinder to contemporary efforts to defend cosmopolitan connection without attending to the racialized forms of power that have defined modern experience. And his suggestion that the ideas undergirding the age of revolution are most fully represented in the figure of the black slave offers an alternative to any cosmopolitanism that proceeds from the view that race—like gender, nationality, religion—is a "morally irrelevant characteristic."[47] On the other hand, Du Bois's insistence on narrating the founding and early years of the United States as a story of the failure to end the transatlantic slave trade alerts readers to the history that is suppressed when American civic nationalism is defended as a kind of healthy particularism.

To be sure, both lines of argument require qualification. Du Bois can be, and has been, persuasively read as a race-transcending cosmopolitan. The outward reach of this writing and his tireless efforts on behalf of victims of repressive political regimes, exploitation, and violence bespeak a concern with the fate of *all* people, regardless of ascriptive identity or location. His convictions about the use and abuse of history in the United States, furthermore, resonate with Nussbaum's caution that "to worship one's country as if it were a god is indeed to bring a curse upon it."[48] At the same time, much of Du Bois's writing can also be summoned in defense of an American civic nationalism. Again and again, he returns to "the underlying principles of the great republic" in order to defend the inclusion of nonwhite men and women within their purview (*SBF*, 43–44). Even Du Bois's last autobiography, which lavishes praise on the Soviet Union and China, gestures toward a division between core American democratic values and their historical perversion and intimates that his own generation would do well to hew to what is best in its civic inheritance: "This is a wonderful America, which the founding fathers dreamed until their sons drowned it in the blood of slavery and devoured it in greed. Our children must rebuild it."[49] Still, I argue, to focus exclusively on those features of his thought that confirm contemporary perspectives is to miss what might be learned from his dissent from those perspectives. At the risk of treading too lightly over difficult terrain, I suggest that we re-view debates about cosmopolitanism and civic nationalism from the vantage offered by *Suppression* and through the lenses of black world and white nation.

Martha Nussbaum's thinking, like that of Du Bois, reaches out, offering an eloquent counterpoint to the self-regard that limits the moral imagination of her fellow Americans. Dismayed by a history of inaction in the face of preventable suffering abroad and by a hardening of distinctions between "us" and "them" in the aftermath of September 11, Nussbaum adds a new introduction to the 1996 volume on cosmopolitanism. The challenges of the post-9/11 world, she writes, intensify the urgency of devising ways to inculcate a substantive commitment to the promise that "all men are created equal."[50] Her prescription is a cosmopolitan education, modeled on the Stoics, that will enable children "to cultivate the factual and imaginative prerequisites for recognizing humanity in the stranger and the other."[51] And she outlines four arguments in favor of such an education: it enhances self-knowledge; it promotes cooperation on matters of international concern; it engenders new awareness of our obligations toward faraway others; and it allows us to defend our egalitarian commitments with consistency.[52]

Surely Du Bois would applaud these ends, and yet he also discloses elements of Nussbaum's approach that may serve ends she would not endorse. Consider, first, the metaphor of concentric circles. Nussbaum draws upon this image to illustrate how we might understand our relationships to "the local community of our birth" and "the community of human argument and aspiration" that is, "fundamentally, the source of our moral obligations."[53] "Our task as citizens of the world," she continues, "will be to 'draw the circles somehow toward the center'" and acknowledge our commonality with the inhabitants of the most expansive circle, that of humanity as a whole.[54] Notably, many of the responses to Nussbaum's argument also adopt this language, whether or not they accept her claims on behalf of world citizenship. In doing so, they draw a map of human affiliation and moral responsibility that is both centered and defined by measures of distance. For example, Sissela Bok maintains that the language of concentric circles can engender a more reflexive orientation, as participants in public policy debates learn to see problems from within and without these circles, and schoolchildren can learn to navigate the responsibilities they will grow into as members of particular communities and of a common world.⁵⁵ *Suppression* raises questions about the neatness and illustrative power of such metaphors. Rendered as a problem of geometry, the question of international concern elides crucial questions about the historical constitution of the world that we now inhabit and the power relations that translate a history of permeable borders and complex influences into neat distinctions of "us" and "them."

Where the essays in *For Love of Country* think through the metaphor of concentric circles to make claims about attachment and obligation at varying levels of distance, Du Bois uses metaphors that allow him to portray a world defined by unequal power. Even when he does proffer circular images, he often does so to indicate enclosure or entrapment. After all, the color line is a cosmopolitan concept and a circle that "belts the world," but it describes a world structured hierarchically by race. Furthermore, Du Bois's account of the "white world" and "colored world within," discussed in chapter 4, suggests the predatory possibilities of encirclement.⁵⁶ Although *Suppression* lacks the figurative power of Du Bois's later work, it nonetheless gestures toward that work by describing the slave trade in the colonial period as "a perfect circle" (*SAST*, 28). My point is not to indict contemporary cosmopolitanism as a cover for a new imperialism but, rather, to ask about the moral and political repercussions of political theory that sidesteps questions about the lingering shadows of old imperialism. In this regard, it is striking that only one of the essays collected in *For Love of Country*—Immanuel Wallerstein's "Neither Patriotism Nor Cosmopolitanism"—begins expressly from the fact of global inequalities and constructs its argument on the basis of differences in "social location."⁵⁷ Because so many of the essays in *For Love of Country* are explicitly animated by concern about these inequalities, the elision effected when historical structures and relationships are translated into abstract, geometrical forms, matters.

A curious detachment from this history also compromises Nussbaum's defense of the obligations of the relatively well-off toward the disadvantaged.⁵⁸ Americans, she warns, should be troubled by the fact that our high standard of living is not universalizable. Indeed, to make our level of comfort and consumption available to all could precipitate an ecological catastrophe.⁵⁹ And she reasons that "we are all going to have to do some tough thinking about the luck of birth and the morality of transfers of wealth from richer to poorer nations."⁶⁰ Nussbaum returns to this idea of sacrifice on the part of richer nations, in a recent essay that rethinks her defense of cosmopolitanism and offers a nuanced account of "'purified' patriotism."⁶¹ Du Bois would, I think, endorse Nussbaum's reminder that it is fortune, not desert, that defines the circumstances into which we are born. With her, he would insist that we reckon with the effects of what we mistakenly understand to be purely personal choices about our own consumption, that we see our duties to others without diminishing their humanity, and that we understand that these effects and these duties do not stop at national borders. Yet he also shows how Nussbaum's argument, for all its power, seems to miss a prior question. It presents extravagant lifestyles and international wealth gaps as though they simply *are*. In contrast, *Suppression* offers a kind of counternarrative, a genesis story which sheds light on the present predicament:

> Here was a rich new land, the wealth of which was to be had in return for ordinary manual labor. Had the country been conceived as existing primarily for the benefit of its actual inhabitants, it might have waited for natural increase or immigration to supply the needed hands; but both Europe and the earlier colonists themselves regarded this land as existing chiefly for the benefit of Europe, and as designed to be exploited as rapidly and ruthlessly as possible, of the boundless wealth of its resources. This was the primary excuse for the rise of the African slave-trade to America (*SAST*, 194).

By calling attention to historical processes through which present inequalities came into being, *Suppression* reverses the logic that asks what we, the relatively well-off, should sacrifice for the sake of the poor; in its stead, he demands an accounting of the historical roots and routes that join our prosperity and their sacrifice.[62] Du Bois thereby indicates that it will only be possible to realize Nussbaum's end of "diversity without hierarchy" by questioning the hierarchical relationships through which our diverse modern world was produced.[63]

Furthermore, the inclusion of Haiti and Toussaint as pivotal elements in the constitution of American democracy hints at an alternative to the color blindness of Nussbaum's cosmopolitanism. *Suppression* does not offer a full-blown account of a revolutionary black world; Du Bois does not conceive such a possibility in the late nineteenth century. But his attunement to the revolutionary implications of Toussaint's campaign for a free Haiti gestures toward a perspective that goes beyond asserting that the moral worth should not be tied to accidents of birth. In Charles Briggs's view, "Du Bois complicates natural identities and contests the notion that they automatically generate political positions at the same time that he casts categories created by racism as the experiential basis for cosmopolitan consciousness."[64] Intimating that Toussaint was representative of the age of revolution *because* he was black and a slave, Du Bois prefigures his later arguments that the chief hope for democracy resides in the concerted action of black laborers around the globe. Whether or not one is persuaded by Du Bois's claims for the broadly emancipatory possibilities of "the darker world," his attention to work of the women and men excluded from the dominant historical consciousness suggests the anticosmopolitan implications of treating all identity categories, equally, as morally irrelevant. As Craig Calhoun remarks, "Some forms of belonging may be crucial to the realization of the sorts of multilayered, multilateral polities that might allow cosmopolitanism to flourish more as democracy than as empire."[65]

This reading of Du Bois thus echoes Judith Butler's alternative to Nussbaum's formulation of the relationship between the universal and the particular. "The universal," Butler observes, "begins to become articulated precisely through challenges to its existing formulation, and this challenge emerges from those who are not covered by it, who have no entitlement to occupy the place of the 'who,' but who nevertheless demand that the universal as such ought to be inclusive of them."[66] Even in its early formulation, Du Bois's treatment of Toussaint and other rebellious slaves generally suggests an amendment to Ross Posnock's observation that Du Bois "insisted on a dialectic between (unraced) universal and (raced) particular."[67] There is ample evidence of such a relationship, perhaps none more famous than Du Bois's stark contrast between the peculiar situation of black Americans in the post-Reconstruction period and his vision of a Kingdom of Culture where all mingle freely in *The Souls of Black Folk*. Still, Du Bois's work invites the supplement of a third term: the raced universal. This term stands in tension with, rather than synthesizing, the other two. Or, as Robert Reid-Pharr remarks, "One might raise 'black' identity to the level of the universal by paying strict attention, as Du Bois himself does, to the fact that blackness is never . . . a final answer but always a site of contradiction, always, in a sense, a question."[68] Du Bois's work, in other words, intimates why efforts to move too precipitously into a postracial future may be hazardous to the cosmopolitan political imagination.

If *Suppression* inaugurates a career that challenges race-blind cosmopolitanism, it is equally incisive in its resistance to the appeal of American civic nationalism. As I note in chapter 3, Du Bois attempts to vindicate the memory of John Brown without endorsing his idea of American mission. Beyond this, my reading of *Suppression* indicates why Du Bois's wrestling with the twinned birth of American freedom and American slavery, and their implication in an international web of relations, defies even the most egalitarian efforts to distill the democratic elements from the U.S. political tradition. One such effort is Benjamin Barber's defense of "constitutional faith."

Responding to Nussbaum's contention that Americans should recognize that their primary allegiance is owed to human beings, in general, rather than to their fellow citizens, Barber distinguishes between healthy or "civic" nationalism and its more dangerous, "ethnic" cousins in order to defend what he calls "a remarkably successful and undogmatic constitutional exercise in American exceptionalism."[69] Not only can such attachment be rendered "safe,"[70] he argues, it is sorely needed in "a world disenchanted in which *Gemeinschaft* and neighborhood have for the most part been supplanted by *Gesellschaft* and bureaucracy."[71] But attachment to what, by whom, and at what cost?

The "what" in Barber's view is American democratic ideals as they are embodied in its founding documents, its defining speeches, and its civic rituals. Good forms of "civic nativism" thus differ from pathological, ethnic forms in their capacity to forge affective ties without relying on violent exclusion. It is just such a capacity that he finds in Americans' "'tribal' sources":

> The American trick was to use the fierce attachments of patriotic sentiment to bond a people to high ideals. Our 'tribal' sources from which we derive our sense of national identity are the Declaration of Independence, the Constitution and the Bill of Rights, the inaugural addresses of our presidents, Lincoln's Gettysburg Address, and Martin Luther King's 'free at last' sermon at the 1963 March on Washington—not so much the documents themselves as the felt sentiments tying us to them, sentiments that are rehearsed at Independence Day parades and in Memorial Day speeches.[72]

Curiously, in an essay that makes no mention of slavery (except in a strange parenthetical gesture quoted below), Barber's choice of examples tacitly bespeaks an interest in reminding readers of slavery's overcoming. Including the Gettysburg Address and "I Have a Dream" speech, it would seem, inoculates him from having to contend with the deliberately narrowed scope of the Declaration of Independence or the omissions that define the Constitution. Read against the backdrop of American debates over the slave trade, however, the distinction between sentimental attachments to some of these democratic sources and the sorts of exclusionary attachments Barber wants to reject appears less obvious. His interpretation might be said to echo Madison's assessment of the constitutional ban on congressional action against the slave trade as a sign of the greatness of American democracy. Although Madison opposed prolonging the trade, he nonetheless describes the clause as "a great point gained in favor of humanity" and concludes that Africans have much for which to be thankful: "Happy would it be for the unfortunate Africans if an equal prospect lay before them of being redeemed from the oppressions of their European brethren!"[73] The irony is not lost on Du Bois, who quotes the entire passage in *Suppression*, including Madison's salvo against anyone who would try to "pervert this clause into an objection against the Constitution" (*SAST*, 65). Like Barber, Du Bois celebrates the achievements of the "Revolutionists of 1776." But he resists the effort to segregate the ideals from the compromises or to forget that they chose not to confront the question of slavery at a moment when it was vulnerable and "a bargain largely of dollars and cents was allowed to open the highway that led straight to the Civil War" (*SAST*, 198).

While Barber's "'tribal' sources" are meant to be purely "civic" in nature, he explains that they grow from the more local attachments of multicultural America. He draws on Woody Guthrie, Walt Whitman, and a carefully redacted selection from Langston Hughes's "Let America Be America Again" to proclaim that "our wise American poets prudently ask us to kindle an affection for the general by reveling in the particular."[74] The particular, in his view, is represented by neighborhood and by ethnic affiliations: "To become an American, women and men must first identify as African Americans or Polish Americans or Jewish Americans or German Americans."[75] Although it may be far from Barber's intention, the list of identities he includes enacts the kind of sleight of hand against which Du Bois struggles throughout his career—one through which African Americans are held to blame for any failure to transform equivalence on paper into substantive equivalence, one through which they stand tacitly accused for their persistent status as a "problem."[76] The description of the "general" offered here is troubling, too. For it is circumscribed by the boundaries of the United States in a way that both elides the significance of the international traffic in human beings to the constitution of the U.S. and disallows the importance of transnational affiliations by women and men who would embrace Toussaint as an American hero or find political solidarity with the wretched of the earth.

Finally, Du Bois's history gives reason for caution about Barber's interpretation of the uprooting that defines American identity. Just as early Americans were able to leave behind the deep animosities of religion and *ethnos* and transfer their allegiance to universal principles, Barber suggests, the heritors of those principles perpetuate the "novel process of uprooting and rerooting."[77] Quoting his earlier book, *An Aristocracy of Everyone*, Barber contends:

> From the outset, then, to be an American was also to be enmeshed in a unique story of freedom, to be free (or to be enslaved) in a novel

sense, more existential than political or legal. Even in colonial times, the new world meant starting over again, meant freedom from rigid and heavily freighted traditional cultures. Deracination was the universal experience.[78]

The parenthetical is puzzling: does he mean that being enslaved in a novel sense offered Africans "freedom from rigid and heavily freighted traditional cultures"?[79] More, it both makes plain and ignores the fact that the experience of deracination he describes was not singular but multiple and that the new start entailed violent uprooting of both African slaves and American Indians.

To present the experience in universal terms, furthermore, is to neglect two considerations. The first is the differentiated ways in which American identities have been understood in relation to citizenship. As Devon Carbado explains, the conflation of American identity and citizenship occludes the processes of *racial* naturalization—de jure and de facto—through which people are interpellated as American.[80] The second omission is how the "story of American freedom" required not only the uprooting of individuals and communities but also the forceful pruning away of counternarratives. Du Bois's careful documentation of the ways that the centuries-old slave trade remained integral to life in the United States through much of the nineteenth century and his attunement to white Americans' persistent efforts to consign that history to oblivion intimate the dangers that inhere in celebrations of deracinated Americanism.

In spite of its emphasis on *our* ancestors and *our* responsibilities, *Suppression* offers a history that points decisively away from the idea that salvation is to be sought in the realization of "American" democracy. Despite Du Bois's assessment that the Founding Fathers might have brought about the end of slavery if they had just had a little more backbone, his narrative defies such neat solutions. Viewing the early years of the republic through the lens of the slave-trade locates the American experiment within the history of the racial contract, a history in which it can neither justify its continued interest in the slave-trade as an inherited imposition (as the deleted paragraph of the Declaration would have it), nor sustain the claim that the United States was forged through a unique break with the past. It adds an important rejoinder that is missing from the pieces collected in *For Love of Country*. Even as Du Bois would embrace Nussbaum's warning about the dangers of a cramped imagination, one structured by the contrast between "us" and "them," he limns a world in which the lines of demarcation are, repeatedly, crossed, blurred, and tangled through the international trade in human beings and its legacies. In place of an abstract conception of world citizenship or a revitalized Americanism, then, my reading of *Suppression* presses us to reconsider the limitations of these alternatives from Du Bois's "ground of disadvantage."

Facing the Worst and Reconstructing Democracy

The final section of *Suppression* reflects back on the argument of the preceding pages and offers what Du Bois calls "The Lesson for Americans." Although Du Bois does not directly address the unraveling of Reconstruction, his concluding paragraphs shift the authorial vantage from the detached stance of the social scientist to the perspective of an American "us" and to Du Bois's own disquiet about the present and future dangers of a national willingness to compromise with evil. Implicating himself along with his fellow citizens as heritors of "the cupidity and carelessness of our ancestors" (*SAST*, 198), Du Bois not only inserts himself into a lineage in which he is not broadly welcome. He also uses that location to discredit the impulse to enclose slavery in the remote past and question the security of boundaries between the American democratic experiment and the international system of subjection in which Americans participated for over 200 years. "In some respects, we as a nation seem to lack this" willingness to engage the most trying political problems, he muses. "We have the somewhat inchoate idea that we are not destined to be harassed with great social questions, and that even if we are, and fail to answer them, the fault is with the question and not with us. Consequently we often congratulate ourselves more on getting rid of a problem than on solving it" (*SAST*, 198–99).[81]

Later, Du Bois wishes that this section had been "less pat and simple"; but it would be a mistake to reduce *Suppression*'s conclusion to mere moralism.[82] Du Bois does not simply examine the historical record and find the founders culpable. When he writes that "no persons would have seen the Civil War with more surprise and horror than the Revolutionists of 1776; yet from the small and apparently dying institution of their day arose the walled and castled Slave Power" (*SAST*, 199), he retells the founding as a tragedy. In Du Bois's narration, the tragedy is not simply that the founders bequeathed a system of racial slavery that only unspeakable violence could overcome but that they bequeathed a political culture of evasion and deferral that would continue to compromise Americans' attachment to liberty and equality.

In other words, we might say that he warns his contemporaries of the continuing consequences of a failure to "face the worst." And, in this sense, Du Bois's "lesson" for Americans also offers a lesson for democratic thought.

It sounds a warning against failures of imagination that limit theorists today from reaching outward, to consider a United States that is entangled with a world it does not always acknowledge, and backward, to the historical processes through which contemporary challenges came to be. These are failings that George Kateb might indict as the effects of an "inactive imagination."[83] Among the greatest of them, Du Bois shows, are the particular blindnesses that prevent us from seeing, fully, the humanity in the African slave or in her descendants and that allow us to construct, anew, a sense of global obligation that does not attend to what is old in the economic misery and political voicelessness of those we would assist. We are not only confronted by the challenges of a "post-Westphalian world," in other words, but also by legacies of racial power that have defied sharp divisions between the domestic and the international from the outset of modernity.[84] To that end, Du Bois urges readers to consider a point that Kateb would not endorse: facing the worst involves thinking within and through identity categories, as well as in opposition to their power to subjugate and degrade.

Thus, even when Du Bois writes as an American and for his fellow Americans, his account of the founding through the history of the slave trade lays groundwork for what Paul Taylor provocatively calls a "post-American perspective."[85] Such a perspective, Taylor writes, entails "a determined skepticism about appeals to the idea of America."[86] If we return to the Virginia resolution discussed in chapter 1, we can now see more clearly why it matters that the expression of regret was revised to begin and end in Jamestown. Although both versions of the resolution address the 400th anniversary of the Jamestown settlement, the initial version situated its commemoration in a global history that highlights the economic underpinnings of the slave trade and its continuation, both domestically and internationally, after 1808. The final version, by contrast, encloses references to the Middle Passage within a larger narrative about Jamestown's legacies, which "include ideas, institutions, a history distinctive to the American experiment in democracy, and a constellation of liberties enshrined in the Virginia Declaration of Rights and the Virginia and United States Constitutions . . ." It enacts a kind of historical and moral isolationism. *Suppression* points toward an alternative. It orients us toward a reading of the United States as, fundamentally, rather than incidentally, constituted through its engagement in the international traffic in slaves, and an understanding of that traffic in light of the larger story of racialized forms of bondage and colonial power that accompanied the spread of new conceptions of equality and freedom. This is not an act of disloyalty and should not be conflated with *anti*-Americanism.[87] (Indeed, even after having been arrested, tried, and acquitted as a foreign agent and nearing the point at which he would leave his U.S. citizenship behind, Du Bois remarkably maintain, "I still believe that some day this nation will become a democracy without a color-line."[88]) Rather, it challenges the omissions that enable appeals to "constitutional faith." At the same time, the term retains the particularity of Du Bois's position as an American, even as his political imagination and his scope of concern encompasses "the darker world," and thus provides a useful foil to the racial transcendence of "cosmopolitanism."

By revisiting the horrors and the triumphs of a suppressed past, remapping the relationship of democracy within the United States and beyond its borders, Du Bois indicates how political theorists today might stretch the boundaries of our thinking. The heavy inheritance of the present-past, he reminds us, imposes responsibilities on each successive generation to eradicate entrenched forms of racial injustice. But it also bequeaths a deep reservoir in the historical examples of slaves and citizens who devised creative ways to oppose racial hierarchy. Across a long and varied career, Du Bois pressed his fellows, and presses us, toward a generative possibility: that the legacies of the many thousands gone may still give rise to establishment of more democratic, and as yet unimagined, norms, practices, and relations of power.

ACKNOWLEDGMENTS

Toward the end of *Beloved*, Toni Morrison offers an arresting image of Denver, a lonely and terrified teenager, standing at the edge of her porch in tattered and gaudy clothes and deciding whether or not to step out into a hostile, unfamiliar world and seek help for her family. Denver's decision to take that step, commentators note, marks one of the pivotal moments of the novel. But I have always been equally moved by what happens next. When Denver ventures into the community from which she has been severed for most of her life, she is repaid, again and again, with unexpected gifts of words and food. Morrison's attentive rendering of the power of baskets of eggs and plates of rabbit, of the way a greeting can be life-changing, reminds us of the unearned gifts that sustain us all. More specifically, for those of us who spend our time teaching and writing, Morrison's account of the offerings that save Denver and her family captures something fundamental about our dependence on the comments or questions, offers of food or childcare that appear unbidden, often when they are needed most. It also suggests the limitation of formal acknowledgments; like the anonymous gifts to Denver, many of the best insights of any scholarly work emerge from the contributions of reviewers and commentators who were always unknown or are now lost to memory.

I owe a special debt to the people who read this manuscript in its entirety, in some cases more than once. For such careful and generous readings, I thank Roxanne Euben, George Shulman, Stephen White, Victor Wolfenstein, and an anonymous reviewer for Oxford University Press. Although I regret that I have almost certainly neglected individuals who have helped in important ways, it is a pleasure to be able to thank: Leora Batnitzky,

Colin Bird, P. J. Brendese, Anna Brickhouse, Michael Dawson, Joshua Dienstag, Lisa Disch, Chad Dodson, Raymond Duvall, Robert Fatton, Bennett Foddy, Jason Frank, William Freehling, Jennifer Geddes, Robert Gooding-Williams, Bonnie Gordon, Erica Gould, Ayten Gündoğdu, Grace Hale, Michael Hanchard, Richard Handler, Frederick Harris, Barnor Hesse, Matthew Holden, Catherine Holland, Alan Houston, James Johnson, George Kateb, David Kim, George Klosko, Sharon Krause, Christopher Lebron, Jill Locke, John Lowe, Nancy Luxon, Stephen Marshall, Wende Marshall, Sidney Milkis, Charles Mills, Laurie Naranch, Jeff Olick, Joel Olson, Carmen Pavel, Eric Porter, Mark Reinhardt, Neil Roberts, Melvin Rogers, Jennifer Rubenstein, Lynn Sanders, Kim Scheppele, Melissa Schwartzberg, Tommie Shelby, Anna Marie Smith, Rogers Smith, Valerie Smith, Jeff Spinner-Halev, Simon Stow, Tracy Strong, Jack Turner, Jerry Watts, Vesla Weaver, Cornel West, Elizabeth Wingrove, and Elizabeth Wittner. The staff and faculty of the Politics Department at the University of Virginia have provided a wonderful home to work in. Many of my ideas were sparked or sharpened through conversations with Virginia undergraduates and graduate students, especially the graduate students in my seminars on "Politics and Memory." I am also thankful for Kiran Banerjee's research assistance and for the suggestions of Andrew Douglas, Molly Farneth, Adom Getachew, Nadim Khoury, Justin Rose, and Greta Snyder. The enthusiasm and patience of series editors Cathy Cohen and Frederick Harris and Oxford University Press editor David McBride were essential.

I am grateful for a fellowship from the National Endowment for the Humanities and for Sesquicentennial and summer research funding from the University of Virginia. In its very earliest stages, this project was supported by a postdoctoral fellowship at the Center for the Study of Values in Public Life at Harvard Divinity School and research grants from Babson College. The faculty, fellows, and staff at the Virginia Foundation for the Humanities and the University Center for Human Values at Princeton provided crucial measures of quiet and stimulation. Earlier versions of chapters 2 and 5 appeared in the *American Political Science Review* 97 (February 2003) and *Hypatia: A Journal of Feminist Philosophy* 20 (Summer 2005), respectively, and I thank the publishers for permission to use the material here.

Over the long course of its development, this project has been nourished by the encouragement of friends and family, both in Charlottesville and across the country. Chad and Reid, most of all, challenge me in the best ways and bring joy to the everyday. Finally, a study of examples and exemplarity would be incomplete without acknowledging the example set by my parents, Dale and Bill Balfour, to whom this book is dedicated.

NOTES

Preface

1. Martin Luther King, Jr., "Honoring Dr. Du Bois," in *Black Titan: W. E. B. Du Bois*, ed. John Henrik Clarke, Esther Jackson, Ernest Kaiser, J. H. O'Dell (Boston: Beacon Press, 1970), 181.
2. King, "Honoring Dr. Du Bois," 176.
3. King, "Honoring Dr. Du Bois," 176.
4. King, "Honoring Dr. Du Bois," 183.
5. King, "Honoring Dr. Du Bois," 183.
6. King, "Honoring Dr. Du Bois," 180.
7. Bruce Western, *Punishment and Inequality in America* (New York: Russell Sage Foundation, 2006), 29.
8. King, "Honoring Dr. Du Bois," 183.

Chapter One

1. Wole Soyinka, *The Burden of Memory, The Muse of Forgiveness* (New York: Oxford University Press, 1999), 81–82.
2. The text of the original and amended resolutions can be found online at: http://leg1.state.va.us/cgi-bin/legp504.exe?071+sum+SJ332. The House of Delegates version (HJR728) is identical.
3. Donald McEachin, quoted in Suzanne Goldenberg, "After 400 Years, Virginia Issues Official Apology for Slavery," *Guardian* (London), February 26, 2007.
4. Maryland, North Carolina, Alabama, Florida, and New Jersey have since passed similar measures, and apologies for slavery have been debated in other state legislatures and city councils. In July 2008, the U.S. House of Representatives passed a resolution (H. Res. 194) apologizing for slavery and Jim

Crow. The Senate followed suit on June 18, 2009. For a comparative analysis of the work performed by state apologies, see Melissa Nobles, *The Politics of Official Apologies* (Cambridge: Cambridge University Press, 2008).

5. Interestingly, a brief survey of the newspaper coverage of the revised resolution indicates that the change of language did little to prevent reporters and commentators from calling it an "apology." See, for example, Stanley Fish, "But I Didn't Do It!" *New York Times*, sec. A, March 21, 2007. Despite the changed wording, the resolution is also included in a list of twentieth- and twenty-first-century apologies in Nobles, *The Politics of Official Apologies*, 161–62.

6. For an eloquent critique of the "tort model" of responsibility, see Roy L. Brooks, *Atonement and Forgiveness: A New Model for Black Reparations* (Berkeley: University of California Press, 2004).

7. The resolution's attention to the psychological legacies of slavery, as well as its material and political harms, responds both to racial grievance and racial grief. See Anne Anlin Cheng, *The Melancholy of Race: Psychoanalysis, Assimilation, and Hidden Grief* (New York: Oxford University Press, 2001).

8. Although there is much to be said on behalf of any acknowledgment that links antiblack racism to the brutal treatment of American Indians, the final version of the resolution does so in a way that intimates that one of the gravest harms suffered by native Virginians was that they were unjustly made to bear the badges of slavery. In the discussion of Virginia's notorious Racial Integrity Act of 1924, the resolution makes reference to "the one-drop rule," not to challenge its insidious effects generally but to regret that native Virginians with African ancestry were denied their rightful recognition as tribal members. W. E. B. Du Bois mocks this logic in a 1930 editorial in *The Crisis*. Noting that some native Virginians responded to white hysteria over "mixed schools" by attempting to differentiate themselves from black Virginians, he writes: "It is a little hard to distinguish between Negro and Indian blood, and these folks want the benefit of the doubt." W. E. B. Du Bois, "Virginia," in *Writings in Periodicals Edited by W. E. B. Du Bois: Selections from the Crisis, Vol. 2 (1926–1934)*, ed. Herbert Aptheker (Millwood, NY: KrausThomson, 1983), 580.

9. For recent surveys of such efforts, see Martha Minow, *Between Vengeance and Forgiveness: Facing History after Genocide and Mass Violence* (Boston: Beacon Press, 1998); *When Sorry Isn't Enough: The Controversy over Apologies and Reparations for Human Injustice* (New York: NYU Press, 1999), ed. Roy L. Brooks; Elazar Barkan, *The Guilt of Nations: Restitution and Negotiating Historical Injustices* (New York: Norton, 2000); *The Handbook of Reparations* (Oxford: Oxford University Press, 2006), ed. Pablo de Greiff.

10. For a critique of this logic, see Rogers M. Smith, "Beyond Tocqueville, Myrdal, and Hartz: The Multiple Traditions in America," *American Political Science Review* 87 (September 1993): 549–66.

11. "In its dominant articulation, the history of slavery exists in a state of civil servitude to the idea of American freedom," observes Walter Johnson, neatly capturing the double gesture of the final Virginia resolution. Walter Johnson, "Slavery, Reparations, and the Mythic March of Freedom," *Raritan* 27 (Fall 2007): 43.
12. Michel-Rolph Trouillot, "Abortive Rituals: Historical Apologies in the Global Era," *Interventions: International Journal of Postcolonial Studies* 2 (2000): 181.
13. William E. Connolly, "Tocqueville, Territory and Violence," *Theory, Culture & Society* 11 (1994): 27.
14. See Judith N. Shklar, *The Faces of Injustice* (New Haven: Yale University Press, 1990).
15. Guyora Binder, "The Slavery of Emancipation," *Cardozo Law Review* 17 (1996): 2071.
16. See Alexis de Tocqueville, *Democracy in America* I, ed. J. P. Mayer, trans. George Lawrence (New York: HarperPerennial, 1988), 316.
17. George Kateb, "The Adequacy of the Canon," in *Patriotism and Other Mistakes* (New Haven: Yale University Press, 2006), 385.
18. Kateb, "The Adequacy of the Canon," 385.
19. As Michel-Rolph Trouillot notes in his study of Euro-American responses to the Haitian Revolution, the failure to recognize the slaves' claim to freedom was not so much ideological as epistemological. It was unthinkable at the time and has been rendered unthinkable still through what Trouillot calls "formulas of erasure" and "formulas of banalization" that keep some elements of the past at bay. Michel-Rolph Trouillot, *Silencing the Past: Power and the Production of History* (Boston: Beacon Press, 1995). One indicator of the forces of these formulas is the regularity with which political theorists limit the "age of revolution" to Philadelphia and Paris. For a critique of the omission of Haiti, and Toussaint, from Hannah Arendt's reading of the age of revolution, see David Scott, *Conscripts of Modernity: The Tragedy of Colonial Enlightenment* (Durham: Duke University Press, 2004), 211–21.
20. John S. Dryzek, Bonnie Honig, and Anne Phillips, "Introduction," *The Oxford Handbook of Political Theory*, ed. John S. Dryzek, Bonnie Honig, and Anne Phillips (Oxford: Oxford University Press, 2006), 5.
21. Along similar lines, Charles Mills asks: "Why is race—in some respects so obvious—so hard for white philosophers to 'see' theoretically?" Charles W. Mills, *Blackness Visible: Essays on Philosophy and Race* (Ithaca: Cornell University Press, 1998), xiii.
22. As a scholar, Du Bois made a career of tearing down barriers: he was the first African American to earn a Ph.D. from Harvard, in 1895; he inaugurated the field of urban sociology with *The Philadelphia Negro* (1999) and oversaw an ambitious series of studies of African American life at Atlanta University; he radically revised the prevailing account of Reconstruction history, most

notably in *Black Reconstruction;* and he offered successive accounts of African contributions to world history. As a writer, he similarly refused to be limited by established forms. He wrote widely in a variety of genres—including, but not limited to, poetry, novels, journalism, scholarly monographs, autobiographies—even as he troubled generic boundaries in the hope of engendering new consciousness in his readers. As an activist, Du Bois's staggering list of achievements includes founding roles or leadership positions in the Niagara Movement, the National Association for the Advancement of Colored People, and the Council on African Affairs; the organization of four Pan-African conferences; and tireless travel on behalf of full equality for all Americans, decolonization, and peace. This summary, too partial and inadequate, offers a glimpse of the commitments and mobility that informed Du Bois's vision as a political thinker.

23. For a compelling account of how Du Bois also strives to make these legacies *audible*, see Alexander G. Weheliye, "The Grooves of Temporality," *Public Culture* 17 (Spring 2005): 319–38.

24. Sheldon S. Wolin, *Politics and Vision: Continuity and Innovation in Western Political Thought*, expanded ed. (Princeton: Princeton University Press, 2004), 17.

25. Wolin, *Politics and Vision*, 18.

26. Thomas C. Holt, "The Political Uses of Alienation: W. E. B. Du Bois on Politics, Race, and Culture, 1903–1940," *American Quarterly* 42 (June 1990): 306. Donna Haraway concurs: "The standpoints of the subjugated are not 'innocent' positions. On the contrary, they are preferred because in principle they are least likely to allow denial of the critical and interpretive core of all knowledge. They are knowledgeable of modes of denial through repression, forgetting, and disappearing acts—ways of being nowhere while claiming to see comprehensively." Donna Haraway, "Situated Knowledges: The Science Question in Feminism and the Privilege of Partial Perspective," *Feminist Studies* 14 (Autumn 1988): 584.

27. In this sense, Du Bois's work exemplifies what Haraway describes as "situated knowledge." Haraway, "Situated Knowledges," 575–99.

28. For an exploration of Ralph Ellison's use of the language of shadows to convey the presence of the past, see W. James Booth, "The Color of Memory: Reading Race with Ralph Ellison," *Political Theory* 36 (October 2008): 683–707.

29. Robert Gooding-Williams, "Du Bois's Counter-Sublime," *The Massachusetts Review* 35 (Summer 1994): 219.

30. Toni Morrison, *Beloved* (New York: Plume, 1987), 275.

31. On Du Bois's treatment of Crummell as a tragic figure, see Gooding-Williams, "Du Bois's Counter-Sublime," 202–24.

32. As Jonathan Flatley comments, "rather than philosophical concepts, Du Bois creates something closer to constellations: the image of the veil is

surrounded by a rhetoric of light and shadows." Jonathan Flatley, *Affective Mapping: Melancholia and the Politics of Modernism* (Cambridge: Harvard University Press, 2008), 121.

33. See Michael C. Dawson, "After the Deluge: Publics and Publicity in Katrina's Wake," *Du Bois Review* 3 (March 2006): 240.

34. Thomas McCarthy, "*Vergangenheitsbewältigung* in the USA: On the Politics of the Memory of Slavery," *Political Theory* 30 (October 2002): 641.

35. See Manning Marable, *Living Black History: How Reimagining the African-American Past Can Remake America's Racial Future* (New York: Basic Books, 2006); Robin D. G. Kelley, *Freedom Dreams: The Black Radical Imagination* (Boston: Beacon Press, 2002).

36. Saidiya Hartman, "The Time of Slavery," *South Atlantic Quarterly* 101 (Fall 2002): 763.

37. Hartman, "The Time of Slavery": 773.

38. As Benedict Anderson notes, Americans have been trained "to remember/forget," to remember the Civil War as fratricide and forget that North and South faced each other as enemy sovereign states. Benedict Anderson, *Imagined Communities: Reflections on the Origin and Spread of Nationalism*, rev. ed. (London: Verso, 1991), 201. See also David W. Blight, "Quarrel Forgotten or a Revolution Remembered? Reunion and Race in the Memory of the Civil War, 1875–1913," in *Union and Emancipation: Essays on Politics and Race in the Civil War Era*, ed. David W. Blight and Brooks D. Simpson (Kent, OH: Kent State University Press, 1997), 151–79. Interestingly, a reference to slavery as a prime cause of the Civil War was omitted from the original text of the Virginia resolution. In the U.S. House of Representatives, H. Res. 194 was similarly amended, eliminating the observation that the Civil War "was fought over the slavery issue." Available at http://www.govtrack.us/congress/billtext.xpd?bill=hr110-194.

39. Tocqueville, *Democracy in America* I, 341.

40. Sheldon S. Wolin, "Injustice and Collective Memory," in *The Presence of the Past: Essays on the State and the Constitution* (Baltimore: Johns Hopkins University Press, 1989), 32–46.

41. Sheldon S. Wolin, *Tocqueville Between Two Worlds: The Making of a Political and Theoretical Life* (Princeton: Princeton University Press, 2001), 147. Wolin's discussion of "tableau" and "spectacle" as metaphors in Tocqueville's repertoire speak to the theorist's aspiration to reorient readers or engender a new vision. Where "a spectacle presents a panorama intended to provoke awe or amazement," "a tableau . . . produces comprehension by revealing unsuspected connections that, at first glance, may have seemed implausible."

42. W. E. B. Du Bois, "The Development of a People" (1904) in *SBF*, 248 (emphasis added). For a reworking of this language, see also W. E. B. Du Bois, *The Negro* (1915; rep., Mineola, NY: Dover, 2001), 95.

43. W. E. B. Du Bois, *The Gift of Black Folk: The Negroes in the Making of America* (1924; repr., New York: Washington Square Press, 1970), 191.
44. See Jane Bennett and Michael J. Shapiro, "Introduction," in *The Politics of Moralizing*, ed. Jane Bennett and Michael J. Shapiro (New York: Routledge, 2002), 1–9.
45. See Martha Biondi, "The Rise of the Reparations Movement," *Radical History Review* 87 (Fall 2003): 17; Michael C. Dawson and Rovana Popoff, "Reparations: Justice and Greed in Black and White," *Du Bois Review* 1 (2004): 55. Robin Kelley explores how reparations activism can provide an avenue for coming to terms with the gendered character of racial exploitation. Kelley, *Freedom Dreams*, 131–32.
46. Although my reading of Du Bois is informed by Hazel Carby's exploration of "highly gendered structures of intellectual and political thought and feeling" in *Souls*, I depart from her interpretation of this passage as an implicit comparison of the "betrayal" of the black mother to the Compromise of 1877. Hazel V. Carby, *Race Men* (Cambridge: Harvard University Press, 2000), 12, 38.
47. David Blight and Robert Gooding-Williams note that the language of clasped hands specifically references and undermines the prevalent image of former enemies "clasping hands across the bloody chasm" in the aftermath of the Civil War (*SBF*, 200, n. 27). See also Blight and Gooding-Williams, "Introduction," 13–16.
48. Frank M. Kirkland, "Modernisms in Black," in *A Companion to African-American Philosophy*, ed. Tommy L. Lott and John P. Pittman (Malden, MA: Blackwell, 2003), 81.
49. As Cheryl Wall summarizes, Du Bois's writing evinces "a tragic sensibility, one that is grounded in history but not bound by it." Cheryl A. Wall, "Resounding *Souls*: Du Bois and the African American Literary Tradition," *Public Culture* 17 (Spring 2005): 234.
50. Mark Reinhardt, *The Art of Being Free: Taking Liberties with Tocqueville, Marx, and Arendt* (Ithaca: Cornell University Press, 1997), x.
51. See the excellent collection of articles in *Du Bois Review* 3 (March 2006); and *After the Storm: Black Intellectuals Explore the Meaning of Hurricane Katrina*, ed. David Dante Troutt (New York: New Press, 2006).
52. Justice Bradley, *Civil Rights Cases* (1883), quoted in Derrick Bell, Race, *Racism and American Law*, 3rd ed. (New York: Aspen Law & Business, 1992), 113.
53. For an extended treatment of this paradox of formal equality, see Patricia J. Williams, *The Alchemy of Race and Rights: Diary of a Law Professor* (Cambridge: Harvard University Press, 1991).
54. Much of the philosophical debate about Du Bois's conception of "race" has emerged in response to Anthony Appiah's 1985 essay "The Uncompleted Argument: Du Bois and the Illusion of Race." Although I do not take up

this debate directly, I hope to show, in contrast to Appiah, why it remains crucial, *politically*, to work with and through a concept of race. Anthony Appiah, "The Uncompleted Argument: Du Bois and the Illusion of Race," *Critical Inquiry* 12 (Autumn 1985): 21–37.

55. Joan Scott nicely captures this concern when she writes: "Being able to grab a piece of the past as our own enables us to hold a meaningful space in the present; there is no future to imagine or behold." Joan Wallach Scott, "After History?" *Common Knowledge* 5 (Winter 1996): 19.

56. As Michael Hanchard notes, the definition of time has functioned as an instrument of racial domination—from the denial that African subjects had a past, to the "time appropriation" of racial slavery, to the temporizing on the part of the powerful that issued in repeated commands to African Americans to "wait" for full citizenship. The experience of the African diaspora has transpired in what Hanchard calls "racial time." Michael Hanchard, "Afro-Modernity: Temporality, Politics, and the African Diaspora," *Public Culture* 11 (Winter 1999): 245–68. For an acute account of temporal politics that focuses on Native American struggles, see Kevin Bruyneel, *The Third Space of Sovereignty: The Postcolonial Politics of U.S.-Indigenous Relations* (Minneapolis: University of Minnesota Press, 2007).

57. Or, as Romand Coles, echoing Bob Dylan, eloquently puts it: "It's not dark yet, but it's gettin' there." Romand Coles, *Beyond Gated Politics: Reflections for the Possibility of Democracy* (Minneapolis: University of Minnesota Press, 2005), xxviii.

58. Cornel West, *Democracy Matters: Winning the Fight Against Imperialism* (New York: Penguin, 2004), 7.

59. Wendy Brown, "Untimeliness and Punctuality: Critical Theory in Dark Times," in *Edgework: Critical Essays on Knowledge and Politics* (Princeton: Princeton University Press, 2005), 10 (emphasis in the original).

60. Shamoon Zamir, *Dark Voices: W. E. B. Du Bois and American Thought, 1888–1903* (Chicago: University of Chicago Press, 1995).

61. Anne Norton, "Seeing in the Dark," *Theory & Event* 10 (2007).

62. Robert Gooding-Williams, "Du Bois, Politics, Aesthetics: An Introduction," *Public Culture* 17 (Spring 2005): 206. Indeed, as Flatley astutely notes, "how modest we think this assessment depends on the meaning and value we give to the word 'fugitive.'" Flatley, *Affective Mapping*, 226, n.7. For detailed discussion of Du Bois's construction of *Souls*, see Eric J. Sundquist, *To Wake the Nations: Race in the Making of American Literature* (Cambridge: Belknap/Harvard University Press, 1998), 457–539; Robert Stepto, *From Behind the Veil: A Study of Afro-American Narrative*, 2nd ed. (Urbana: University of Illinois Press, 1991); Eugene Victor Wolfenstein, *A Gift of the Spirit: Reading The Souls of Black Folk* (Ithaca: Cornell University Press, 2007).

63. In his introduction to the Oxford edition of Du Bois's single-authored books, Henry Louis Gates, Jr., remarks that "Du Bois was, in the end, an essayist, an essayist of the first order." Henry Louis Gates, Jr., "The Black Letters on the Sign: W. E. B. Du Bois and the Canon," in W. E. B. Du Bois, *The Suppression of the African Slave-Trade to the United States of America, 1638–1870* (1896; repr., New York: Oxford University Press, 2007), xii.
64. Sheldon S. Wolin, "Fugitive Democracy," in *Democracy and Difference: Contesting the Boundaries of the Political*, ed. Seyla Benhabib (Princeton: Princeton University Press, 1996), 39.
65. Samira Kawash, *Dislocating the Color Line: Identity, Hybridity, and Singularity in African-American Narrative* (Stanford: Stanford University Press, 1997), 83.
66. Stephen Best and Saidiya Hartman, "Fugitive Justice," *Representations* 92 (Fall 2005): 9. See also Jacques Rancière's comment that "whoever is nameless *cannot* speak"; their utterances are registered instead as "fugitive sound." Jacques Rancière, *Dis-Agreement: Politics and Philosophy*, trans. Julie Rose (Minneapolis: University of Minnesota Press, 1999), 23–24 (emphasis in the original). Donna Haraway makes a similar point through optic, rather than aural, metaphor: "Struggles over what will count as rational accounts of the world are struggles over *how* to see. Haraway, "Situated Knowledges," 587 (emphasis in the original).
67. Toni Morrison, "Unspeakable Things Unspoken: The Afro-American Presence in American Literature," *Michigan Quarterly Review* 28 (Winter 1989): 5.
68. In other words, it is crucial that the wide range of African American political thought not be confined to "the shadow of Du Bois," as Gooding-Williams rightly warns. Robert Gooding-Williams, *In the Shadow of Du Bois: Afro-Modern Political Thought in America* (Cambridge: Harvard University Press, 2009).
69. My approach to Du Bois borrows from the model adopted by Iris Young, when she draws upon Jean-Paul Sartre to understand the category of gender. Young allows that she writes in the spirit of a "Bandita" or outlaw (here, too, one might employ the language of the "fugitive"), appropriating those aspects of Sartre's work that can spur the imagination without embracing everything he thought. Iris Marion Young, "Gender as Seriality: Thinking about Women as a Social Collective," in *Intersecting Voices: Dilemmas of Gender, Political Philosophy, and Policy* (Princeton: Princeton University Press, 1997), 22–23.

Chapter Two

1. This essay, entitled "Of the Dawn of Freedom," is a moderately revised version of an essay entitled "The Freedmen's Bureau," which appeared in the *Atlantic Monthly* in 1901.
2. Rayford W. Logan, *The Negro in American Life and Thought: The Nadir, 1877–1901* (New York: The Dial Press, 1954).

3. See Meizhu Lui, Bárbara Robles, Betsy Leondar-Wright, Rose Brewer, and Rebecca Adamson, with United for a Fair Economy, *The Color of Wealth: The Story Behind the U.S. Racial Divide* (New York: The New Press, 2006).
4. Two figures at the heart of Du Bois's critique of the historical misrepresentation of black citizenship, John W. Burgess and William A. Dunning of Columbia University, were also founders of the profession of political science in the United States. See Judith N. Shklar, *Redeeming American Political Thought*, ed. Stanley Hoffman and Dennis F. Thompson (Chicago: University of Chicago Press, 1998), 104.
5. Charles Lemert, "The Race of Time: Du Bois and Reconstruction," *boundary 2* 27 (Fall 2000): 232.
6. Thomas Holt elaborates on this disjunction between the expectations of the former slaves and the planters and Northern industrialists who sought to control them. Using C. B. Macpherson's notion of possessive individualism, Holt argues that the aim of the Northern "emancipators" was to transform the former slaves into a working class; freedom would thus mean the opportunity to compete in the market, and inequality would be accepted as a "natural" consequence of supply and demand. Thomas C. Holt, "'An Empire over the Mind': Emancipation, Race, and Ideology in the British West Indies and the American South," *Region, Race, and Reconstruction: Essays in Honor of C. Vann Woodward*, ed. J. Morgan Kousser and James M. McPherson (New York: Oxford University Press, 1982), 283–313.
7. Hayden White, *Figural Realism: Studies in the Mimesis Effect* (Baltimore: Johns Hopkins University Press, 2000), viii.
8. Judith N. Shklar, *American Citizenship: The Quest for Inclusion* (Cambridge: Harvard University Press, 1991), 15.
9. David W. Blight, "W. E. B. Du Bois and the Struggle for American Historical Memory," *History and Memory in African-American Culture*, ed. Geneviève Fabre and Robert O'Meally (New York: Oxford University Press, 1994), 46.
10. David W. Blight, *Race and Reunion: The Civil War in American Memory* (Cambridge, MA: Harvard/Belknap, 2001), 253.
11. W. E. B. Du Bois, "From the Boston 'Globe,'" *Crisis* 9 (January 1915): 131–32. Although the central point of Du Bois's editorial is to make a passionate case for empowering the broadest possible group of citizens, one could also say that he anticipates Lani Guinier and Gerald Torres's argument that the condition of racially vulnerable citizens serves as the "miner's canary" that indicates the health of democracy in the United States. Lani Guinier and Gerald Torres, *The Miner's Canary: Enlisting Race, Resisting Power, Transforming Democracy* (Cambridge: Harvard University Press, 2002).
12. It provides, for example, the starting point for Du Bois's Black Flame trilogy—*The Ordeal of Mansart*, *Mansart Builds a School*, and *Worlds of Color*—published between 1957 and 1961.

13. David Brion Davis, "At the Heart of Slavery" *New York Review of Books* 43 (October 17, 1996): 51–54.
14. Du Bois uses this term in *Black Reconstruction* in connection with those activists who understood that eliminating slavery was the primary end of the war and, over time, recognized that political rights without capital would be insufficient to protect black and white workers. Recently, Angela Davis has applied the concept to a critical assessment of the American prison system. Angela Y. Davis, *Abolition Democracy: Beyond Empire, Prisons, and Torture* (New York: Seven Stories Press, 2005).
15. This point is an extension of Martha Minow's effort "to develop and deepen a vocabulary" for considering responses to historic injustice." Martha Minow, *Between Vengeance and Forgiveness: Facing History after Genocide and Mass Violence* (Boston: Beacon Press, 1998), 4.
16. This is not to say that Du Bois was alone in challenging white norms of reading and writing Reconstruction history. See Daniel Savage Gray, "Bibliographic Essay: Black Views on Reconstruction," *The Journal of Negro History* 58 (January 1973): 73–85.
17. On this last point, the fate of *Brown v. Board of Education* (1954) provides a forceful example. After unanimously outlawing segregation in public schools, the Supreme Court issued a second decision concerning implementation, *Brown* II (1955), in which it ordered that desegregation proceed "with all deliberate speed," thereby subordinating the constitutional rights of black schoolchildren to other considerations. In her essay on "whiteness as property," Cheryl Harris notes that this decision "articulated a new and heretofore unknown approach to rectifying violations of constitutional rights—an approach that invited defiance and delay." Cheryl I. Harris, "Whiteness as Property," *Harvard Law Review* 106 (June 1993): 1755. For a more thorough treatment of the parallels between the two periods of reconstruction, see Philip A. Klinkner, with Rogers M. Smith, *The Unsteady March: The Rise and Decline of Racial Equality in America* (Chicago: University of Chicago Press, 1999), 317–45.
18. See Donald R. Kinder and Lynn M. Sanders, *Divided by Color: Racial Politics and Democratic Ideals* (Chicago: University of Chicago Press, 1996); Lawrence D. Bobo and Ryan A. Smith, "From Jim Crow Racism to Laissez-Faire Racism: The Transformation of Racial Attitudes," in *Beyond Pluralism: The Conception of Groups and Group Identities in America*, ed. Wendy F. Katkin, Ned Landsman, Andrea Tyree (Urbana: University of Illinois Press, 1998), 182–220.
19. Du Bois indicates the stakes of this kind of recovery when he relates that he was commissioned by *Encyclopedia Britannica* to write "a history of the American Negro," and the editors insisted on deleting any references to Reconstruction. When they refused to publish even a short statement about the different ways the period was remembered by black and white Americans,

Du Bois withdrew his article (*BR*, 713); see also David Levering Lewis, *W. E. B. Du Bois: The Fight for Equality and the American Century, 1919–1963* (New York: Henry Holt, 2000), 232–35.

20. Here, Du Bois echoes Alexis de Tocqueville's assertion that "there is no intermediate state that can be durable between the excessive inequality created by slavery and the complete equality which is the natural result of independence." Alexis de Tocqueville, *Democracy in America* I, trans. George Lawrence, ed. J.P. Mayer (New York: HarperCollins, 1969), 362.

21. For an analysis of *Black Reconstruction*'s innovations with respect to both the historiography of the period and Marxian theory, see Cedric J. Robinson, *Black Marxism: The Making of a Black Radical Tradition* (London: Zed Books, 1983), 266–348.

22. Du Bois does not call for complete economic equality in *Souls*. His meaning is closer to Rousseau's conception of a society in which "no citizen should be so opulent that he can buy another, and none so poor that he is constrained to sell himself." Jean-Jacques Rousseau, *On the Social Contract*, ed. Roger D. Masters, trans. Judith R. Masters (New York: St. Martin's Press, 1978), 75. In *Black Reconstruction*, Du Bois goes further, maintaining that economically stratified democracies must find ways of redistributing wealth and income.

23. As the language of "guardianship" and "guidance" attests, even at the time of *Black Reconstruction*, Du Bois does not view the freedmen and women as ready to inhabit the mantle of citizenship without assistance from above. Indeed, Robert Gooding-Williams makes a powerful case that Du Bois's work through *Souls* conceives African American politics as "leadership and rule." Although I am not persuaded that this element of Du Bois's thinking is as determinative as Gooding-Williams contends, his meticulous reconstruction of Du Bois's political thought warns against conflating the democratic insights that Du Bois's work makes possible with positions he would himself have embraced. Robert Gooding-Williams, *In the Shadow of Du Bois: Afro-Modern Political Thought in America* (Cambridge: Harvard University Press, 2009). For an overview and critique of the conception of racial uplift that informs Du Bois's views at the turn of the twentieth century, see Kevin K. Gaines, *Uplifting the Race: Black Leadership, Politics, and Culture in the Twentieth Century* (Chapel Hill: University of North Carolina Press, 1996).

24. W. E. B. Du Bois, "Reconstruction and Its Benefits," *American Historical Review* 15 (July 1910): 785.

25. For example, Andrew Johnson's 1866 veto of the Freedmen's Bureau bill appeals to the American Assumption in its criticism of the bureau for offering aid not enjoyed by "the thousands, not to say millions, of the white race who are honestly toiling from day to day for their subsistence." Andrew Johnson, "Veto Message of February 19, 1866," in *A Compilation of the Messages and Papers of the Presidents 1789–1907*, Vol. VI, ed. James D. Richardson (Washington, DC: Bureau of National Literature and Art, 1908), 401.

26. See also Eric Foner, *Reconstruction: America's Unfinished Revolution, 1863–1877* (New York: Harper & Row, 1988), 50–60; Leon F. Litwack, *Been in the Storm So Long: The Aftermath of Slavery* (New York: Vintage, 1979), 387–408.
27. Representative Thaddeus Stevens (R-PA) and Senator Charles Sumner (R-MA) were two important exceptions.
28. Economist William Darity, Jr., notes that *every* case of compensation related to losses incurred under slavery in the Western Hemisphere has concerned reparations for slave owners, not the slaves or their descendants. William Darity, Jr., "Forty Acres and a Mule: Placing a Price Tag on Oppression," in *The Wealth of Races: The Present Value of Benefits from Past Injustices*, ed. Richard F. America (New York: Greenwood Press, 1990), 5.
29. Recapitulating this logic, recent Supreme Court decisions have, according to Gary Orfield, treated school desegregation plans as a form of punishment for past segregation rather than a means of securing adequate schooling for children of color. The most pernicious aspect of this reasoning is that it redescribes the effort to reconstruct educational opportunities as a short-term fix for a problem of the past. Gary Orfield, Susan E. Eaton, and the Harvard Project on School Desegregation, *Dismantling Desegregation: The Quiet Reversal of Brown v. Board of Education*, (New York: W. W. Norton, 1996), 2.
30. According to Arnold Rampersad, at the time *Souls* was published, Du Bois held that "to limit life to the achievement of what is called the American dream was teleological pessimism of the most sordid kind." Arnold Rampersad, *The Art and Imagination of W. E. B. Du Bois* (1976; repr., New York: Schocken Books, 1990), 86.
31. Jennifer L. Hochschild, *Facing Up to the American Dream: Race, Class, and the Soul of the Nation* (Princeton: Princeton University Press, 1995), xviii. For further discussion of the reluctance of African Americans—across a wide ideological spectrum—to embrace all of the tenets of what Du Bois calls the American Assumption, see Michael C. Dawson, *Black Visions: The Roots of Contemporary African-American Political Ideologies* (Chicago: University of Chicago Press, 2001).
32. David Levering Lewis links Du Bois's treatments of racial gifts in books that include *The Negro* (1915) and *The Gift of Black Folk* (1924) to the racial theory he begins to articulate with "The Conservation of Races" (1897) and continues to develop throughout his career. David Levering Lewis, *W. E. B. Du Bois: Biography of a Race, 1868–1919* (New York: Henry Holt, 1993), 286, 446.
33. For an interpretation of the slaves' actions as a massive and (apart from Du Bois's work) unappreciated insurrection, see Steven Hahn, "Did We Miss the Greatest Slave Rebellion in Modern History?" in *The Political Worlds of Slavery and Freedom* (Cambridge: Harvard University Press, 2009), 55–114.
34. As the language suggests, *Souls* does not make the kind of strong case for the political agency of the slaves that Du Bois will elaborate in *Black Reconstruction*.

Nonetheless, I contend that it is crucial to recognize the germ of that argument in Du Bois's nod to the effects of the slaves' persistence in forcing the Union hand. In this regard, I depart from Gooding-Williams's view that *Souls* describes black political agency narrowly as a matter of rule and obedience. Gooding-Williams persuasively highlights the antidemocratic dimensions of Du Bois's early political thought but sometimes does so by downplaying those dimensions that are closer to the model of democratic politics he draws from his reading of Frederick Douglass's *My Bondage and My Freedom*. Robert Gooding-Williams, *In the Shadow of Du Bois: Afro-Modern Political Thought in America* (Cambridge: Harvard University Press, 2009). I should also note that Du Bois's recognition of the effect of the fugitives' flight is likely influenced by his Harvard teacher, Albert Bushnell Hart, who made a similar claim in an 1891 article. However, while Hart writes that the slaves played a role in turning the tide of the war by assisting the Union, running to Union lines, and, eventually, serving as soldiers, he does not emphasize this point. I am grateful to Victor Wolfenstein for calling this article to my attention. See Albert Bushnell Hart, "Why the South Was Defeated in the Civil War," *New England Magazine* 11 (November 1891): 363–76.

35. W. E. B. Du Bois, "The Negro and Social Reconstruction" [1936], in W. E. B. Du Bois, *Against Racism: Unpublished Essays, Papers, Addresses, 1887–1961*, ed. Herbert Aptheker (Amherst: University of Massachusetts Press, 1985), 105–06.

36. Peter Kolchin, *American Slavery, 1619–1877* (New York: Hill and Wang, 1993), 204.

37. W. E. B. Du Bois, *The Gift of Black Folk: The Negroes in the Making of America* (1924; repr., New York: Washington Square Press, 1970), ch. 5.

38. Du Bois, "Reconstruction and Its Benefits": 781–99.

39. For an account of the continued devaluation of "raced bodies" and its roots in slavery and modern imperialism, see Thomas McCarthy, *Race, Empire, and the Idea of Human Development* (Cambridge: Cambridge University Press, 2009).

40. A. Leon Higginbotham, Jr., *Shades of Freedom: Racial Politics and Presumptions of the American Legal Process* (New York: Oxford University Press, 1998).

41. For further discussion of the political implications of the "wages of whiteness," see Joel Olson, *The Abolition of White Democracy* (Minneapolis: University of Minnesota Press, 2004).

42. Boris I. Bittker, *The Case for Black Reparations* (New York: Random House, 1973).

43. Bill E. Lawson, "Moral Discourse and Slavery," in *Between Slavery and Freedom: Philosophy and American Slavery*, ed. Howard McGary and Bill E. Lawson (Bloomington: Indiana University Press, 1992), 71–89. Charles Henry writes that this gap has deep historical roots. During the Revolutionary period, he

observes, there was no consideration of reparations to freed slaves, even after their service in the military. Charles P. Henry, *Long Overdue: The Politics of Racial Reparations* (New York: New York University Press, 2007), 39.

44. Robert Westley, "The Accursed Share: Genealogy, Temporality, and the Problem of Value in Black Reparations Discourse," *Representations* 92 (Fall 2005): 83.
45. Robin Kelley links reparations, and progressive social movements more broadly, to poetry or "an emancipation of language." Robin D. G. Kelley, *Freedom Dreams: The Black Radical Imagination* (Boston: Beacon Press, 2002), 9.
46. Walter Johnson, "Slavery, Reparations, and the Mythic March of Freedom," *Raritan* 27 (Fall 2007): 55.
47. Melvin L. Oliver and Thomas M. Shapiro, *Black Wealth/White Wealth: A New Perspective on Racial Inequality*, 2nd ed. (New York: Routledge, 2006), 264.
48. Wole Soyinka, *The Burden of Memory, the Muse of Forgiveness* (New York: Oxford University Press, 1999), 39.
49. Dominick LaCapra's distinction between two senses of commensurability helps to clarify this point. Whereas reparations, or any form of compensation for historic injustice, clearly fails the test of commensurability insofar as it cannot equal the suffering wrought by the original wrong, it can nonetheless serve as a "necessarily imperfect translation." "Thus," writes LaCapra, "certain acts, including reparations and the public acknowledgment of injustice on the part of perpetrators or those taking up their dire legacy, may be acknowledged by victims as acceptable even if never fully satisfactory or adequate." Dominick LaCapra, *History and Memory after Auschwitz* (Ithaca: Cornell University Press, 1998), 197, n. 13.
50. See Roy L. Brooks, "The Age of Apology," in *When Sorry Isn't Enough: The Controversy over Apologies and Reparations for Human Injustice*, ed. Roy L. Brooks (New York: New York University Press, 1999), 3–11.
51. One indicator of the proliferation of reparations movements and their new seriousness as a subject of scholarly inquiry is the publication, in 2006, of the 1,000-page *The Handbook of Reparations*, ed. Pablo de Greiff, The International Center for Transitional Justice (Oxford: Oxford University Press, 2006).
52. For an overview of the history of these efforts, see Vincene Verdun, "If the Shoe Fits, Wear It: An Analysis of Reparations to African Americans," *Tulane Law Review* 67 (February 1993): 600–07.
53. The text of the Black Manifesto is reprinted in Bittker, *The Case for Black Reparations*, 167–75.
54. Randall Robinson, *The Debt: What America Owes to Blacks* (New York: Dutton, 2000).
55. Michael C. Dawson and Rovana Popoff, "Reparations: Justice and Greed in Black and White," *Du Bois Review* 1 (2004): 61–62.

56. Alfred L. Brophy, *Reparations: Pro & Con* (New York: Oxford University Press, 2006), 4.
57. For a discussion of the Tulsa suit, see Brophy, *Reparations*, 127–33.
58. W. E. B. Du Bois, "The Latest Craze," *Crisis* 11 (January 1916): 133.
59. My argument dovetails with Ira Katznelson's brief for a reinvigorated commitment to racially just affirmative action policies. See Ira Katznelson, *When Affirmative Action Was White: An Untold History of Racial Inequality in Twentieth-Century America* (New York: Norton, 2005).
60. Oliver and Shapiro, *Black Wealth, White Wealth*, 193. Taking institutional barriers to black home ownership as just one measure of the policies and practices that perpetuated racial inequality until well after the passage of the civil rights legislation of the 1960s, Oliver and Shapiro estimate that African Americans living today have sustained approximately $82 billion in losses (this figure appears in the 1996 edition of Oliver and Shapiro's book, and the second edition notes a *growth* in the wealth gap between 1996 and 2002). Oliver and Shapiro, *Black Wealth, White Wealth*, 8–9, 204.
61. George Lipsitz, *The Possessive Investment in Whiteness: How White People Profit from Identity Politics* (Philadelphia: Temple University Press, 1998), vii. See also Michael K. Brown and David Wellman, "Embedding the Color Line: The Accumulation of Racial Advantage and the Disaccumulation of Opportunity in Post-Civil Rights America," *Du Bois Review* 2 (2005): 187–207; Katznelson, *When Affirmative Action Was White;* Olson, *The Abolition of White Democracy;* David R. Roediger, *The Wages of Whiteness: Race and the Making of the American Working Class* (London: Verso, 1999); Harris, "Whiteness as Property."
62. This is not to say that the establishment of causal connections between slavery and its legacies is simple. For a careful account of this question, see Robert C. Lieberman, "Legacies of Slavery? Race and Historical Causation in American Political Development," in *Race and American Political Development*, ed. Joseph Lowndes, Julie Novkov, and Dorian T. Warren (New York: Routledge, 2008), 206–33.
63. In this regard, Du Bois's analysis provides a response to Adolph Reed's concern that arguments for reparations, which he characterizes as a political "nonstarter," reinforce perceptions of poor and working-class blacks as culturally "defective." Adolph L. Reed, Jr., "The Case Against Reparations" *The Progressive* 64 (December 2000): 15–17.
64. Ida B. Wells-Barnett discerns and decries the power of this fear as one of the causes of lynching. See Ida B. Wells-Barnett, "Southern Horrors," in *On Lynchings* (Amherst, NY: Humanity Books, 2002), 44–46. Recent attention to the assault on prosperous African Americans in the Tulsa riot of 1921 reinforces this point. See Alfred L. Brophy, *Reconstructing the Dreamland: The Tulsa Riot of 1921: Race, Reparations, and Reconciliation* (New York: Oxford University Press, 2002); James S. Hirsch, *Riot and Remembrance: The Tulsa*

Race War and Its Legacy (Boston: Houghton Mifflin, 2002); Brent Staples, "Unearthing a Riot," *New York Times Magazine* (December 19, 1999): 64–69.

65. Eric K. Yamamoto, "Racial Reparations: Japanese American Redress and African American Claims," *Boston College Law Review* 40 (December 1998): 486. Guinier and Torres make an analogous point by exposing the limitations of conventional interest-group politics and showing how multiracial coalitions have succeeded in achieving broad social benefits by "enlisting race." Guinier and Torres, *The Miner's Canary*.

66. Judith Butler, *Precarious Life: The Powers of Mourning and Violence* (London: Verso, 2004), 21 (emphasis in the original).

67. For an acute examination of the phenomenon of unconscious racism and its effects on American law, see Charles R. Lawrence III, "The Id, the Ego, and Equal Protection: Reckoning with Unconscious Racism," *Stanford Law Review* 39 (January 1987): 317–88.

68. Theodor W. Adorno, "What Does Coming to Terms with the Past Mean?" trans. Timothy Bahti and Geoffrey Hartman, in *Bitburg in Moral and Political Perspective*, ed. Geoffrey H. Hartman (Bloomington: Indiana University Press, 1986), 117.

69. W. James Booth, *Communities of Memory: On Witness, Identity, and Justice* (Ithaca: Cornell University Press, 2006).

70. Any program of reparations would require public engagement with the question of how American national identity has been constituted. It would also require that Americans as a group address the question of *black* national identity. Although questions about the nature and boundaries of black identity are far too complex to be adequately explored here, it is worth noting Westley's observation that "the irony posed by the very question of Black national group status is that in ordinary social and political discourse, Blacks are treated as a group for every purpose other than rights-recognition." Robert Westley, "Many Billions Gone: Is It Time to Reconsider the Case for Black Reparations?" *Boston College Law Review* 40 (December 1998): 469. Sheldon Wolin and David Blight provide powerful accounts of the ways in which American national identity has been constructed, to a significant degree, by the active forgetting of slavery. See Sheldon S. Wolin, "Injustice and Collective Memory," in *The Presence of the Past: Essays on the State and the Constitution* (Baltimore: Johns Hopkins University Press, 1989), 32–46; Blight, *Race and Reunion*. Of course, the case of African Americans and the institution of slavery do not provide the only example of the intimate relationship between racial and national identity in the United States. For a discussion of the relationship between race and nation in the case of Mexican Americans, see Thomas C. Holt, *The Problem of Race in the 21st Century* (Cambridge: Harvard University Press, 2000), 49–55.

71. Hannah Arendt, *Eichmann in Jerusalem: A Report on the Banality of Evil* (New York: Penguin Books, 1963), 298. See also Hannah Arendt, "Collective Responsibility," in *Responsibility and Judgment*, ed. Jerome Kohn (New York: Schocken Books, 2003), 147–58. Jürgen Habermas makes a similar point in the context of the Historians' Debate about the relationship between contemporary Germany and the Nazi past: "There is first of all the obligation that we in Germany have—even if no one else any longer assumes it—to keep alive the memory of the suffering of those murdered by German hands, and to keep it alive quite openly and not just in our own minds" (quoted in LaCapra, *History and Memory after Auschwitz*, 198). Thomas McCarthy, who also quotes from this text, considers how the Historians' Debate sheds light on the politics of memory in the United States. Thomas McCarthy, "*Vergangenheitsbewältigung* in the USA: On the Politics of the Memory of Slavery," *Political Theory* 30 (October 2002): 623–48.

72. Minow, *Between Vengeance and Forgiveness*, 5. For an incisive critique of attempts to restrict the responsibility to address the slave past to those descendants, see McCarthy, "*Vergangenheitsbewältigung* in the USA."

73. Westley, "The Accursed Share": 85.

74. See Anne Anlin Cheng, *The Melancholy of Race: Psychoanalysis, Assimilation, and Hidden Grief* (New York: Oxford University Press, 2001).

75. For an account of the belatedness of reparations claims, see Westley, "The Accursed Share"; and Stephen Best and Saidiya Hartman, "Fugitive Justice," *Representations* 92 (Fall 2005): 1–15.

76. Wendy Brown, *Edgework: Critical Essays on Knowledge and Politics* (Princeton: Princeton University Press, 2005), 4.

77. *Alexander v. Oklahoma*, No. 03- C-133-E, 2004 U.S. Dist. LEXIS 5131 (D. Okla. Mar. 19, 2004), aff'd, 382 F.3d 1206 (10th Cir. 2004).

78. Rousseau, *On the Social Contract*, 69.

79. Alan Keenan, *Democracy in Question: Democratic Openness in a Time of Political Closure* (Stanford: Stanford University Press, 2003), 52. For an elaboration on Rousseau's dilemma and on Keenan's reading of it in the context of the reparations debate, see Lawrie Balfour, "Act and Fact: Reparations as a Democratic Politics of Reconciliation," in *The Politics of Reconciliation in Multicultural Societies*, ed. Will Kymlicka and Bashir Bashir (New York: Oxford University Press, 2008), 94–113.

80. Joe R. Feagin and Eileen O'Brien, "The Growing Movement for Reparations," in *When Sorry Isn't Enough: The Controversy over Apologies and Reparations for Human Injustice*, ed. Roy L. Brooks (New York: New York University Press, 1999), 343.

81. Yamamoto, "Racial Reparations," 520.

82. George Shulman, *American Prophecy: Race and Redemption in American Political Culture* (Minneapolis: University of Minnesota Press, 2008), 210.

Chapter Three

1. Barack Obama, *The Audacity of Hope: Thoughts on Reclaiming the American Dream* (New York: Vintage, 2006), 116.
2. W. E. B. Du Bois, "The Niagara Movement: Address to the Country," in *W. E. B. Du Bois: A Reader*, ed. David Levering Lewis (New York: Henry Holt, 1995), 369.
3. On the riot and Du Bois's response, see David Levering Lewis, *W. E. B. Du Bois: Biography of a Race, 1868–1919* (New York: Henry Holt, 1993), 333–37; David Fort Godshalk, *Veiled Visions: The 1906 Atlanta Race Riot and the Reshaping of American Race Relations* (Chapel Hill: University of North Carolina Press, 2005).
4. As William Cain observes, this period marked the height of "Negrophobia," when the black image in white imaginations was unrulable, violent, and sexually dangerous. William E. Cain, "Violence, Revolution, and the Cost of Freedom: John Brown and W. E. B. Du Bois," *boundary 2* 17 (Spring 1990): 317.
5. Many scholars—and Du Bois himself—note the significance of this period for Du Bois's career. For an account of the impact of the riot specifically, see Domenic J. Capeci, Jr., and Jack C. Knight, "Reckoning with Violence: W. E. B. Du Bois and the 1906 Atlanta Race Riot," *Journal of Southern History* 62 (November 1996): 727–66.
6. David W. Blight, *Race and Reunion: The Civil War in American Memory* (Cambridge: Belknap/Harvard University Press, 2001), 111.
7. Thomas McCarthy, "*Vergangenheitsbewältigung* in the USA: On the Politics of the Memory of Slavery," *Political Theory* 30 (October 2002): 634. My understanding of this phenomenon has been enlarged by the work of P. J. Brendese.
8. Benjamin Quarles, *Allies for Freedom* (1974; repr., New York: Da Capo Press, 2001), 170–98.
9. For instance, each of these figures is the subject of a biographical series of paintings by Jacob Lawrence. For a discussion of one artist who has dissented from the embrace of Brown—Kara Walker—see Gwendolyn Dubois Shaw, *Seeing the Unspeakable: The Art of Kara Walker* (Durham: Duke University Press, 2004), 67–101.
10. Quarles, *Allies for Freedom*, no page.
11. Gary Alan Fine, "John Brown's Body: Elites, Heroic Embodiment, and the Legitimation of Political Violence," *Social Problems* 46 (May 1999): 242.
12. David S. Reynolds, *John Brown, Abolitionist: The Man Who Killed Slavery, Sparked the Civil War, and Seeded Civil Rights* (New York: Alfred A. Knopf, 2005), 489.
13. David Howard, "The View from Torrington," *New York Times*, December 1, 1996.
14. Derrick Bell, *Faces at the Bottom of the Well: The Permanence of Racism* (New York: Basic Books, 1992), 7.

15. James Baldwin, quoted in Russell Banks, "John Brown's Body: James Baldwin and Frank Shatz in Conversation," *Transition* 81/82 (2000): 255 (emphasis in the original).
16. Marita Sturken, *Tangled Memories: The Vietnam War, the AIDS Epidemic, and the Politics of Remembering* (Berkeley: University of California Press, 1997), 7.
17. Sacvan Bercovitch, *The American Jeremiad* (Madison: University of Wisconsin Press, 1978), 160. William Connolly's account of "fundamentalism" provides another way of understanding this impulse to incorporate evidence of internal conflict into a vision of redeemed Americanism with the effect that genuine opposition is demonized. See William E. Connolly, *The Ethos of Pluralization* (Minneapolis: University of Minnesota Press, 1995).
18. Nonetheless, it is also worth noting that the money that paid for the statue came from African American communities in New York and Philadelphia. Ellen Barry, "John Brown's Ghost," *Boston Globe*, February 21, 1999.
19. Lerone Bennett, Jr., quoted in Benjamin Quarles, *Blacks on John Brown* (1972; repr., New York: Da Capo, 2001), 139.
20. For a powerful examination and critique of the relationship of vindicationism and Romanticism, see David Scott, *Conscripts of Modernity: The Tragedy of Colonial Enlightenment* (Durham: Duke University Press, 2004). My interpretation of Du Bois is informed by Scott's interpretation of C. L. R. James. Where Scott makes a case for the displacement of romance by tragedy, my approach to Du Bois's text focuses on what Scott calls the "agonistic juxtaposition" of different modes of emplotment. I also emphasize what Bonnie Honig calls "the *reading* practices of political theorists." Bonnie Honig, *Democracy and the Foreigner* (Princeton: Princeton University Press, 2001), 109 (emphasis in the original).
21. Epithets from Richard O. Boyer, *The Legend of John Brown: A Biography and History* (New York: Alfred A. Knopf, 1973), 138–61; and Lewis, *W. E. B. Du Bois: Biography of a Race*, 358, respectively.
22. Daniel C. Littlefield, "Blacks, John Brown, and a Theory of Manhood," in *His Soul Goes Marching On: Responses to John Brown and the Harpers Ferry Raid*, ed. Paul Finkelman (Charlottesville: University Press of Virginia, 1995), 72.
23. Quarles, *Allies for Freedom*, 111.
24. Michael Walzer, *The Revolution of the Saints: A Study in the Origins of Radical Politics* (Cambridge: Harvard University Press, 1965).
25. John Brown, quoted in Stephen B. Oates, *To Purge This Land with Blood: A Biography of John Brown*, 2nd ed. (Amherst: University of Massachusetts Press, 1984), 197.
26. Russell Banks, *Cloudsplitter* (New York: HarperPerennial, 1998), 254–55.
27. While it is beyond the scope of this chapter to consider Brown as a political thinker, there is promising work to be done on the Chatham "constitution," which was intended to govern the independent state of freed slaves that Brown hoped to establish in the Appalachians, and on Brown's letters from

prison, which provide insight into his conception of revolution and his vision of a redeemed American democracy. John Brown, *Provisional Constitution and Ordinances for the People of the United States* (Weston, MA: M&S Press, 1969).

28. Jack Turner, "Performing Conscience: Thoreau, Political Action, and the Plea for John Brown," *Political Theory* 33 (August 2005): 451.

29. Franny Nudelman, "'The Blood of Millions': John Brown's Body. Public Violence, and Political Community," *American Literary History* 13 (Winter 2001): 642.

30. For a description of the second Niagara Movement meeting, see Lewis, *W. E. B. Du Bois: Biography of a Race*, 328–30; and Quarles, *Allies for Freedom*, 3–14.

31. Herbert Aptheker notes that, even as Du Bois pursued nonviolent forms of protest in this period, "the main thing . . . was his conviction in the truth of the principle enunciated in the Declaration of Independence—and that was not a call to vote but rather a call to arms." Herbert Aptheker, "Introduction," W. E. B. Du Bois, *John Brown* (1962; repr., Millwood, NY: Kraus-Thomson, 1973), 8.

32. For an account of the exchange between Du Bois and Ellis Paxson Oberholtzer, the editor at George W. Jacobs & Co., see Aptheker, "Introduction," *John Brown*, rev. ed., 5–7; and Lewis, *W. E. B. Du Bois: Biography of a Race*, 356–57.

33. I am grateful to Robert Gooding-Williams for pointing out that Du Bois's view of Turner and Brown as part of a single tradition represents a shift from the language of *Souls*. In the earlier book, Du Bois delineates three successive traditions of black political leadership. Turner, in this account, is identified with an early period of revolt and revenge. After an intervening period defined by accommodation and adjustment, a third tradition emerges. It is to this tradition, which is exemplified by Douglass and other black leaders who seek inclusion through self-assertion, that Du Bois connects Brown's raid.

34. See Du Bois, "Address to the Country," 367–69. In the "Address," Du Bois extends this lineage to include such figures as William Lloyd Garrison, Charles Sumner, Robert Gould Shaw, and Wendell Phillips, and everyone who died fighting slavery.

35. Du Bois's positive gloss on Brown's economic failings supports Keith Byerman's contention that *John Brown* is a hagiography. Keith E. Byerman, *Seizing the Word: History, Art, and Self in the Work of W. E. B. Du Bois* (Athens: University of Georgia Press, 1994), 162–78. For an alternative view of Brown's financial troubles, one that attributes them to a "scorn for calculation," see William W. Freehling, *The Road to Disunion, Volume II: Secessionists Triumphant, 1854–1861* (New York: Oxford University Press, 2007), 207.

36. In this regard, according to Herbert Aptheker, he anticipated developments in the study of history by 30 or 40 years. Aptheker, "Introduction," *John Brown*, rev. ed., 11.

37. Arnold Rampersad, *The Art and Imagination of W. E. B. Du Bois* (1976; repr., New York: Schocken Books, 1990), 112, 5–6.
38. In fact, Eric Sundquist proposes that John Brown be thought of as a "white Black Christ," for he embodies the revolutionary spirit that the Black Christ represents. Eric J. Sundquist, *To Wake the Nations: Race in the Making of American Literature* (Cambridge: Harvard/Belknap, 1993), 598. Adding to the list of apt biblical comparisons, William Cain argues that "Samson is . . . likely the most compelling prototype for the violent Brown, for he dwells, arrogantly and destructively, in the sacred Old Testament text that Brown deeply absorbed and trusted." Cain, "Violence, Revolution, and the Cost of Freedom," 314.
39. Oates, *To Purge This Land with Blood*, 329–34. Its continuing force is reflected in the attention devoted to Brown's sanity in a recent PBS documentary. Ken Chowder, *John Brown's Holy War*, directed by Robert Kenner (PBS Home Video, 2000).
40. Historian James O. Horton emphasizes this point in *John Brown's Holy War;* see also Quarles, *Allies for Freedom*, 118–19.
41. Edward J. Blum, *W. E. B. Du Bois: American Prophet* (Philadelphia: University of Pennsylvania Press, 2007), 113.
42. For a fascinating discussion of the difficulties of authenticating this exchange, see Nell Irvin Painter, *Sojourner Truth: A Life, A Symbol* (New York: Norton, 1996), 160–62.
43. By contrast, commendations of Brown by Ralph Waldo Emerson and Henry David Thoreau do not address the killings. This omission may be traceable to Brown himself, who, according to biographer Stephen Oates, denied his role in the Pottawatomie killings when he visited Transcendentalist supporters in Concord. On the other hand, Reynolds contends that there is evidence that the Transcendentalists knew about the massacre and indeed relished the violence of Brown's campaign. Whether or not the neglect of this event represents his defenders' ignorance, it makes the meaning of Brown's martyrdom less problematic. Oates, *To Purge This Land with Blood*, 196; Reynolds, *John Brown, Abolitionist*, 206–38. For an insightful treatment of the political implications of Thoreau's memorial to Brown, see Turner, "Performing Conscience," 448–71.
44. Du Bois, *John Brown*, rev. ed., 5.
45. Du Bois, *John Brown*, rev. ed., 395.
46. I explore this book and this quotation more fully in chapter 6.
47. See Ralph Ellison, "What America Would Be Like without Blacks," in *Going to the Territory* (New York: Vintage, 1986), 104–12.
48. For an extended critique of the linkage between the myth of American nationhood and white supremacy, see George Shulman, "Race and the Romance of American Nationalism in Martin Luther King, Norman Mailer, and James Baldwin," in *Cultural Studies and Political Theory*, ed. Jodi Dean (Ithaca: Cornell University Press, 2000), 209–27.

49. Bercovitch, *American Jeremiad*, 132–75.
50. In Du Bois's speech at Harpers Ferry, by contrast, he cloaks his demands in the language of "true Americans" and calls for a return to founding principles. Du Bois, "Address to the Country," 367.
51. Du Bois, *John Brown* (rev. ed.), 144.
52. Obama, *Audacity of Hope*, 116.
53. For an incisive account of fanaticism as a political strategy, see Joel Olson, "The Freshness of Fanaticism: The Abolitionist Defense of Zealotry," *Perspectives on Politics* 5 (December 2007): 685–701.
54. Lynn M. Sanders, "Against Deliberation," *Political Theory* 25 (June 1997): 353.
55. One example Sanders offers is that of the congressional testimony of Japanese-Americans interned during World War II. Sanders, "Against Deliberation," 361.
56. Michael Hanchard "Afro-Modernity: Temporality, Politics and the African Diaspora," *Public Culture* 11 (Winter 1999): 245–68.
57. Martin Luther King, Jr., "Letter from Birmingham City Jail," in *A Testament of Hope: The Essential Writings and Speeches of Martin Luther King, Jr.*, ed. James Melvin Washington (San Francisco: HarperCollins, 1986), 296.
58. Bruce Western, *Punishment and Inequality in America* (New York: Russell Sage Foundation, 2006), 16, 193. On gender and mass incarceration, see Angela Y. Davis, *Are Prisons Obsolete?* (Toronto: Open Media, 2003), 60–83.
59. On the rise of the carceral system as a "'race making' institution" see Loïc Wacquant, "From Slavery to Mass Incarceration: Rethinking the 'Race Question' in the US," *New Left Review* 13 (January/February 2002): 41–60.
60. Glenn C. Loury, *Race, Incarceration, and American Values* (Cambridge: MIT Press, 2008), 27.
61. Du Bois, *John Brown* (rev. ed.), 402.
62. For a critical look at how such a Manichean framework was mobilized to expand state power after September 11, 2001, see Elizabeth Anker, "Villains, Victims and Heroes: Melodrama, Media, and September 11, *Journal of Communication* 55 (March 2005): 22–37. On the connections between Brown and modern terrorism, see Reynolds, *John Brown, Abolitionist*, 500–03; Jerry Zremski, "Anti-Abortion Radical Fringe Considers Doctor's Cold-Blooded Killing Justifiable," *Buffalo News*, October 26, 1998. However, to assimilate Brown's story into a generic tradition of American terrorism is to do an injustice to the memory of slavery by either ignoring it altogether or making it one among many interchangeable causes. See George Will, "Terror from the Fringe," *Atlanta Constitution*, April 25, 1995.
63. Wendy Brown, *Manhood and Politics: A Feminist Reading in Political Theory* (Totowa, N.J.: Rowman & Littlefield, 1988).
64. This connection is also explored by Philip Klinkner and Rogers Smith, who identify the involvement of the United States in a major war as one of the

three factors that have been present at each moment of substantial improvement in the situation of African Americans. They do not, however, address the gendering of citizenship that follows from this connection and say nothing specifically about the status of women in their proposal for a reinstituted draft and the creation of a "universal national service." Philip A. Klinkner, with Rogers M. Smith, *The Unsteady March: The Rise and Decline of Racial Equality in America* (Chicago: University of Chicago Press, 1999), 349–51.

65. Du Bois anticipates his mature analysis in his Harvard commencement address on "Jefferson Davis as a Representative of Civilization" (1890). There he notes the incompleteness of the martial civilization that Davis exemplifies, a civilization defined by "individualism coupled with the rule of might." W. E. B. Du Bois, "Jefferson Davis as a Representative of Civilization," in *W. E. B. Du Bois: A Reader*, ed. David Levering Lewis (New York: Henry Holt, 1995), 17–19.

66. Lewis, *W. E. B. Du Bois: Biography of a Race*, 358. William Cain and Nahum Chandler offer alternative readings, indicating that Du Bois's narrative *does* focus on "the inner development of the Negro American." See Cain, "Violence, Revolution, and the Cost of Freedom"; Nahum D. Chandler, "The Souls of an Ex-White Man," *CR: The New Centennial Review* 3 (Spring 2003): 179–95.

67. The ease with which black participation in the antislavery struggle can be overshadowed by the legendary Brown is borne out in the PBS documentary *John Brown's Holy War*. Although generally balanced in its assessment of Brown himself, the film's focus on the "Secret Six," prominent white men who supported Brown's activities, and its failure to mention the Chatham Convention reinforce the perception of the abolitionist struggle as a white one.

68. Iris Marion Young, "The Logic of Masculinist Protection: Reflections on the Current Security State," *Signs* 29 (Autumn 2003): 1–25.

69. J. Peter Euben, *The Tragedy of Political Theory: The Road Not Taken* (Princeton: Princeton University Press, 1990), 34.

70. George Shulman, "Thinking Authority Democratically: Prophetic Practices, White Supremacy, and Democratic Politics," *Political Theory* 36 (October 2008): 709–10.

71. Linda Alcoff offers a recent example of how the burden of white antiracist acts of resistance can fall disproportionately on African Americans associated with them—whether directly or indirectly. Examining *Race Traitor: A Journal of the New Abolitionism* (which explicitly takes inspiration from Brown), Alcoff notes the journal's hopeful interpretation of a group of white students in Indiana, who risked censure and violence at their nearly all-white high school by wearing dreadlocks and adopting the dress of hip-hop artists. Yet, she remarks, "the most violence was suffered by the black families in the

school, families that were not consulted and probably unprepared for the attack." Linda Martín Alcoff, "What Should White People Do?" *Hypatia: A Journal of Feminist Philosophy* 13 (Summer 1998): 14–16.

72. Cain, "Violence, Revolution, and the Cost of Freedom": 330.
73. For a critical appraisal of Thoreau's celebration of Brown, see Shulman, *American Prophecy*, 75–88.
74. Relatedly, Kathy Ferguson shows how a discourse that made anarchist Emma Goldman "dangerous" not only obscures the history of antilabor violence in the United States but also limits the conceptual resources available to understand and challenge the violence of contemporary capitalism. Kathy E. Ferguson, "Discourses of Danger: Locating Emma Goldman," *Political Theory* 36 (October 2008): 735–61. Ali Behdad makes a similar point about the relationship between historical amnesia about violence against immigrants and foreigners and the repetition of such violence. Ali Behdad, *A Forgetful Nation: On Immigration and Cultural Identity in the United States* (Durham: Duke University Press, 2006).
75. John Ashcroft, quoted in, Karen Hosler, "Ashcroft Rebuts Racial-Bias Charges," *Baltimore Sun*, January 18, 2001. Contrast this view with a Confederate defense of the practice of slaughtering captured black soldiers, rather than holding them as prisoners: "We cannot treat negroes . . . as prisoners of war without a destruction of the social system for which we contend." Arkansas newspaper, quoted in Drew Gilpin Faust, *This Republic of Suffering: Death and the Civil War* (New York: Alfred A. Knopf, 2008), 45. On a similar controversy surrounding Gale Norton, Bush's nominee to head the Department of the Interior, see E. J. Dionne, "Unsettled Questions," *Denver Post*, January 17, 2001. For a critical account of the history and significance of the "Lost Cause" tradition to which Ashcroft and Norton subscribe, see David W. Blight, "A Confederacy of Denial," *Washington Post*, January 29, 2001.
76. Behdad, *A Forgetful Nation*, 6.

Chapter Four

1. William E. Connolly, "Confessing Identity\Belonging to Difference," *Identity\Difference: Democratic Negotiations of Political Paradox*, expanded edition (Minneapolis: University of Minnesota Press, 2002), xxiii.
2. This acute formulation, which captures the tenor of much recent democratic thought, belongs to Thomas Dumm. Thomas Dumm, *Loneliness as a Way of Life* (Cambridge: Harvard University Press, 2008), 159.
3. Nahum D. Chandler, "The Figure of W. E. B. Du Bois as a Problem for Thought," *CR: The New Centennial Review* 6 (2007): 46–47.
4. W. E. B. Du Bois, "The Talented Tenth," in *The Negro Problem: A Series of Articles by Representative Negroes of To-day* (1903; repr., New York: AMS Press, 1970), 33.

5. It is a generous assessment as well, for Du Bois might justifiably complain that his life was prevented from realizing its potential significance—for instance, the influence he could have wielded had he held a chair at a historically white university—because "it was part of a Problem."
6. In his early work, in particular, Du Bois's commitment to scientific study and meliorative public policy bespeaks an orientation toward *solving* social problems. W. E. B. Du Bois, "The Study of the Negro Problems," *The Annals of the American Academy of Political and Social Science* 11 (January 1898): 1–23. See Robert Gooding-Williams, *In the Shadow of Du Bois: Afro-Modern Political Thought in America* (Cambridge: Harvard University Press, 2009).
7. William L. Andrews, *To Tell a Free Story: The First Century of Afro-American Autobiography, 1760–1865* (Champaign: University of Illinois Press, 1988), 11. By focusing on the work that the "problem" performs as a metaphor, I do not deny its metonymic function. But I do contend that to read the relationship between Du Bois and "the Problem" solely metonymically disguises their misfit.
8. While there is considerable overlap between the two words, the OED highlights the etymological link between example and "sample," both indicating "something taken out." "Exemplar," by contrast, is related to "sampler" or pattern. Oxford English Dictionary Online (http://dictionary.oed.com/). Consulted December 11, 2008.
9. Alexander Gelley, "Introduction," *Unruly Examples: On the Rhetoric of Exemplarity*, ed. Alexander Gelley (Stanford: Stanford University Press, 1995), 1–3.
10. Gelley, "Introduction," *Unruly Examples*, 14.
11. Kirstie M. McClure, "The Odor of Judgment: Exemplarity, Propriety, and Politics in the Company of Hannah Arendt," in *Hannah Arendt and the Meaning of Politics*, ed. Craig Calhoun and John McGowan (Minneapolis: University of Minnesota Press, 1997), 53–57. For an alternative approach to exemplarity that emphasizes the capacity of political institutions, concepts, and movements "to set the *political* imagination in motion," see Alessandro Ferrara, *The Force of the Example: Explorations in the Paradigm of Judgment* (New York: Columbia University Press, 2008), 22 (emphasis in the original).
12. It is not surprising, then, that *Dusk of Dawn* raises pointed questions about Du Bois's enthusiasm for the Talented Tenth as the engine of racial uplift. Although he continues to argue for the role of an educated leadership, he also allows that "my own panacea of earlier days was flight of class from mass" (*DOD*, 216), and he emphasizes the importance of "intelligent democratic control" over leaders (*DOD*, 212).
13. This chapter will not directly engage the debate about whether the "turn to ethics" by Connolly and other theorists constitutes a retreat from politics. For a thoughtful intervention into this debate, see Paul Apostolidis, "Politics and Connolly's Ethics: Immigrant Narratives, Racism, and Identity's Contingency," *Theory & Event* 11 (2008).

14. Arnold Rampersad, "Biography, Autobiography, and Afro-American Culture," *The Yale Review* 73 (Autumn 1983): 12.
15. Toni Morrison, "Rootedness: The Ancestor as Foundation," in *Black Women Writers (1950–1980): A Critical Evaluation*, ed. Mari Evans (Garden City, NY: Anchor Press, 1984), 339.
16. Toni Morrison, *Beloved* (New York: Plume, 1987), 275.
17. William L. Andrews, "Introduction," *Black American Literature Forum* 24 (Summer 1990), 197.
18. Thomas C. Holt, "The Political Uses of Alienation: W. E. B. Du Bois on Politics, Race, and Culture, 1903–1940," *American Quarterly* 42 (June 1990): 307.
19. William L. Andrews, "Checklist of Du Bois's Autobiographical Writings," in *Critical Essays on W. E. B. Du Bois*, ed. William L. Andrews (Boston: G. K. Hall, 1985), 226.
20. Sidonie Smith and Julia Watson, "Introduction," *Getting a Life: Everyday Uses of Autobiography*, ed. Sidonie Smith and Julia Watson (Minneapolis: University of Minnesota Press, 1996), 1–24.
21. Sidonie Smith, "Who's Talking/Who's Talking Back? The Subject of Personal Narrative," *Signs* 18 (Winter 1993): 393.
22. See Lee Quinby, "The Subject of Memoirs: *The Woman Warrior*'s Technology of Ideographic Selfhood," in *De/Colonizing the Subject: The Politics of Gender in Women's Autobiography*, ed. Sidonie Smith and Julia Watson (Minneapolis: University of Minnesota Press, 1992), 297–320.
23. Arnold Rampersad, *The Art and Imagination of W. E. B. Du Bois* (1976; repr., New York: Schocken, 1990), 244.
24. Ira Reid, Du Bois's colleague at Atlanta University, offers a helpful accounting of some key missing elements in *Dusk of Dawn*. See letter from Ira Reid to W. E. B. Du Bois, February 15, 1940, in *The Correspondence of W. E. B. Du Bois, Volume II: Selections, 1934–1944*, ed. Herbert Aptheker (Amherst: University of Massachusetts Press, 1976), 215–18. For a critique of Du Bois's failure to acknowledge black women's leadership, see Hazel V. Carby, *Race Men* (Cambridge: Harvard University Press, 1998); for an account of the constraints of exemplarity and its relationship to "the burdens of masculinity," see Ross Posnock, *Color and Culture: Black Writers and the Making of the Modern Intellectual* (Cambridge: Harvard University Press, 1998), 84. I address questions of gender and leadership more directly in chapter 5.
25. Nathan Huggins, *Revelations: American History, American Myths*, ed. Brenda Smith Huggins (New York: Oxford University Press, 1995), 80. Rampersad observes that, despite the influence of his dissertation advisor, Alfred Bushnell Hart at Harvard, and Gustav von Schmoller in Berlin, Du Bois retained a strong attraction to "Carlyle's way, cherishing the power of the irresistible individual and the small band of natural leaders of intellect and vision." Rampersad, *Art and Imagination of W. E. B. Du Bois*, 45. Among the

individuals who captured Du Bois's imagination as a young man, he notes with some chagrin, was Otto von Bismarck (*DOD* 32).

26. Kathryne V. Lindberg, "W. E. B. Du Bois's *Dusk of Dawn* and James Yates's *Mississippi to Madrid* Or 'What Goes Around Comes Around and Around and Around' in Autobiography," *Massachusetts Review* 35 (Summer 1994): 284.

27. It bears remembering that Du Bois also demonstrated a keen ability to employ the great in the service of social criticism. His college valedictory address, for example, undercut the self-satisfaction of an audience of Harvard faculty, students, and parents in a subversive portrait of Jefferson Davis as "representative of civilization." W. E. B. Du Bois, "Jefferson Davis as a Representative of Civilization" [1890] in *W. E. B. Du Bois: A Reader*, ed. David Levering-Lewis (New York: Henry Holt, 1995), 17–19. See Shamoon Zamir, *Dark Voices: W. E. B. Du Bois and American Thought, 1888–1903* (Chicago: University of Chicago Press, 1995), 23–67.

28. Rampersad, *The Art and Imagination of W. E. B. Du Bois*, 241.

29. Zamir, *Dark Voices*, 3.

30. W. E. B. Du Bois, *The Autobiography of W. E. B. Du Bois: A Soliloquy on Viewing My Life from the Last Decade of Its First Century*, ed. Herbert Aptheker (New York: International Publishers, 1968), 12.

31. W. E. B. Du Bois, "Criteria of Negro Art" [1926] in *W. E. B. Du Bois: A Reader*, ed. David Levering-Lewis (New York: Henry Holt, 1995), 511.

32. Du Bois heightens this sense of expectation by contrasting the blood and tears that defined his earlier autobiographical efforts with the "more benign fluid" in which this book was written (*DOD*, xxx). At the same time, his eloquent account of the false dawn of Reconstruction in the second chapter of *The Souls of Black Folk* shadows even this confident assertion of the beginning of a new day.

33. This discussion of dimness and vision is indebted to Scott's reading of Samuel Delany's autobiography, *The Motion of Light in Water*. Joan W. Scott, "'Experience,'" in *Feminists Theorize the Political*, ed. Judith Butler and Joan W. Scott (New York: Routledge, 1992), 35.

34. Caren Kaplan, "Resisting Autobiography: Out-Law Genres and Transnational Feminist Subjects," in *De/Colonizing the Subject: The Politics of Gender in Women's Autobiography*, ed. Sidonie Smith and Julia Watson (Minneapolis: University of Minnesota Press), 115–68.

35. Kaplan, "Resisting Autobiography," 119.

36. Michel Foucault, "Nietzsche, Genealogy, History," in *Language, Counter-Memory, Practice: Selected Essays and Interviews*, ed. Donald F. Bouchard, trans. Donald F. Bouchard and Sherry Simon (Ithaca: Cornell University Press, 1977), 142. I do not mean to equate Du Bois's and Foucault's conceptions of genealogy but simply to highlight the critical, unsettling work that Du Bois undertakes in *Dusk of Dawn*.

37. Aptly, Kenneth Mostern observes that "Du Bois . . . writes his autobiography *as a Negro man*, and scare quotes would be particularly inappropriate around this phrase." Kenneth Mostern, *Autobiography and Black Identity Politics: Racialization in Twentieth-Century America* (Cambridge: Cambridge University Press, 1999), 59 (emphasis in the original).
38. Elizabeth W. Bruss, *Autobiographical Acts: The Changing Situation of a Literary Genre* (Baltimore: Johns Hopkins University Press, 1976), 128.
39. For an earlier, largely identical, version of this dialogue that appeared in *Smart Set* in 1923, see W. E. B. Du Bois, "The Superior Race," in *W. E. B. Du Bois: A Reader*, ed. David Levering Lewis (New York: Henry Holt, 1995), 470–77.
40. Patricia J. Williams, *The Alchemy of Race and Rights: Diary of a Law Professor* (Cambridge: Harvard University Press, 1991), 113.
41. Joseph R. Biden, Jr., quoted in Adam Nagourney, "Biden Unwraps '08 Bid with an Oops!" *New York Times*, February 1, 2007.
42. Lawrie Balfour, "'A Most Disagreeable Mirror': Race Consciousness as Double Consciousness," *Political Theory* 26 (June 1998): 346–69.
43. For a recent argument that makes similar claims on behalf of black solidarity, see Tommie Shelby, *We Who Are Dark: The Philosophical Foundations of Black Solidarity* (Cambridge: Belknap/Harvard University Press, 2005).
44. Cathy J. Cohen, *The Boundaries of Blackness: AIDS and the Breakdown of Black Politics* (Chicago: University of Chicago Press, 1999).
45. Mostern, *Autobiography and Black Identity Politics*, 81.
46. William E. Connolly, "Then and Now: Participant-Observation in Political Theory," in *The Oxford Handbook of Political Theory*, ed. John S Dryzek, Bonnie Honig, and Anne Phillips (Oxford: Oxford University Press, 2006), 839.
47. William E. Connolly, *The Ethos of Pluralization* (Minneapolis: University of Minnesota Press, 1995), xii. Connolly's criticism of pluralism is as concerned with its territorial boundaries and the violence that those boundaries engender as it is with the constitution of identities. Although this chapter does not address this aspect of Connolly's work directly, I return to it indirectly through an inquiry into the global scope of Du Bois's political thought in chapter 6.
48. Connolly, "Confessing Identity\Belonging to Difference," xvi.
49. Connolly, *Ethos of Pluralization*, 19.
50. Connolly, *Ethos of Pluralization*, 74.
51. Connolly, *Ethos of Pluralization*, 184.
52. William E. Connolly, *Neuropolitics: Thinking, Culture, Speed* (Minneapolis: University of Minnesota Press, 2002), 18.
53. Connolly, *Ethos of Pluralization*, 69.
54. Judith Butler and William E. Connolly, "Power, Politics and Ethics: A Discussion between Judith Butler and William Connolly," *Theory & Event* 4 (2000): par. 16.

55. Connolly, *Ethos of Pluralization*, 70.
56. Du Bois, "Criteria of Negro Art." See Posnock, *Color and Culture*, 138–45.
57. Frantz Fanon's account of the effect of being looked upon as "a Negro" vivifies this conception of responsibility: "I was responsible at the same time for my body, for my race, for my ancestors. I subjected myself to an objective examination, I discovered my blackness, my ethnic characteristics; and I was battered down by tom-toms, cannibalism, intellectual deficiency, fetishism, racial defects, slave-ships, and above all else, above all: 'Sho' good eatin.'" Frantz Fanon, *Black Skin, White Masks*, trans. Charles Lam Markmann (New York: Grove Weidenfeld, 1967), 112.
58. Connolly, *Ethos of Pluralization*, 46.
59. Rampersad astutely says of *Dusk of Dawn*: "This self-portrait is distinguished by its author's compassion, founded on his own admission of complicity as a human being in the human criminality against which he took a stand." Rampersad, *The Art and Imagination of W. E. B. Du Bois*, 244. For one such example, see Du Bois's admission that his early critique of the white world did not question the rightness of that world but rather felt that "what was wrong was that I and people like me and thousands of others who might have my ability and aspiration, were refused permission to be a part of this world" (*DOD*, 27).
60. In his discussion of European incursions in the Americas in *Identity\Difference*, for instance, Connolly worries that "words like 'conquest' and 'colonization' underplay the effects of the encounter upon the self-identities of the initiating power." The alternative Du Bois offers is to show that it is possible to formulate an account of "the encounter" as conquest without losing sight of the effects on those "self-identities" that Connolly rightly addresses. Connolly, *Identity\Difference*, 36–40.
61. Connolly, *Identity\Difference*, 64.
62. See Cheryl I. Harris, "Whiteness as Property," *Harvard Law Review* 106 (June 1993): 1707–91; George Lipsitz, *The Possessive Investment in Whiteness: How White People Profit from Identity Politics* (Philadelphia: Temple University Press, 1998).
63. Toni Morrison, *Playing in the Dark: Whiteness and the Literary Imagination* (Cambridge: Harvard University Press, 1992), 38 (emphasis in the original).
64. Connolly, "Confessing Identity\Belonging to Difference," xiv.
65. Fanon makes a related point about asymmetry in the colonial context: "The Negro suffers in his body quite differently from the white man." Fanon, *Black Skin, White Masks*, 138. For an elaboration of the asymmetrical expectations attached to white and black bodies, see Lewis R. Gordon, *Bad Faith and Antiblack Racism* (Atlantic Highlands, NJ: Humanities Press, 1995), 97–103.
66. Connolly, *Ethos of Pluralization*, xxvi.

67. Devon Carbado offers an illuminating extension of this point. For women and men identified as "black," he observes, "the pressure to be polite, and the self-discipline and self-regulation it engenders, is often experienced as a survival strategy." Devon Carbado, "Racial Naturalization," *American Quarterly* 57 (September 2005): 650.
68. My understanding of shared vulnerability was enlarged by conversations with P. J. Brendese and by Greta Snyder's exploration, in a seminar paper, of the "equal distribution of risk."
69. For an incisive account of "*asymmetrical* reciprocity," see Iris Marion Young, *Intersecting Voices: Dilemmas of Gender, Political Philosophy, and Policy* (Princeton: Princeton University Press, 1997), 38–59. For critical perspective on Connolly's account of working-class resentment of the "underclass," see Joel Olson, *The Abolition of White Democracy* (Minneapolis: University of Minnesota Press, 2004), 82–87.
70. Although my reading of *Dusk of Dawn* emphasizes how Du Bois's autobiographical practice resembles Connolly's critical self-reflection, these concerns dovetail with George Shulman's account of the differences between democratic theories of ethos and cultivation, on the one hand, and prophetic critics of white supremacy, on the other. George Shulman, *American Prophecy: Race and Redemption in American Political Culture* (Minneapolis: University of Minnesota Press, 2008), 240–43.
71. Connolly, "Confessing Identity\Belonging to Difference," xiv. For a critique of Connolly's work that attributes this individualism to his focus on Foucault's writings on the "care of the self" and neglect of Foucault's defense of pluralistic or "associative" practices of freedom, see Ella Myers, "Resisting Foucauldian Ethics: Associative Politics and the Limits of the Care of the Self," *Contemporary Political Theory* 7 (May 2008): 125–46.
72. Stuart Hall, quoted in Linda Martín Alcoff, *Visible Identities: Race, Gender, and the Self* (New York: Oxford University Press, 2006), 115.
73. Robert Gooding-Williams, "Race, Multiculturalism and Democracy," *Constellations* 5 (March 1998): 33.
74. For a powerful argument along these lines, see Lani Guinier and Gerald Torres, *The Miner's Canary: Enlisting Race, Resisting Power, Transforming Democracy* (Cambridge: Harvard University Press, 2002).
75. Connolly, *Identity\Difference*, 222.
76. As Dumm notes, Du Bois concludes *Souls* with the same words—"THE END"—and the absence of a period at the finish of the earlier book encourages readers to move forward. Dumm, *Loneliness as a Way of Life*, 164–65.

Chapter Five

1. Hortense J. Spillers, "Mama's Baby, Papa's Maybe: An American Grammar Book," *Diacritics* (Summer 1987): 65.

2. Marlon B. Ross, *Manning the Race: Reforming Black Men in the Jim Crow Era* (New York: New York University Press, 2004), 49.
3. See Ross, *Manning the Race*, 50; Hazel V. Carby, *Race Men* (Cambridge: Harvard University Press, 1998), 9–41.
4. This approach is reinforced by Angela Davis, who credits slave women with "spelling out standards for a new womanhood." Angela Y. Davis, *Women, Race, and Class* (New York: Vintage, 1981), 29.
5. In an illuminating reading of "Damnation" as an adaptation of *The Star of Ethiopia*, Du Bois's pageant of black world history, Susan Gillman shows how "Damnation" revises both the pageant culture of the day and the masculinism of his own contribution to that culture. Susan Gillman, "Pageantry, Maternity, and World History," in *Next to the Color Line: Gender, Sexuality, and W. E. B. Du Bois*, ed. Susan Gillman and Alys Eve Weinbaum (Minneapolis: University of Minnesota Press, 2007), 378–415.
6. Will Kymlicka and Wayne Norman, "Return of the Citizen: A Survey of Recent Work on Citizenship Theory," *Ethics* 104 (January 1994): 352–81.
7. Mary G. Dietz, *Turning Operations: Feminism, Arendt, and Politics* (New York: Routledge, 2002), 5.
8. Ruth Lister, *Citizenship: Feminist Perspectives*, 2nd ed. (New York: Palgrave Macmillan, 2003), 1–3.
9. See Clarissa Rile Hayward, "Binding Problems, Boundary Problems: The Trouble with 'Democratic Citizenship,'" in *Identities, Affiliations, and Allegiances*, ed. Seyla Benhabib, Ian Shapiro, and Danilo Petranović (Cambridge: Cambridge University Press, 2007), 181–205.
10. My use of the phrase "languages of citizenship" is informed by: Bill E. Lawson, "Moral Discourse and Slavery," in Howard McGary and Bill E. Lawson, *Between Slavery and Freedom: Philosophy and American Slavery* (Bloomington: Indiana University Press, 1992), 71–89; Susan Bickford, "Anti-Anti-Identity Politics: Feminism, Democracy, and the Complexities of Citizenship," *Hypatia* 12 (Fall 1997): 111–31; Catherine A. Holland, *The Body Politic: Foundings, Citizenship, and Difference in the American Political Imagination* (New York: Routledge, 2001). For a forceful account of the ways citizenship laws were used to exclude on the basis of race, gender, national origin, and religion from the colonial period to 1912, see Rogers M. Smith, *Civic Ideals: Conflicting Visions of Citizenship in U.S. History* (New Haven: Yale University Press, 1997).
11. Patricia Hill Collins, "Producing Mothers of the Nation: Race, Class and Contemporary US Population Policies," in *Women, Citizenship and Difference*, ed. Nira Yuval-Davis and Pnina Werbner (London: Zed Books, 1999), 118–29.
12. Wahneema Lubiano, "Black Ladies, Welfare Queens, and State Minstrels: Ideological War by Narrative Means," in *Race-ing Justice, En-gendering Power: Essays on Anita Hill, Clarence Thomas, and the Construction of Social Reality*, ed. Toni Morrison (New York: Pantheon, 1992), 350; see also Rhonda M.

Williams and Carla L. Peterson, "The Color of Memory: Interpreting Twentieth-Century U.S. Social Policy from a Nineteenth-Century Perspective," *Feminist Studies* 24 (Spring 1998): 7–25.

13. See, Gwendolyn Mink, "Aren't Poor Single Mothers Women? Feminists, Welfare Reform, and Welfare Justice," in *Whose Welfare?* ed. Gwendolyn Mink (Ithaca: Cornell University Press, 1999), 171–88. There are, of course, other examples, the most significant of which may be the distinctions between citizens and foreigners and between citizens and criminals.

14. Leslie Rout, quoted in Michael Hanchard, *Party/Politics: Horizons in Black Political Thought* (New York: Oxford University Press, 2006), 214.

15. Judith N. Shklar, *American Citizenship: The Quest for Inclusion* (Cambridge: Harvard University Press, 1991), 22.

16. Joel Olson, *The Abolition of White Democracy* (Minneapolis: University of Minnesota Press, 2004), 53–59.

17. Elizabeth V. Spelman, *Inessential Woman: Problems of Exclusion in Feminist Thought* (Boston: Beacon, 1988), 13.

18. See Kevin K. Gaines, *Uplifting the Race: Black Leadership, Politics, and Culture in the Twentieth Century* (Chapel Hill: University of North Carolina Press, 1996).

19. Spillers, "Mama's Baby, Papa's Maybe," 80.

20. I adapt this formulation from Judith Butler's assessment of "the question of postmodernism." Judith Butler, "Contingent Foundations," in *Feminists Theorize the Political*, ed. Judith Butler and Joan W. Scott (New York: Routledge, 1992), 3.

21. Kimberlé Crenshaw, "Whose Story Is It, Anyway? Feminist and Antiracist Appropriations of Anita Hill," in *Race-ing Justice, En-gendering Power: Essays on Anita Hill, Clarence Thomas, and the Construction of Social Reality*, ed. Toni Morrison (New York: Pantheon, 1992), 403. For an inquiry into Du Bois's thought as a precursor to the critical theoretical work that is described as "intersectional," see Ange-Marie Hancock, "W. E. B. Du Bois: Intellectual Forefather of Intersectionality?" *Souls* 7 (2005): 74–84.

22. Jean Fagin Yellin, "Du Bois' *Crisis* and Woman's Suffrage," *Massachusetts Review* 14 (Spring 1973): 365–75; Garth E. Pauley, "W. E. B. Du Bois on Woman Suffrage: A Critical Analysis of his *Crisis* Writings," *Journal of Black Studies* 30 (January 2000): 383–410.

23. Cheryl Townsend Gilkes, "The Margin as the Center of a Theory of History: African-American Women, Social Change, and the Sociology of W. E. B. Du Bois," *W. E. B. Du Bois on Race and Culture*, ed. Bernard W. Bell, Emily R. Grosholz, and James B. Stewart (New York: Routledge, 1996), 134.

24. David Levering Lewis, *W. E. B. Du Bois: The Fight for Equality and the American Century, 1919–1963* (New York: Henry Holt, 2000), 11. Lewis also notes the disjuncture between the arguments of "Damnation" and the tightly circumscribed, patriarchal world inhabited by Nina Gomer Du Bois, Du Bois's wife.

25. Arnold Rampersad, *The Art and Imagination of W. E. B. Du Bois* (1976; repr., New York: Schocken Books, 1990), 170. This chapter does not dispute Lister's claim that "a feminist citizenship theory and praxis must be internationalist in its outlook and scope." Indeed, attention to the international dimensions of white supremacy is a hallmark of Du Bois's thought and, according to Jean Fagin Yellin, "Du Bois consistently placed the struggle for woman's rights within an international historical context." Because "Damnation" focuses on conditions in the United States, however, this chapter does not directly address the array of moral and political questions raised by the restriction of citizenship to people born or naturalized in the United States. Lister, *Citizenship*, 43; Yellin, "Du Bois' *Crisis* and Woman's Suffrage": 371.
26. Hazel V. Carby, *Reconstructing Womanhood: The Emergence of the Afro-American Woman Novelist* (New York: Oxford University Press, 1989).
27. Anna Julia Cooper, *A Voice from the South* (1892; repr., New York: Oxford University Press, 1988), 31.
28. Carby, *Race Men*, 12, 10. On Du Bois's failure to give credit to Ida B. Wells-Barnett's work and her exclusion from the NAACP's list of its "Founding Forty," see Paula J. Giddings, *Ida: A Sword Among Lions* (New York: Amistad, 2008). For an example of this kind of willful elision of black women's leadership much later in Du Bois's career, see Brenda Gayle Plummer's account of his efforts, along with Walter White, to marginalize Mary McLeod Bethune at the U.N. Conference on International Organization in San Francisco in 1945. Brenda Gayle Plummer, *Rising Wind: Black Americans and U.S. Foreign Affairs, 1935–1960* (Chapel Hill, University of North Carolina Press, 1996), 135–36.
29. Mark Reinhardt, "Who Speaks for Margaret Garner? Slavery, Silence, and the Politics of Ventriloquism," *Critical Inquiry* 29 (Autumn 2002): 84.
30. My focus on Du Bois's use of Cooper, rather than her own *A Voice From the South*, is not meant to diminish the importance of Cooper's text. For an overview of contemporary debates about Cooper's feminist thought, see Charles Lemert, "Anna Julia Cooper: The Colored Woman's Office," *The Voice of Anna Julia Cooper*, ed. Charles Lemert and Esme Bhan (Lanham, MD: Rowman and Littlefield, 1998), 1–43.
31. See Gayatri Chakravorty Spivak, "Can the Subaltern Speak?" *Marxism and the Interpretation of Culture*, ed. Cary Nelson and Lawrence Grossberg (Urbana: University of Illinois Press, 1988), 271–313; Reinhardt, "Who Speaks for Margaret Garner?" Sherley Anne Williams's novel *Dessa Rose* provides an exemplary exploration of this question in its telling of the story of a white man's appropriation of an escaped slave's story and the slave's subversion of his efforts. Sherley Anne Williams, *Dessa Rose* (New York: William Morrow, 1986). See also Deborah E. McDowell, "Negotiating between Tenses: Witnessing Slavery after Freedom—Dessa Rose," in *Slavery and the Literary*

Imagination, ed. Deborah E. McDowell and Arnold Rampersad (Baltimore: The Johns Hopkins University Press, 1989), 144–63.

32. Ann DuCille, *Skin Trade* (Cambridge: Harvard University Press, 1996), 118.
33. Joy James, *Transcending the Talented Tenth: Black Leaders and American Intellectuals* (New York: Routledge, 1997), 53–55.
34. Farah Jasmine Griffin, "Black Feminists and Du Bois: Respectability, Protection, and Beyond," *Annals of the American Academy of Political and Social Science* 568 (March 2000): 28–41.
35. Crucially, the "politics of respectability" is double-edged. In making claim to the title of true womanhood, black women both subverted the racial basis of that ideal and perpetuated damning assumptions about the character of women who did not live up to that ideal. Evelyn Brooks Higginbotham, *Righteous Discontent: The Women's Movement in the Black Baptist Church, 1880–1920* (Cambridge: Harvard University Press, 1993). This tension between agency and discipline inherent in a politics of respectability is not unique to African American aspirations in the early twentieth century. For an account of a similar tension in gay and lesbian campaigns for full citizenship, see Shane Phelan, *Sexual Strangers: Gays, Lesbians, and Dilemmas of Citizenship* (Philadelphia: Temple University Press, 2001).
36. See Frances Foster, "'In Respect to Females . . . ': Differences in the Portrayals of Women by Male and Female Narrators," *Black American Literature Forum* 15 (Summer 1981): 66–70; Carby, *Reconstructing Womanhood*, 20–39; McDowell, "Reading Between Tenses," 146.
37. See Davis, *Women, Race, and Class*, 3–29; bell hooks, *Ain't I a Woman: Black Women and Feminism* (Boston: South End, 1981), 15–49; Jacqueline Dowd Hall, "'The Mind that Burns in Each Body': Women, Rape, and Racial Violence," in *Powers of Desire: The Politics of Sexuality*, ed. Ann Snitow, Christine Stansell, and Sharon Thompson (New York: Monthly Review Press, 1983), 328–49.
38. Lauren Berlant, *The Queen of America Goes to Washington City: Essays on Sex and Citizenship* (Durham: Duke University Press, 1997), 221.
39. On the exclusion of black women from rape law, see Evelyn Brooks Higginbotham, "African-American Women's History and the Metalanguage of Race," *Signs* 17 (Winter 1992): 251–74.
40. Crenshaw, "Whose Story Is It, Anyway?" 418.
41. Hazel V. Carby, "Policing the Black Woman's Body in an Urban Context," *Cultures in Babylon: Black Britain and African America* (London: Verso, 1999), 22–39. Even as Du Bois challenges what Carby describes as the "moral panic" that greeted the northern migration of African American women, his praise for their "efficiency" partakes of the same discourse that Carby criticizes.
42. Dorothy Roberts, *Killing the Black Body: Race, Reproduction, and the Meaning of Liberty* (New York: Vintage, 1997), 86.

43. Stuart Hall, "New Ethnicities," in *Stuart Hall: Critical Dialogues in Cultural Studies*, ed. David Morley and Kuan-Hsing Chen (New York: Routledge, 1996), 448.
44. See Patricia Morton, *Disfigured Images: The Historical Assault on Afro-American Women* (New York: Greenwood Press, 1991), 58–59; Gaines, *Uplifting the Race*, 152–78; Tera W. Hunter, "'The 'Brotherly Love' for Which this City is Proverbial Should Extend to All': The Everyday Lives of Working-Class Women in Philadelphia and Atlanta in the 1890s," *W. E. B. Du Bois, Race, and the City: The Philadelphia Negro and Its Legacy*, ed. Michael B. Katz and Thomas J. Sugrue (Philadelphia: University of Pennsylvania Press, 1998); Cathy J. Cohen, "Deviance as Resistance: A New Research Agenda for the Study of Black Politics," *Du Bois Review* 1 (2004): 27–45.
45. Kenneth W. Warren, "An Inevitable Drift? Oligarchy, Du Bois, and the Politics of Race between the Wars," *boundary 2* 27 (Fall 2000): 160.
46. For a discussion of Du Bois's "innocence" with regard to homosexuality, see Ross, *Manning the Race*, 254–55.
47. Spillers, "Mama's Baby, Papa's Maybe," 74.
48. Roberts, *Killing the Black Body*, 9.
49. Felicia Kornbluh, "The Goals of the National Welfare Rights Movement: Why We Need Them Thirty Years Later," *Feminist Studies* 24 (Spring 1998): 71–74.
50. Uma Narayan, "Towards a Feminist Vision of Citizenship: Rethinking the Implications of Dignity, Political Participation, and Nationality," in *Reconstructing Political Theory: Feminist Perspectives*, ed. Mary Lyndon Shanley and Uma Narayan (University Park: Pennsylvania State University Press, 1997), 51–52.
51. W. E. B. Du Bois, "The Black Mother" (1912) in *W. E. B. Du Bois: A Reader*, ed. David Levering Lewis (New York: Henry Holt, 1995), 294. For an account of congressional debates in which white dependence on (black women's) domestic work was explicitly offered as an argument against expanding welfare benefits, see Dorothy Roberts, "Welfare's Ban on Poor Motherhood," in *Whose Welfare?* ed. Gwendolyn Mink (Ithaca: Cornell University Press, 1999), 160–61.
52. Eileen Boris, "The Power of Motherhood: Black and White Activist Women Redefine the 'Political,'" *Yale Journal of Law and Feminism* 2 (Fall 1989): 25–50.
53. For an analysis of the ways in which black women's achievement, particularly vis-à-vis black men, has been narrated as the flip side of the "pathologies" of single motherhood, see Lubiano, "Black Ladies, Welfare Queens, and State Minstrels."
54. In *The Gift of Black Folk*, which appeared four years after "Damnation," he goes still further, concluding that "the Negro woman more than the women of any other group in America is the protagonist in the fight for an economically independent womanhood in modern countries." W. E. B. Du Bois, *The Gift of Black Folk* (1924; repr., New York: Washington Square Press, 1970), 142.

55. In this regard, Du Bois's arguments resemble claims about care as a practice, rather than a trait associated exclusively or primarily with women. See Joan Tronto, *Moral Boundaries: A Political Argument for an Ethic of Care* (New York: Routledge, 1993).
56. This point is developed by Wendy Sarvasy, who looks to women activists of the early twentieth century as a model for feminist social citizenship. Although she does not offer Du Bois as one of her examples, she quotes "The Servant in the House" to illustrate her notion of "a vision of politics as centrally concerned with nurturing human life." Wendy Sarvasy, "Social Citizenship from a Feminist Perspective," *Hypatia: A Journal of Feminist Philosophy* 12 (Fall 1997): 54–73.
57. Susan Gillman and Alys Eve Weinbaum argue that this comment reflects Du Bois's tendency toward "simple and straightforward juxtaposition" and reveals an "additive logic" that treats these causes as distinct. Although I agree that Du Bois exhibits such a tendency, he also explores the kind of expressly interactive linkages described by Stuart Hall as "articulation." See Susan Gillman and Alys Eve Weinbaum, "Introduction: W. E. B. Du Bois and the Politics of Juxtaposition," in *Next to the Color Line: Gender, Sexuality, and W. E. B. Du Bois* (Minneapolis: University of Minnesota Press, 2007), 1–34. For an account of "articulation," see Stuart Hall, "On Postmodernism and Articulation: An Interview with Stuart Hall," ed. Lawrence Grossberg, in *Stuart Hall: Critical Dialogues in Cultural Studies*, ed. David Morley and Kuan-Hsing Chen (London: Routledge, 1996), 141–45.
58. For a thoughtful exploration of the sources and implications of Du Bois's mother ideal, see Reiland Rabaka, "W. E. B. Du Bois and 'The Damnation of Women': An Essay on Africana Anti-Sexist Critical Social Theory," *Journal of African American Studies* 7 (2003): 37–60.
59. Vilashini Cooppan, "Move on Down the Line: Domestic Science, Transnational Politics, and Gendered Allegory in Du Bois," in *Next to the Color Line: Gender, Sexuality, and W. E. B. Du Bois*, ed. Susan Gillman and Alys Eve Weinbaum (Minneapolis: University of Minnesota Press, 2007), 59.
60. Holloway Sparks, "Dissident Citizenship: Democratic Theory, Political Courage, and Activist Women," *Hypatia: A Journal of Feminist Philosophy* 12 (Fall 1997): 74–111.
61. See Black Public Sphere Collective, ed., *The Black Public Sphere: A Public Culture Book* (Chicago: University of Chicago Press, 1995); Nancy Fraser, "Rethinking the Public Sphere: A Contribution to the Critique of Actually Existing Democracy," *Justice Interruptus: Critical Reflections on the "Postsocialist" Condition* (New York: Routledge, 1997), 69–98.
62. Michael C. Dawson, *Black Visions: The Roots of Contemporary African-American Political Ideologies* (Chicago: University of Chicago Press, 2001), 27 (emphasis in the original).
63. Higginbotham, *Righteous Discontent*.

64. This is not to say that Du Bois does not assign to black women a peculiarly important spiritual role in the community. As early as "The Conservation of Races" (1897), he refers to "the Divine faith of our black mothers" as crucial to the advance of the black race. W. E. B. Du Bois, "The Conservation of Races," in *The Souls of Black Folk*, ed. David W. Blight and Robert Gooding-Williams (Boston: Bedford, 1997), 235.
65. Danielle S. Allen, *Talking to Strangers: Anxieties of Citizenship since Brown v. Board of Education* (Chicago: University of Chicago Press, 2004).
66. Jacques Rancière, *Dis-Agreement: Politics and Philosophy*, trans. Julie Rose (Minneapolis: University of Minnesota Press, 1999), 25.
67. Bonnie Honig, *Democracy and the Foreigner* (Princeton: Princeton University Press, 2001), 101.
68. Dietz, *Turning Operations*, 34.
69. Dietz, *Turning Operations*, 33.
70. For a compelling call to build new research agendas from the actions of "deviant" citizens that challenges the boundaries of what Du Bois would recognize as "normal," see Cohen, "Deviance as Resistance."
71. Jean Bethke Elshtain, "Antigone's Daughters," *Feminism and Politics*, ed. Anne Phillips (New York: Oxford University Press, 1998 [1982]), 363.
72. Elshtain, "Antigone's Daughters," 369.
73. Elshtain, "Antigone's Daughters," 372.
74. Elshtain, "Antigone's Daughters," 369.
75. Elshtain, "Antigone's Daughters," 375.
76. Sharon Hays's study of the effects of welfare reform documents the ways that the incoherence of American attitudes to motherhood vis-à-vis work outside the home in the case of poor (and mostly nonwhite) women is expressed in public policy. Sharon Hays, *Flat Broke with Children: Women in the Age of Welfare Reform* (New York: Oxford University Press, 2003).
77. Warning about the dangers of "womanism," for example, Dietz provides a convincing rejoinder to claims for women's inherent moral superiority. Yet another common usage of the term, coined by Alice Walker to describe black women's challenge to conventional feminism is not mentioned. Dietz, *Turning Operations*, 40–41; Alice Walker, *In Search of Our Mothers' Gardens: Womanist Prose* (New York: Harcourt Brace Jovanovich, 1983), xi–xii.
78. Dietz, *Turning Operations*, 57.
79. Dietz, *Turning Operations*, 58.
80. For critiques of the political usefulness of the metaphor of family that consider race in conjunction with gender, see Patricia Hill Collins, "It's All in the Family: Intersections of Gender, Race, and Nation," *Hypatia* 13 (Summer 1998): 62–83; Paul Gilroy, "It's a Family Affair," *Black Popular Culture*, ed. Gina Dent (Seattle: Bay Press, 1992), 303–16.
81. Dietz, *Turning Operations*, 58.

82. The publicity of motherhood for the poor is illustrated, devastatingly, by Patricia Williams's retelling of the story of a homeless woman who delivered a baby on the subway and then lost that child because her poverty rendered her "unfit" in the view of the state. Patricia J. Williams, *The Alchemy of Race and Rights: Diary of a Law Professor* (Cambridge: Harvard University Press, 1991), 25.
83. Anna Marie Smith, *Welfare Reform and Sexual Regulation* (Cambridge: Cambridge University Press, 2007), 253.
84. Griffin, "Black Feminists and Du Bois," 33.

Chapter Six

1. Toni Morrison, quoted in Paul Gilroy, "Living Memory: A Meeting with Toni Morrison," *Small Acts: Thoughts on the Politics of Black Cultures* (London: Serpent's Tail, 1993), 178.
2. W. E. B. Du Bois, "Worlds of Color," *Foreign Affairs* 3 (April 1925): 423.
3. Brent Hayes Edwards' essay on anti- and intercolonial literature and politics in post–World War I Paris first drew my attention to Du Bois's use of the shadow in this piece. See Brent Hayes Edwards, "The Shadow of Shadows," *positions* 11 (Spring 2003): 11–49.
4. W. E. B. Du Bois, "The Negro Mind Reaches Out," *The New Negro*, ed. Alain Locke (1925; rep., New York: Atheneum, 1992), 413.
5. For a close examination of the connections Du Bois draws—politically, philosophically, and aesthetically—between African and Asian liberation, see Bill V. Mullen, "W. E. B. Du Bois, *Dark Princess*, and the Afro-Asian International," in *Left of the Color Line: Race, Radicalism, and Twentieth-Century Literature of the United States*, ed. Bill V. Mullen and James Smethurst (Chapel Hill: University of North Carolina Press, 2003), 87–106.
6. Du Bois, "Worlds of Color," 423. Du Bois revises these words in the second version, replacing "the ground of disadvantage" with "this wide perspective" and adding that such a perspective reminds that "empire is the heavy hand of capital abroad." Du Bois, "The Negro Mind Reaches Out," 386.
7. The literature on Du Bois's global orientation is, happily, growing apace, as more scholars turn to his anti-imperial and anticolonial work, and closer attention is paid to his writings from World War I until his death. A partial list of books that deal centrally with these aspects of Du Bois's career includes Gerald Horne, *Black and Red: W. E. B. Du Bois and the Afro-American Response to the Cold War, 1944–1963* (Albany: State University of New York Press, 1986); Penny M. Von Eschen, *Race against Empire: Black Americans and Anticolonialism, 1937–1957* (Ithaca: Cornell University Press, 1997); Nikhil Pal Singh, *Black Is a Country: Race and the Unfinished Struggle for Democracy* (Cambridge: Harvard University Press, 2004); Susan Gillman and Alys Eve Weinbaum, eds., *Next to the Color Line: Gender,*

Sexuality, and W. E. B. Du Bois (Minneapolis: University of Minnesota Press, 2007).

8. See Wilson Jeremiah Moses, *The Golden Age of Black Nationalism, 1850–1925* (Oxford: Oxford University Press, 1978), 156–69.

9. See *The Negro* (1915); *Black Folk Then and Now: An Essay in the History and Sociology of the Negro Race* (1939); and *The World and Africa: An Inquiry into the Part Which Africa Has Played in World History* (1946).

10. For two important exceptions within political science, see Manning Marable, *W. E. B. Du Bois: Black Radical Democrat* (Boston: G. K. Hall, 1986); and Adolph L. Reed, Jr., *W. E. B. Du Bois and American Political Thought: Fabianism and the Color Line* (New York: Oxford University Press, 1997). In calling this omission into question, my intention is not to reinforce scholarly boundaries or to disregard the political theoretical contributions of thinkers from other disciplines. To the contrary, my concern is the comfort with which many political theorists engage in debates about the relative merits of various forms of statism and cosmopolitanism without asking how the legacies of slavery and colonialism might affect "our" responsibilities toward impoverished others.

11. Nancy Fraser, "Reframing Justice in a Globalizing World," *New Left Review* 36 (November/December 2005): 78.

12. Amy Kaplan, *The Anarchy of Empire in the Making of U.S. Culture* (Cambridge: Harvard University Press, 2002), 199.

13. For an illuminating discussion of Du Bois's "worldliness," see Paul Gilroy, *Postcolonial Melancholy* (New York: Columbia University Press, 2005), 33–38. It is possible, I think, to learn from and concur with Gilroy's view without accepting his implication that defending a constructive account of American blackness commits one to a "totemic concept of race." Gilroy, *Postcolonial Melancholy*, 145.

14. W. E. B. Du Bois, "To the Nations of the World," in *W. E. B. Du Bois: A Reader*, ed. David Levering Lewis (New York: Henry Holt, 1995), 639.

15. W. E. B. Du Bois, "The Present Outlook for the Dark Races of Mankind," in *The Oxford W. E. B. Du Bois Reader*, ed. Eric J. Sundquist (New York: Oxford University Press, 1996), 53. Drawing on Du Bois's early work and on this essay, in particular, Nahum Chandler remarks that "Du Bois's discourse at the turn of the twentieth century bespeaks a powerful sense of the way that the question of the African American is a question about the possibilities of a global modernity in general." Nahum D. Chandler, "The Figure of W. E. B. Du Bois as a Problem for Thought," *CR: The New Centennial Review* 6 (Winter 2006): 44.

16. Nikhil Pal Singh, "Culture/Wars: Recoding Empire in an Age of Democracy," *American Quarterly* 50 (September 1998): 514. See also Singh, *Black Is a Country*.

17. Etienne Balibar, "Ambiguous Universality," *differences: A Journal of Feminist Cultural Studies* 7 (Spring 1995): 48–75.
18. Du Bois goes further in the 1930s, figuring the dark world as a universal class akin to Marx's proletariat. It is not necessary, however, to embrace a view of the dark world as humanity's salvation in order to learn from examples of transnational black solidarity. See Thomas C. Holt, "The Political Uses of Alienation: W. E. B. Du Bois on Politics, Race, and Culture, 1903–1940," *American Quarterly* 42 (June 1990): 301–23; Joel Olson, "W. E. B. Du Bois and the Race Concept," *Souls* 7 (June 2005): 124–26.
19. W. E. B. Du Bois, "A Negro Nation within the Nation," in *W. E. B. Du Bois Speaks: Speeches and Addresses 1920–1963*, ed. Philip S. Foner (New York: Pathfinder, 1970), 77–86.
20. See Gary Gerstle, *American Crucible: Race and Nation in the Twentieth Century* (Princeton: Princeton University Press, 2001).
21. One might also usefully invert these phrases and speak of a "black nation" and "white world" as a framework for thinking about the development of black communities in a world dominated by whites. The critical promise of such a reversal is apparent in Charles Mills's suggestion that there is a "transnational white polity" bound together by the racial contract, and by Du Bois's language of "the white world" and "the colored world within" in *Dusk of Dawn*. Charles W. Mills, *The Racial Contract* (Ithaca: Cornell University Press, 1997), 29.
22. W. E. B. Du Bois, "Apologia," *The Suppression of the African Slave-Trade to the United States of America, 1638–1870* (1954; repr., New York: Schocken Books, 1969), xxxi. David Levering Lewis notes that subsequent scholarship has proved Du Bois wrong in one regard—he overestimated the number of slaves imported to the United States through the international trade in the years before the Civil War. Lewis also notes that such a mistake makes little difference to the larger thrust of the argument. David Levering Lewis, *W. E. B. Du Bois: Biography of a Race, 1868–1919* (New York: Henry Holt, 1993), 156–57.
23. See, for example, Kaplan, *Anarchy of Empire*, 175–76; William E. Cain, "From Liberalism to Communism: The Political Thought of W. E. B. Du Bois," in *Cultures of United States Imperialism*, ed. Amy Kaplan and Donald E. Pease (Durham: Duke University Press, 1993), 456–73.
24. Manning Marable, "The Pan-Africanism of W. E. B. Du Bois," in *W. E. B. Du Bois on Race and Culture: Philosophy, Politics, and Poetics*, ed. Bernard W. Bell, Emily R. Grosholz, and James B. Stewart (New York: Routledge, 1996), 196.
25. Reed, *W. E. B. Du Bois and American Political Thought*, 78–79. Assessing Du Bois's response to U.S. actions in Liberia, Cedric Robinson offers evidence that this developmental perspective shaped Du Bois's thought well into the twentieth century. Cedric J. Robinson, "W. E. B. Du Bois and Black

Sovereignty," in *Imagining Home: Class, Culture and Nationalism in the African Diaspora*, ed. Sidney J. Lemelle and Robin D. G. Kelley (London: Verso, 1994), 145–57.

26. W. E. B. Du Bois, "The Wounded World," unpublished manuscript quoted in Jennifer D. Keene, "W. E. B. Du Bois and the Wounded World: Seeking Meaning in the First World War for African-Americans," *Peace & Change* 26 (April 2001): 146.

27. For an exploration of *Suppression* in relation to American historiography and wider social scientific trends of its time, see Shamoon Zamir, *Dark Voices: W. E. B. Du Bois and American Thought, 1888–1903* (Chicago: University of Chicago Press, 1995), 68–109.

28. Arnold Rampersad, *The Art and Imagination of W. E. B. Du Bois* (1976; repr., New York: Schocken Books, 1990), 50. As Priscilla Wald points out, this confidence was misplaced; neither of Du Bois's first two books "sufficiently compelled white America to confront its own image in the mirroring gaze that Du Bois had exposed." Priscilla Wald, *Constituting Americans: Cultural Anxiety and Narrative Form* (Durham: Duke University Press, 1995), 191.

29. Du Bois, "Apologia," xxxi-ii. William Cain offers an alternative to Du Bois's assessment. Contrasting Du Bois's final book, the posthumously published autobiography with *Suppression*, Cain argues that "though the *Autobiography* announces its acceptance of Marxist-Leninist ideology, it is *The Suppression of the African Slave Trade* that arguably shows greater insight into the relationship between politics and economics, and that more resourcefully demystifies pure notions of American destiny." William E. Cain, "W. E. B. Du Bois's Autobiography and the Politics of Literature," *Black American Literature Forum* 24 (Summer 1990): 310.

30. Only under Lincoln, Du Bois writes, was the work of suppressing the trade unified in one department, and the first slave trader was hanged for the crime in 1862 (*SAST*, 191). In Appendix C, which lists "typical cases of vessels engaged in the American slave-trade," the last ship mentioned, the *Huntress*, flew the American flag when it delivered slaves to Cuba in 1864 (*SAST*, 298).

31. Du Bois quotes this passage in its entirety, noting that "the clique of political philosophers to which Jefferson belonged never imagined the continued existence of the country with slavery." Without impugning the passion of their efforts to criticize and curtail the trade, Du Bois describes the attempt to lay the blame for slavery beyond the bounds of the colonies themselves as "radical and not strictly truthful" (*SAST*, 48–49). Du Bois records Jefferson's continued opposition to the trade, citing an 1806 statement from the pulpit of the presidency: "I congratulate you, fellow-citizens, on the approach of the period at which you may interpose your authority constitutionally, to withdraw the citizens of the United States from all further participation in those violations of human rights which have been so long continued on the

unoffending inhabitants of Africa, and which the morality, the reputation, and the best interests of our country, have long been eager to proscribe" (*SAST*, 95). As Du Bois observes, this view did not capture the views of the *whole* country, whose preparation for the approach of 1808 witnessed not only the development of antitrade legislation but also the emergence of more robust proslavery arguments in the South (*SAST*, 95–96).

32. Patricia J. Williams, *The Alchemy of Race and Rights: Diary of a Law Professor* (Cambridge: Harvard University Press, 1991), 121. Contrast this view with Abraham Lincoln's, as expressed in his speech on the Kansas-Nebraska Act in 1854. Lincoln also notes the omissions that defined the Founders' allusions to slavery in the Constitution and the unsteady trajectory of efforts to halt the international trade. Yet, in contrast to Du Bois, he attributes their willingness to extend the trade and the institutional life of slavery to "necessity." Abraham Lincoln, "From Speech on the Kansas-Nebraska Act at Peoria, Illinois," in *Lincoln: Selected Speeches and Writings* (New York: Vintage Books/The Library of America, 1992), 96–97.

33. W. E. B. Du Bois, "The Enforcement of the Slave Trade Laws" (1891), in *Writings by W. E. B. Du Bois in Periodicals Edited by Others* I (1891–1909), ed. Herbert Aptheker (Millwood, NY: Kraus-Thomson, 1982), 27.

34. Perhaps the most notable recent articulation of this claim is Barack Obama's March 2008 speech in Philadelphia. Barack Obama, "A More Perfect Union." Available at: http://www.barackobama.com/2008/03/18/remarks_of_senator_barack_obam_53.php; downloaded on September 24, 2008.

35. In no way does this imply that *Suppression* paints a homogeneous picture of American responses to the trade. Indeed, Du Bois takes pains to trace the forces of moral opposition, particularly among the Quakers, and to provide a nuanced account of when and to what extent their views had an effect on policy.

36. Du Bois was far from alone among African American political thinkers to recognize and respond to the Haitian Revolution. See Ifeoma Kiddoe Nwankwo, *Black Cosmopolitanism: Racial Consciousness and Transnational Identity in the Nineteenth-Century Americas* (Philadelphia: University of Pennsylvania Press, 2005).

37. This denial may be most obvious in the withholding of diplomatic relations with Haiti until 1862. Laurent Dubois, *Avengers of the New World: The Story of the Haitian Revolution* (Cambridge: Belknap/Harvard, 2004), 303.

38. Michel-Rolph Trouillot, *Silencing the Past: Power and the Production of History* (Boston: Beacon Press, 1995), 88.

39. W. E. B. Du Bois, *The Gift of Black Folk: Negroes in the Making of America* (1924; repr. New York: Washington Square Press, 1970), 77.

40. W. E. B. Du Bois, *Color and Democracy: Colonies and Peace* (New York: Harcourt, Brace and Co., 1945), 67–68.

41. W. E. B. Du Bois, *The Negro* (1915; repr., Mineola, NY: Dover, 2001), 103.

42. Bonnie Honig, *Democracy and the Foreigner* (Princeton: Princeton University Press, 2001).
43. My comments here are informed by William Connolly's notion of "a politics of *nonterritorial democratization of global issues.*" William E. Connolly, *Identity\Difference: Democratic Negotiations of Political Paradox* (Ithaca: Cornell University Press, 1991), 218 (emphasis in the original).
44. Eric Lott, "After Identity, Politics: The Return of Universalism," *New Literary History* 31 (2000): 677.
45. For a helpful overview of the colonization movement, see Eric Foner, "Lincoln and Colonization," in *Our Lincoln: New Perspectives on Lincoln and His World*, ed. Eric Foner (New York: W. W. Norton, 2008), 135–66.
46. Du Bois, *The Negro*, 146. See also a slightly amended version of this claim in "The Souls of White Folk," in *Darkwater* (*DW* 27). Of course, the depth of the challenge Du Bois poses here is qualified by the masculinism of the formulation.
47. Martha C. Nussbaum, "Patriotism and Cosmopolitanism," in Martha C. Nussbaum, *For Love of Country: Debating the Limits of Patriotism*, ed. Joshua Cohen (Boston: Beacon Press, 1996), 5.
48. Nussbaum, "Patriotism and Cosmopolitanism," 16.
49. W. E. B. Du Bois, *The Autobiography of W. E. B. Du Bois: A Soliloquy on Viewing My Life from the Last Decade of Its First Century* (New York: International Publishers, 1968), 422.
50. Martha C. Nussbaum, "Introduction: Cosmopolitan Emotions?" in Nussbaum, *For Love of Country?*, ix-xiv. This introduction was added to the 2002 edition of the collection, and the title was slightly amended. All references to essays from the original edition will be cited as such.
51. Martha C. Nussbaum, "Reply," in Nussbaum, *For Love of Country*, 133.
52. Nussbaum, "Patriotism and Cosmopolitanism," 11–15.
53. Nussbaum, "Patriotism and Cosmopolitanism," 7.
54. Nussbaum, "Patriotism and Cosmopolitanism," 9.
55. Sissela Bok, "From Part to Whole," in Nussbaum, *For Love of Country*, 38–44.
56. Du Bois's defense of "A Negro Nation within the Nation" during the same period similarly suggests a nested relationship in which the development of the smaller African American community (economically, socially, educationally, politically) would pave the way for more equal participation in the United States more generally. Du Bois, "A Nation within the Nation," 77–86.
57. Immanuel Wallerstein, "Neither Patriotism Nor Cosmopolitanism," in Martha C. Nussbaum, *For Love of Country* 122–24. Although not explicitly framed in terms of entrenched global inequalities, Richard Falk's critique of neoliberalism and his defense of "globalization-from-below" offer resources through which to address such inequalities. Richard Falk, "Revisioning Cosmopolitanism," in Nussbaum, *For Love of Country*, 53–60.

58. It is curious, in part, because much of Nussbaum's work is marked by an elegant use of history.
59. Nussbaum, "Patriotism and Cosmopolitanism," 12–14.
60. Nussbaum, "Reply," 135.
61. Martha C. Nussbaum, "Toward a Globally Sensitive Patriotism," *Daedalus* 137 (Summer 2008): 78–93.
62. In *The World and Africa*, he develops this claim against the backdrop of the "catastrophe" of World War II. Offering as an example "a blameless, cultured beautiful young woman in a London suburb," Du Bois asks: "How far is such a person responsible for the crimes of colonialism?" In reply, he allows that "it will in all probability not occur to her that she has any responsibility whatsoever, and that may well be true." Yet, he continues, "Equally, it may be true that her income is the result of starvation, theft, and murder; that it involves ignorance, disease, and crime on the part of thousands; that the system which sustains the security, leisure, and comfort she enjoys is based on the suppression, exploitation, and slavery of the majority of mankind." Du Bois, *The World and Africa*, 41–42.
63. Nussbaum, "Reply," 138.
64. Charles L. Briggs, "Genealogies of Race and Culture and the Failure of Vernacular Cosmopolitanisms: Rereading Franz Boas and W. E. B. Du Bois," *Public Culture* 17 (Winter 2005): 87.
65. Craig Calhoun, "Social Solidarity as a Problem for Cosmopolitan Democracy," in *Identities, Affiliations, and Allegiances*, ed. Seyla Benhabib, Ian Shapiro, and Danilo Petranović (Cambridge: Cambridge University Press, 2007), 287.
66. Judith Butler, "Universality in Culture," in Nussbaum, *For Love of Country*, 48. This argument also resonates with the idea of "democratic takings" discussed in chapter 5. See Bonnie Honig, *Democracy and the Foreigner* (Princeton: Princeton University Press, 2001).
67. Ross Posnock, *Color and Culture: Black Writers and the Making of the Modern Intellectual* (Cambridge: Harvard University Press, 1998), 13.
68. Robert Reid-Pharr, *Once You Go Black: Choice, Desire, and the Black American Intellectual* (New York: New York University Press, 2007), 17.
69. Benjamin R. Barber, "Constitutional Faith," in Nussbaum, *For Love of Country*, 31. For a thoughtful, critical examination of recent arguments for "civic" nationalism, see Patchen Markell, "Making Affect Safe for Democracy? On 'Constitutional Patriotism,'" *Political Theory* 28 (February 2000): 38–63. For a helpful critique of the distinction between ethnic and civic nationalism, see Will Kymlicka, "Misunderstanding Nationalism," in *Politics in the Vernacular: Nationalism, Multiculturalism, and Citizenship* (Oxford: Oxford University Press, 2001), 242–53. Although Kymlicka dismisses the idea that African Americans constitute a national minority, his observations about the cultural component of "civic" nationalism, on the one hand, and his refutation

of claims about the backwardness of "minority cultural nationalism," on the other, dovetails with the argument I draw from Du Bois.

70. Barber, "Constitutional Faith," 36.
71. Barber, "Constitutional Faith," 31.
72. Barber, "Constitutional Faith," 32–33.
73. *The Federalist Papers*, ed. Clinton Rossiter, no. 42 (New York: New American Library, 1961), 266. Du Bois identifies the source of this quotation as *The Federalist*, no. 41 (*SAST*, 65).
74. Barber, "Constitutional Faith," 35.
75. Barber, "Constitutional Faith," 34. In this passage, Barber effectively reproduces the image of concentric circles.
76. For a critical account of the collapse of distinctions between race and ethnicity, see Ian F. Haney Lopez, "'A Nation of Minorities': Race, Ethnicity, and Reactionary Colorblindness," *Stanford Law Review* 59 (February 2007): 985–1063.
77. Barber, "Constitutional Faith," 31.
78. Barber, "Constitutional Faith," 32.
79. In the larger argument from which the quotation is taken, Barber does dedicate a good deal of attention to slavery and to the importance of unfreedom to any understanding of American history. Nonetheless, his insistence on American identity as "rooted in principle" suggests that the treatment slavery might be read as a variation on what Trouillot calls a "formula of banalization," a mechanism for acknowledging historical atrocity but trivializing its distinctive significance. Benjamin R. Barber, *An Aristocracy of Everyone: The Politics of Education and the Future of America* (New York: Ballantine, 1992), 46. Trouillot, *Silencing the Past*, esp. 96–97.
80. Devon Carbado, "Racial Naturalization," *American Quarterly* 57 (2005): 633–58.
81. Du Bois's claim resonates with what Ellison calls "the fantasy of a blackless America": "the recurring fantasy of solving one basic problem of American democracy by 'getting shut' of the blacks through various wishful schemes that would banish them from the nation's bloodstream, from its social structure, and from its conscience and historical consciousness." Ralph Ellison, "What America Would Be Like without Blacks," in *Going to the Territory* (New York: Vintage, 1986), 104–05.
82. Du Bois, "Apologia," xxxii.
83. George Kateb, "The Adequacy of the Canon," in *Patriotism and Other Mistakes* (New Haven: Yale University Press, 2006), 384–407.
84. See Fraser, "Reframing Justice in a Globalizing World," 69–88. Thomas McCarthy challenges the image of a modern world divided among self-contained national units and calls for a retroactive conception of global justice. See Thomas McCarthy, *Race, Empire, and the Idea of Development* (Cambridge: Cambridge University Press, 2009), 226–27.

85. Building on Du Bois's remarks just before leaving the United States for Ghana ("Chin up and fight on, but realize that American Negroes can't win."), Taylor argues that Du Bois is not evincing despair so much as identifying the limits of any anti-racist politics that is confined to "the idea of America, at least as it stands." Paul Taylor, "What's the Use of Calling Du Bois a Pragmatist?" *Metaphilosophy* 35 (January 2004): 101–02.
86. Taylor, "What's the Use of Calling Du Bois a Pragmatist?" 102.
87. Another approach follows Homi Bhabha, for whom "post" indicates movement "beyond." As Bhabha explains, it is not a refutation but "a space of intervention in the here and now." Homi Bhabha, *The Location of Culture* (London: Routledge, 1994), 7.
88. W. E. B. Du Bois, *In Battle for Peace: The Story of My 83rd Birthday* (New York: Masses and Mainstream, 1952), 163.

INDEX OF WRITINGS OF W. E. B. DU BOIS

The Autobiography of W. E. B. Du Bois, 129–30, 169n30

"The Black Mother," 177n51
Black Reconstruction in America, 13, 18–20, 23–45, 65–66, 107, 110, 122

Color and Democracy: Colonies and Peace, 184n40
"The Conservation of Races," 154n32, 179n64
"Criteria of Negro Art," 169n31, 171n56

"The Damnation of Women," 21, 72, 97–114
Darkwater: Voices from Within the Veil, 78, 100, 107, 108
"The Development of a People," 10–11
Dusk of Dawn, 9, 18, 33, 48, 55, 71–95, 119, 121

"The Enforcement of the Slave Trade Laws," 184n33

"From the Boston 'Globe,'" 151n11

The Gift of Black Folk, 11, 33, 154n32, 155n37, 177n54, 184n39

In Battle for Peace, 187n88

"Jefferson Davis as a Representative of Civilization," 165n65, 169n27
John Brown, 20–21, 47–70

"The Latest Craze," 157n58
"A Litany at Atlanta," 48

The Negro, 154n32, 185n46
"The Negro and Social Reconstruction," 155n35
"The Negro Mind Reaches Out," 115–16
"A Negro Nation within the Nation," 119, 185n56
"The Niagara Movement: Address to the Country," 47, 162n34, 164n50

"Of the Dawn of Freedom," 23, 123–24
"Of the Ruling of Men," 108

"The Present Outlook for the Dark Races of Mankind," 181n15

"Reconstruction and Its Benefits," 153n24, 155n38

"The Servant in the House," 107, 178n56
The Souls of Black Folk, 7–20, 23–34, 39–40, 43, 45, 47, 54, 72, 78, 84–85, 108, 115, 119, 125, 129, 133

"The Souls of White Folk," 119, 185n46
"The Study of the Negro Problems," 167n6
"The Superior Race," 170n39
The Suppression of the African Slave-Trade to the United States of America, 1638–1870, 18–19, 21–22, 59, 115–38

"The Talented Tenth," 166n4, 167n12
"To the Nations of the World," 181n14

"Virginia," 144n8

The World and Africa, 186n62
"Worlds of Color," 115–16
"The Wounded World," 183n26

INDEX

abolition democracy, 26, 152n14
Adams, John, 50
Adorno, Theodor, 42
affirmative action, 15
Africa
    contributions to world history of, 8, 117, 126, 146n22
    Du Bois and 81–82, 115–17
    Du Bois, gender, and, 107–09
    link between U.S. and, 60, 125
    shadows and, 8, 115–16
African Americans, contributions of. *See* contributions of African Americans
Alcoff, Linda, 165–66n71
Allen, Danielle, 110
American Assumption, 30–31, 40, 107
American Dream, 31–32
American exceptionalism, 43, 125, 126, 134
Anderson, Benedict, 147n38
Andrews, William, 72, 77
Anker, Elizabeth, 164n62
anti-slave trade law (1794), 127, 128
apologies for slavery and/or Jim Crow, 1–4, 10, 12, 36, 37, 38, 40, 143n4, 143n5
Apostolidis, Paul, 167n13
Appiah, Anthony, 148–49n54
Aptheker, Herbert, 162n31, 162n36
Arendt, Hannah, 42, 145n19, 159n71
Aristotle, 73
Ashcroft, John, 69–70, 166n75

autobiography, 75–80, 83
The Autobiography of W. E. B. Du Bois, 129–30, 169n30

Baldwin, James, 50
Balibar, Etienne, 93, 119
Banks, Russell, 53
Barber, Benjamin, 118, 133–36
Behdad, Ali, 70, 166n74
Bell, Derrick, 50
Bennett, Lerone, Jr., 50–51
Bercovitch, Sacvan, 50, 51, 60
Berlant, Lauren, 103
Best, Stephen, 20, 159n75
Bhabha, Homi, 187n87
Bible, 52–53, 55–56
Bickford, Susan 173n10
Binder, Guyora, 145n15
Bismark, Otto von, 168–69n25
Bittker, Boris, 36
"black counterpublic," 110
Black Flame trilogy, 151n12
black humanity, 26, 28, 33–35, 41, 76, 80, 91, 116, 129, 138
Black Manifesto, 37
"The Black Mother," 177n51
"black noise," 20
Black Public Sphere Collective, 110
Black Radical Congress (BRC), 37–38
Black Reconstruction in America, 13, 18–20, 23–45, 65–66, 107, 110, 122

black worldliness, 118–20, 129–37
Blight, David, 25, 49, 147n38, 148n47, 151n10, 158n70, 166n75
Blum, Edward, 56
Bobo, Lawrence, 38, 152n18
Bok, Sissela, 130–31
Booth, W. James, 42, 146n28
Boris, Eileen, 177n52
Briggs, Charles, 132
Brooks, Roy, 144n6, 156n50
Brophy, Alfred, 157n57
Brown, John, 71, 133. *See also John Brown*
   activism of, 51–53
   overview of, 47–51
   terror in "postracial" America and, 61–70
Brown, Owen, 53
Brown, Wendy, 16–17, 159n76, 164n63
Bruce, Blanche K., 41
Bruss, Elizabeth, 170n38
Bruyneel, Kevin, 149n56
Bush, George W., 3, 38, 69
Butler, Judith, 133, 158n66, 174n20
Byerman, Keith, 162n35

Cain, William, 68, 160n4, 163n38, 165n66, 183n29
Calhoun, Craig, 133
capitalism, 29, 76, 93, 114, 120–21
Carbado, Devon, 136, 172n67
Carby, Hazel, 101, 148n46, 168n24, 176n41
Carlyle, Thomas, 168n25
caste segregation, 79–80
Chandler, Nahum, 72, 165n66, 181n15
charity, 40
Cheng, Anne Anlin, 144n7
citizenship
   American, 24–25, 36, 99, 110, 136
   democratic, 19, 21, 29, 71–72, 98–100, 110, 113
   economic independence and, 28–32, 106
   exclusion and, 93, 99, 113–14
   feminist theories of, 72, 98, 102, 111–14, 175n25, 178n56
   former slaves and, ix, 7, 15, 23–24, 27, 30, 43, 47, 151n4, 153n23
   gender and, 21, 65–66, 98, 106, 107–8, 165n64
   multiracial, 90
   prison and, 64
   world, 118, 130, 137

civic nationalism, 129–36
Civil Liberties Act (1988), 37, 41
civil rights, ix–xi, 13, 14–16, 26–27, 30, 36, 39, 41, 66, 67, 157n60
Civil Rights Act (1964), 15
Civil War
   Amendments, 14, 39, 41
   black contributions to, 3, 13, 32–33, 40, 70, 109
   loss and, 11–12, 25
   slavery and, 25–26, 27–28, 135
   violence of, 53, 69, 122
class divisions, 16, 30–31, 39–40, 131–32
Clinton, Bill, 38
Cohen, Cathy, 170n44, 177n44, 179n70
Coles, Romand, 149n57
Collins, Patricia Hill, 98, 179n80
colonialism, 6, 37, 60–61, 71, 76, 88, 116, 118, 120–21, 171n60, 181n10
color line, 7, 81, 86, 103, 108, 115, 131, 139
Color and Democracy: Colonies and Peace, 184n40
communism, 76
Connolly, William, 4, 21, 71, 72, 74–75, 81, 88–95, 161n17, 170n47, 171n60, 172n70, 172n71, 185n43
"The Conservation of Races," 154n32, 179n64
Constitution, 14, 123, 124, 134–35
constitution, of John Brown, 53, 161n27
contemporary racial conditions
   as crisis, 63–64
   reparations and, 41–42
   slavery and, 2, 13
contributions of African Americans
   to emancipation, 2–3, 32–33, 121, 126–27
   reparations and, 40–41
   to United States, 26, 28
   women and, 109–10
Conyers, John, 37
Cooper, Anna Julia, 100–101, 102, 108, 175n30
Cooppan, Vilashini, 109
cosmopolitanism, 22, 118, 129–33, 139, 181n10
Council on African Affairs, 146n22
Crenshaw, Kimberlé, 103, 174n21
"Criteria of Negro Art," 169n31, 171n56

Cromwell, Oliver, 52
Crummell, Alexander, 8, 146n31

"The Damnation of Women," 21, 72, 97–114
Darity, William, 154n28
Darkwater: Voices from Within the Veil, 78, 100, 107, 108
"darker world," 116–19, 133, 139, 182n18
Darwinism, social, 61
Davis, Angela, 152n14, 164n58, 173n4
Davis, David Brion, 152n13
Davis, Jefferson, 69, 165n65, 169n27
Dawson, Michael, 38, 110, 154n31
Declaration of Independence, 3, 53, 124, 134, 162n31
Delany, Martin, 57
Delany, Samuel, 169n33
deliberative theory, 62–63
"The Development of a People," 10–11
Dietz, Mary, 98, 100, 111–13, 179n77
    Turning Operations, 111–13
Dionne, E. J., 166n75
double-consciousness, 7, 34, 73–74, 86, 116
Douglass, Frederick, 28, 54, 155n34
    John Brown and, 49, 51, 57, 62, 67–68
Du Bois, Alexander, 81
Dubois, Laurent, 184n37
DuCille, Ann, 101
Duke, David, 67
Dumm, Thomas, 166n2, 172n76
Dusk of Dawn, 9, 18, 33, 48, 55, 71–95, 119, 121

economic independence, of women, 106–7
economic reconstruction, 28–32
education,
    development and, 29–30, 87, 109, 185n56
    inequality and, 2, 9, 14, 154n29
    Reconstruction and, 31, 33
Edwards, Brent Hayes, 180n3
Ellison, James, 43
Ellison, Ralph Waldo, 146n28, 163n47, 187n81
Elshtain, Jean Bethke, 100, 111, 112
emancipation
    black contributions to, 2–3, 32–33, 121, 126–27

King and, ix–x
    realities of, 23
    reparations and, 41
    as unintended event, 27–28
Emerson, Ralph Waldo, 53, 163n43
"The Enforcement of the Slave Trade Laws," 184n33
equality,
    absolute, 28
    formal, 14–15, 20, 26, 28, 39, 148n53
    gender, 21, 100
essays, 18–19, 78, 150n63
"ethic of care," 107
Ethiopianism, 117
Euben, Peter, 67
exception, 21, 84–86
exemplarity, 20–21, 71–75, 83–87, 167n11, 168n24
    of African American women, 97–114
expansionism, 60

Falk, Richard, 185n57
Fanon, Frantz, 171n57, 171n65
Faust, Drew Gilpin, 166n75
feminist theory. *See also* women
    of citizenship, 111–14
    in "The Damnation of Women," 100–102
    democratic citizenship and, 97–100
Ferguson, Kathy, 166n74
Ferrara, Alessandro, 167n11
Fine, Gary Alan, 49
Fish, Stanley, 144n5
Flatley, Jonathan, 146–47n32, 149n62
Foner, Eric, 154n26, 185n45
For Love of Country (Nussbaum), 117–20, 129–37
Forman, James, 37
"forty acres and a mule," 2, 31
Foster, Frances, 176n36
Foucault, Michel, 81, 89, 169n36
Franklin, Benjamin, 50
Fraser, Nancy, 110, 117, 187n84
Freedmen's Bureau, 23, 29–30, 31, 34, 39
freedom, contending meanings of, 24–25
Freehling, William, 162n35
French Revolution, 60
Freud, Sigmund, 121
"From the Boston 'Globe,'" 151n11
"fugitive pieces," 17–20

Fugitive Slave Act (1850), 19, 52
fugitive slaves, 13, 19, 27–28, 32–33, 56, 76

Gaines, Kevin, 153n23, 174n18, 177n44
Garnet, Henry Highland, 57
Garrison, William Lloyd, 63
Gates, Henry Louis, Jr., 150n63
Gelley, Alexander, 73
gender, 16, 21, 77, 97–114
genealogy, 80–83, 87–88, 108–9
"General Strike," 13, 32–33
generosity, Connolly and, 91, 93
German reparations, 37
Gerstle, Gary, 182n20
Gettysburg Address, 134
Ghana, 6, 117, 188n85
Giddings, Paula, 175n28
The Gift of Black Folk, 11, 33, 154n32, 177n54, 184n39
Gilkes, Cheryl Townsend, 100
Gillman, Susan, 173n5, 178n57
Gilroy, Paul, 179n80, 181n13
global political imagination
　of Du Bois, 20, 21–22, 25, 116–29
　John Brown and, 60
　For Love of Country and, 129–37
　Suppression and, 120–29
Gooding-Williams, Robert, 18, 94, 146n29, 146n31, 148n47, 150n68, 153n23, 155n34, 162n33, 167n6
Griffin, Farah Jasmine, 176n34, 180n84
Guinier, Lani, 151n11, 158n65, 172n74
Guthrie, Woody, 135

Habermas, Jürgen, 110, 159n71
Hahn, Steven, 154n33
Haitian Revolution, 52, 60, 122, 123, 126–28, 132–33, 145n19
Hall, Jacqueline Dowd, 176n37
Hall, Stuart, 94, 177n43, 178n57
Hanchard, Michael, 63, 149n56
Hancock, Ange-Marie, 174n21
Haraway, Donna, 146n26, 146n27, 150n66
Hargrove, Frank, 1
Harpers Ferry, 52–54, 57, 67–68
Harris, Cheryl, 152n17, 171n62
Hart, Albert Bushnell, 155n34
Hartman, Saidiya, 10, 20, 159n75
Hays, Sharon, 179n76
Hayward, Clarissa Rile, 173n9

Henry, Charles, 155–56n43
heroic politics, 66–67
Higginbotham, A. Leon, 155n40
Higginbotham, Evelyn Brooks, 102, 176n39
Hochschild, Jennifer, 31
Holland, Catherine, 173n10
Holt, Thomas, 7, 77, 151n6, 158n70, 182n18
Honig, Bonnie, 110–11, 161n20, 186n66
hooks, bell, 176n37
Horsley, Neal, 64
Horton, James O., 163n40
Hose, Sam, 48
H.R. 40, 37
Huggins, Nathan, 168n25
Hughes, Langston, 135
Hunter, Tera, 177n44
Hyman, John A., 41

identity. *See also* racial identity
　American, 3, 98, 120, 132–36, 158n70, 187n79
　categories, 15–16, 21, 74–75, 88, 91, 92, 94, 95, 138
　whiteness and, 119
　women and, 112–13
identity politics, 13, 15–16, 71, 87
ignorance, overcoming, ix, 9, 76, 121
In Battle for Peace, 187n88
incarceration, racial inequality and, xi, 9, 41, 63–64, 88
indigenous people, reparations for, 37
intersectionality, 12, 16, 100, 174n21

Jackson, Stonewall, 69
James, Joy, 101
"Jefferson Davis as a Representative of Civilization," 165n65, 169n27
Jefferson, Thomas, 50, 124, 183–84n31
Jim Crow, x, 7, 8, 12, 19, 20, 27, 35, 39, 43, 85, 107, 113, 119
John Brown. 20–21, 47–70. *See also* Brown, John
John Brown's Holy War, 163n39, 165n67
Johnson, Andrew, 153n25
Johnson, Walter, 36, 145n11

Kaplan, Amy, 118
Kaplan, Caren, 79
Kateb, George, 5, 138

Katznelson, Ira, 157n59
Kawash, Samira, 150n65
Katrina (Hurricane), 14, 40–41
Keenan, Alan, 159n79
Kelley, Robin D. G., 147n35, 148n45, 156n45
Kinder, Donald, 152n18
King, Martin Luther, Jr., ix–x, 14, 63, 134
Kirkland, Frank, 13
Klinkner, Philip, 152n17, 164–65n64
Kolchin, Peter, 32
Kornbluh, Felicia, 177n49
Ku Klux Klan, 26, 49
Kymlicka, Will, 173n6, 186–87n69

LaCapra, Dominick, 156n49
land distribution, 30–32
"The Latest Craze," 157n58
Lawrence, Charles R., III, 158n67
Lawrence, Jacob, 160n9
Lawson, Bill, 36, 173n10
Lee, Robert E., 69
Lemert, Charles, 24
Lewis, David Levering, 66, 100, 154n32, 174n24, 182n22
Lieberman, Robert, 157n62
Lincoln, Abraham, 19, 31–32, 128, 134, 184n32
Lindberg, Kathryne, 78
Lipsitz, George, 157n61, 171n62
Lister, Ruth, 98, 175n25
"A Litany at Atlanta," 48
Littlefield, Daniel, 161n22
Litwack, Leon, 154n26
Locke, Alain, 115
Logan, Rayford, 23
Lopez, Ian Haney, 187n76
Lost Cause, 8, 35, 69, 166n75
Lott, Eric, 185n44
Loury, Glenn, 64
L'Ouverture, Toussaint, 49, 52, 54, 121, 126–27, 132–33, 135
Lubiano, Wahneema, 173n12, 177n53
lynching, 2, 12, 18, 26, 48, 64, 74, 101

Madison, James, 134–35
manhood, 16, 65–66, 106
Marable, Manning, 120, 147n35, 181n10
Markell, Patchen, 186n69

Marx, Karl, 17, 29, 76, 121, 153n21, 182n18
McCarthy, Thomas, 9, 155n39, 159n71, 159n72, 160n7, 187n84
McClure, Kirstie, 73
McDowell, Deborah, 175n31, 176n36
McEachin, Donald, 2
McVeigh, Timothy, 64
memory
  "black counter-memory," 25, 27, 68
  of John Brown, 51, 53, 62, 67, 69, 70, 133
  "one long," 82, 94
  reparations and, 36–37
  "segregated historical memory," 49, 59
  of slavery, 10–12, 19, 42, 68, 164n62
  Wole Soyinka on, 1
metaphors, 7–9, 72–73, 131, 167n7
micropolitics, 88–90
militancy, 64–66
Mill, John Stuart, 108
Mills, Charles, 121, 145n21, 182n21
Mink, Gwendolyn, 174n13
Minow, Martha, 152n15, 159n72
moral absolutism, 64
moralism, 121, 137
Morrison, Toni, 22, 76, 92, 115, 141, 146n30
Morton, Patricia, 177n44
Moses, Wilson Jeremiah, 181n8
Mostern, Kenneth, 87, 170n37
motherhood, 12, 98–99, 104–6, 111–13, 177n53, 179n76, 180n82
"mother idea," 108–9
Moynihan Report, 104
Mullen, Bill, 180n5
Myers, Ella, 172n71

Narayan, Uma, 177n50
National Association for the Advancement of Colored People (NAACP), 146n22
National Coalition of Blacks for Reparations in America (N'COBRA), 37
National Welfare Rights Organization, 113
Native Americans
  genocide of, 91
  reparations for, 15, 37
  theft of land from, 60
  Virginia resolution and, 1, 3

The Negro, 154n32, 185n46
"The Negro and Social Reconstruction," 155n35
"The Negro Mind Reaches Out," 115–16
"A Negro Nation within the Nation," 119, 185n56
neoslavery, 26, 39
Niagara Movement, 53–54, 146n22
"The Niagara Movement: Address to the Country," 47, 162n34, 164n50
Nietzsche, Friedrich, 81, 89
Nobles, Melissa, 144n4, 144n5
Norman, Wayne, 173n6
Norton, Anne, 17
Norton, Gale, 166n75
Nudelman, Franny, 162n29
Nussbaum, Martha, 22, 118, 129–36
Nwankwo, Ifeoma Kiddoe, 184n36

Oates, Stephen, 163n39, 163n43
Obama, Barack, x, 14, 41, 47, 62, 84, 184n34
"Of the Dawn of Freedom," 23, 123–24
"Of the Ruling of Men," 108
Oliver, Melvin, 36, 40, 157n60
Olson, Joel, 155n41, 164n53, 172n69, 174n16, 182n18
Orfield, Gary, 154n29
original sin, slavery as America's, 125, 128
"out-law" genre, 79

Painter, Nell Irvin, 163n42
Pan-African conferences, 146n22
Pan-Africanism, 95, 117, 118
parenthood, 104–6. *See also* motherhood
Parks, Rosa, 14
Pauley, Garth, 174n22
Personal Responsibility and Work Opportunity Act (1996), 99
Phelan, Shane, 176n35
Plato, 73
Plummer, Brenda Gayle, 175n28
political activity, black women and, 107–10
political theory
 canon, 5–6
 critical, 13, 17, 24
 global framing of, 21, 116–20, 129–37
 in shadow of deep disappointment, 7–17
 race and, 5–7, 74–75, 91, 122

Posnock, Ross, 133, 168n24, 171n56
post-civil rights era, x, 14–15, 24, 51, 64, 71, 94
"postracial" era, x, 16, 61, 133
Pottawatomie, 52, 58, 163n43
presentism, 13
"The Present Outlook for the Dark Races of Mankind," 181n15
present-past
 "fugitive pieces" and, 17–22
 idea of, 20, 26, 56
 political theory and, 7–17, 139
 two passing figures of, 11–13, 16, 25, 28, 97
prisons, racial inequality and, xi, 9, 41, 63–64, 88
"problem," 11, 18, 21, 71–75, 84–87, 89, 135, 167n5, 167n7
propaganda, 90
"public sphere," 110

Quarles, Benjamin, 49

Rabaka, Reiland, 178n58
race
 contemporary attitudes on, 9, 41–42, 63
 modernity and, 5–7, 42, 60, 81, 116, 129, 131, 138, 155n39
 political theory and, 5–7, 145n21, 148–49n54
 slavery and, 4–5, 10, 16
 violence and, 48, 51, 61, 103, 137
Race Concept, 18, 21, 74–80, 79, 81–91
racial identity, 15–16, 74–75, 81–83, 87–95, 129, 158n70
racial injustice
 acknowledgment of, x–xi, 35–45, 90
 contemporary, 14–15, 21, 43–44, 49, 55, 61–64, 94
 following Reconstruction, 17, 26, 36, 65
 ignorance and, ix, 9, 76, 121
 Martin Luther King Jr. and, ix–xi
 memory of, 10–12
 reparations and, 35–45
racial justice, 14–15, 27, 43, 67, 69, 76
racial time, 63
racial resentment, 90–92
Rampersad, Arnold, 55–56, 76–77, 121, 154n30, 168n25, 171n59
Rancière, Jacques, 110, 150n66

rape, 103, 111, 176n39
reconciliation, 1–4
Reconstruction, ix, 7, 19, 76, 137
    correcting history of, 7–9, 20, 23–45, 47–49, 70, 123–24, 152n16
    reparations and, 35–45
"Reconstruction and Its Benefits," 153n24, 155n38
Reed, Adolph, 157n63, 181n10, 182n25
Reid, Ira, 168n24
Reid-Pharr, Robert, 133
Reinhardt, Mark, 13, 175n29
reparations, 1–2, 12, 20, 35–45
reproductive liberty, 104–6, 114
resentment, racial, 90–92
respectability, politics of, 102, 176n35
revolution, 58–59, 69, 126–27, 129, 132
Reynolds, David, 160n12, 164n62
Roberts, Dorothy, 105, 176n42, 177n51
Robinson, Cedric, 182–83n25
Robinson, Randall, 37
Rosewood massacre, 37
Ross, Marlon, 97, 177n46
Rousseau, Jean-Jacques, 43–44, 153n22
Rout, Leslie, 174n14

Sanders, Lynn, 63, 152n18
Sarvasy, Wendy, 178n56
Scott, David, 145n19, 161n20
Scott, Joan, 79, 149n55
second-sight, 7, 34
"segregated historical memory," 49
self-fashioning, 89–90
self-help, 27
September 11, 61, 130, 164n62
"The Servant in the House," 107
sexual freedom, 103–6
Shadd, Mary, 101
shadow, metaphor of, 7–9, 78, 115–16
Shapiro, Thomas, 36, 40, 157n60
Shaw, Gwendolyn Dubois, 160n9
Shelby, Tommie, 170n43
Shklar, Judith, 24–25, 145n14, 151n4, 174n15
Shulman, George, 67–68, 159n82, 163n48, 166n73, 172n70
Singh, Nikhil, 119
slave mother, 12
slavery
    abolition of, 120–29

acknowledgment and reparations for, 35–45
black exemplarity and, 21
Civil War and, 25–26, 27–28, 32–33
"fugitive pieces" and, 19–20
legacies of, 92, 111–14
memory of, 1–4, 9–12
modernity and, 5–7, 13
sexual violence of, 12, 103
shadows of, 19, 21, 41, 88, 115–16
in study of modern life, 5–7, 13
women and, 97–100
slave trade, abolishing, 120–29
Smith, Anna Marie, 113
Smith, Gerrit, 52
Smith, Rogers, 144n10, 152n17, 164–65n64, 173n10
Smith, Ryan, 152n18
Smith, Sidonie, 77
social Darwinism, 16, 61
Sorrow Songs, 13
The Souls of Black Folk, 7–20, 23–34, 39–40, 43, 45, 47, 54, 72, 78, 84–85, 108, 115, 119, 125, 129, 133
"The Souls of White Folk," 119, 185n46
Soyinka, Wole, 1, 156n48
Sparks, Holloway, 178n60
Spelman, Elizabeth, 174n17
Spillers, Hortense, 97, 100, 105
Spivak, Gayatri Chakravorty, 175n31
Stepto, Robert, 149n62
Stevens, Thaddeus, 154n27
"The Study of the Negro Problems," 167n6
Sturken, Marita, 50
Sumner, Charles, 154n27
Sundquist, Eric, 149n62, 163n38
"The Superior Race," 170n39
The Suppression of the African Slave-Trade to the United States of America, 1638–1870, 18–19, 21–22, 59, 115–38

Talented Tenth, 87, 166n4
"The Talented Tenth," 166n4, 167n12
Taylor, Paul, 138
terror,
    John Brown and, 21, 61–70, 164n62
    racial, 7, 26, 49, 51
Thoreau, Henry David, 53, 56, 69, 163n43
"To the Nations of the World," 181n14
Tocqueville, Alexis de, 10, 147n41, 153n20

Torres, Gerald, 151n11, 158n65, 172n74
Tronto, Joan, 178n55
Trouillot, Michel-Rolph, 126, 145n12, 145n19, 187n79
Truth, Sojourner, 57, 101
Tubman, Harriet, 49, 57, 65, 101, 109
Tulsa, Oklahoma, race riot, 38, 43
Turner, Jack, 53, 163n43
Turner, Nat, 54, 162n33
Tuskegee syphilis experiment, 37

United States
  civic nationalism and, 129–36
  Congress, regret for slavery, 2, 143–44n4, 147n38
  contributions of African Americans to, 2–3, 26, 28, 32–33
  link between Africa and, 60
  reparation movements in, 37–38
  revolutionary period, 120–29, 135, 137
  as white nation, 119–20
universal/universalism, x, 119, 133
uplift, racial, 73, 84, 87, 99, 153n23, 167n12

Van Dieman, Roger, 83, 84–86, 94
Veil, 7, 8, 17, 146–47n32
Verdun, Vincene, 156n52
victimhood, 3
"Virginia," 144n8
Virginia General Assembly, resolution on slavery, 1–4, 23, 37, 138
Voting Rights Act (1965), 15

Wacquant, Loïc, 164n59
Wald, Priscilla, 183n28
Walker, Kara, 160n9
Wall, Cheryl, 148n49
Wallerstein, Immanuel, 131
Walzer, Michael, 52
Warren, Kenneth, 104
Washington, Booker T., 29, 30, 54
Watson, Julia, 77

wealth, 30–31, 39–40, 131–32
welfare, 98, 99, 105, 113, 177n51, 179n76
Weheliye, Alexander, 146n23
Weinbaum, Alys Eve, 178n57
Wells-Barnett, Ida B., 101, 157n64
West, Cornel, 149n58
Western, Bruce, 63–64, 143n7
Westley, Robert, 36, 158n70, 159n73, 159n75
Wheatley, Phillis, 101
White, Hayden, 24
white Americans
  black humanity and, 34–35, 79–80
  African American liberation of, 41
  identity and, 35, 86, 92
  views on John Brown, 49–50
white nation, 118–20, 127–28, 129–37
white supremacy, 4, 7–9, 60, 63, 67, 85, 112, 117, 119
Whitman, Walt, 135
Will, George, 164n62
Williams, Patricia, 84, 148n53, 180n82, 184n32
Williams, Sherley Anne, 175–76n31
Wolfenstein, Eugene Victor, 149n62
Wolin, Sheldon, 6–7, 19, 147n41, 158n70
Womanism, 179n77
women. *See also* feminist theory
  "The Damnation of Women" and, 21, 103–11
  democratic citizenship and, 97–100
The World and Africa, 186n62
"Worlds of Color," 115–16
"The Wounded World," 183n26

Yamamoto, Eric, 44, 158n65
Yellin, Jean Fagin, 174n22, 175n25
Young, Iris Marion, 150n69, 165n68, 172n69

Zamir, Shamoon, 78, 149n60, 169n27, 183n27